CANNING AND PRESERVING FOOD FOR BEGINNERS

The Essential Guide to Preserving,

Water Bath and Pressure Canning.

With Many Easy, Healthy, And Tasty

Recipes to Prepare at Home

Norma F. Reed

© **Copyright 2021 - Norma F. Reed - All rights reserved.**

This document is geared towards providing exact and reliable information in regard to the topic and issue covered.

- From a Declaration of Principles which was accepted and approved equally by a Committee of the American Bar Association and a Committee of Publishers and Associations.

In no way is it legal to reproduce, duplicate, or transmit any part of this document in either electronic means or in printed format. All rights reserved.

The information provided herein is stated to be truthful and consistent, in that any liability, in terms of inattention or otherwise, by any usage or abuse of any policies, processes, or directions contained within is the solitary and utter responsibility of the recipient reader. Under no circumstances will any legal responsibility or blame be held against the publisher for any reparation, damages, or monetary loss due to the information herein, either directly or indirectly.

Respective authors own all copyrights not held by the publisher.

The information herein is offered for informational purposes solely and is universal as so. The presentation of the information is without contract or any type of guarantee assurance.

The trademarks that are used are without any consent, and the publication of the trademark is without permission or backing by the trademark owner. All trademarks and brands within this book are for clarifying purposes only and are owned by the owners themselves, not affiliated with this document.

TABLE OF CONTENTS

INTRODUCTION 10
    Canning: a little bit of history 11

HOMEMADE PRESERVING AND CANNING: BASICS AND INGREDIENTS 13

Basics Of Preserving: What Is It and How It Works? 14
    Why Preserve Food? 14
    What are Preserves? 14
    How to Prepare Preserves: Step-by-step Instructions 15
    Pickled and Fermented foods 16

Ingredients 17
    Pectin 17
    Lemon juice 17
    Sweetener 17
    Vinegar 17
    Spices 18
    Pickled salt 18

Main types of canned food 19
    Jams, jellies and marmalades 19
    Pickled and fermented vegetables 20
    Vegetables in oil 21

Pressure Canning and Water Bath Canning .. 22
    Canning and Storage Supplies: What Do You Need to Get Started Safely? 23
    Tools for canning 23

Jars for canning 24
    Jars Sanification 25

Water Bath Canning 26
    Water Bath Canning method: a step-by-step guide 26

Pressure Canning 28
    The basic structure of a domestic Pressure Canner 28
    Necessary tools for the production of canned goods with pressure canning 29
    Pressure canning method: a step-by-step guide 29
    How do choose the right canning method for different foods? 31

PRESERVES RECIPES: JAMS, MARMALADES AND JELLIES 32
1. Cinnamon Blueberry Jam 33
2. Apricot Habanero Jam 33
3. Over-The-Top Cherry Jam 34
4. Raspberry and Mint Jam 34
5. Flavorful Strawberry-Rhubarb Jam ... 34
6. Pineapple-Rhubarb Jam 35
7. Roasted Beet Jam 35
8. Ginger Pears Jam 36
9. Rhubarb Jelly 36
10. Rhubarb Raisin Marmalade 37
11. Blackberry Apple Jelly 37
12. Strawberry Jam and Balsamic Vinegar .. 38
13. Luscious Blueberry Jam 38
14. Lemon-Rosemary Marmalade 39
15. Red Onion Apricot Jelly 39
16. Easy Blood Orange Marmalade 40
17. Pink Grapefruit Marmalade 40
18. Apricot Amaretto Jam 41
19. Raspberry Peach Jam 41
20. Blueberry Cinnamon Jam 42
21. Carrot Pineapple Pearl Jam 42
22. Green Tomato Jam 43
23. Pineapple Rhubarb Jam 43
24. Plum Orange Jam 44
25. Pina Colada Zucchini Jam 44
26. Strawberry Mint Jam 45
27. Caramel Apple Jam 45
28. Christmas Raspberries Jam 46
29. Candy Apple Jelly 46
30. Lime Mint Jelly 46
31. Watermelon Jelly 47
32. Cucumber Jelly 47
33. Three-Fruit Marmalade 48
34. Orange Pineapple Marmalade 48
35. Pear Pineapple Jam 49
36. Tomato Lemon Marmalade 49
37. Mixed Citrus Marmalade 50
38. Blackberries Orange Marmalade ... 50
39. Jalapeño Pepper Jelly 51
40. Just Jalapeño Blackberry Jelly 51
41. Savory Ruby Port Vinegar Jelly 52
42. Rosy Jelly Retreat 52

WATER BATH CANNING RECIPES: VEGETABLE PICKLES 54

43. Bread and Butter Pickles 55
44. Roasted Beet Pickles 55
45. Orange and Golden Beets with Roasted Garlic 56
46. Eight-Hour Cortado (Cabbage Slaw) 56
47. Carrot and Daikon Radish 57
48. Ginger-Spiked Carrot and Apple Pickle.... 57
49. Rainbow Chard Stems 58
50. Corn and Chile Pickle 58
51. Russian-Inspired Pickled Mushrooms 59
52. Mushrooms Pickled in White Wine 59
53. Kosher-NYC Style Dill Pickles 60
54. Smoky Full-Sour Pickles 61
55. Half-Sour Dill Pickles 62
56. Dilly and Mustardy Kohlrabi Pickles 63
57. Pickled Cherry Tomatoes 63
58. Canned Garlic Dill Pickles 64
59. Pickled Cauliflower 64
60. Pickled Red Grapes 65
61. Mustard Pickled Vegetables 66
62. Pickled Snap Pea with Carrot 66
63. Pickled Onions 67
64. Lime Jalapeño Pickles 67

WATER BATH CANNING RECIPES: SALSAS AND SAUCES 69

65. Zesty Salsa 70
66. Homemade Pizza Sauce 70
67. Red Tomato Ketchup 71
68. Unripe Tomato Salsa 71
69. Cucumber Relish 72
70. Hot Pepper Mustard Butter 72
71. Asian Plum Sauce 72
72. Peaches and Vanilla Syrup 73
73. Corn Relish 73
74. Green Salsa 74
75. Simple Salsa 74
76. Mango Salsa 75
77. Pineapple Chipotle 75
78. Hot Green Sauce 75
79. Corn & Cherry Tomato Salsa 76
80. Italian Tomatoes Pepper Spread 76
81. Roasted Tomato Chipotle Sauce 77
82. Fiesta Tomatoes Sauce 78
83. Spicy Corn Sauce 78
84. Spicy Tomato Sauce 79
85. Pears and Peaches Salsa 80
86. Zesty Yellow Tomato Spread 80
87. Horseradish Tomato Sauce 81
88. Cherry Chutney 82
89. Mint Chutney 82
90. Christmas Chutney 83
91. Spiced Apple Chutney 83
92. Spiced Cranberry Apple Chutney 84
93. Spiced Cranberry Chutney 85
94. Mango-Pineapple Chutney 85
95. Tomato And Peach Chutney 86
96. Sweet Tamarind Chutney 86
97. Cilantro Chutney 86
98. Lemon Strawberry Sauce 87
99. Peach Chili Sauce 87
100. Pear Barbecue Sauce 88
101. Honey Mustard 88
102. Pickled Pullet Eggs 89
103. Spaghetti Sauce 89
104. Pepper Sauce with Tomato 90
105. Homestyle Spaghetti Sauce 91
106. Roasted Garlic Pasta Sauce 91
107. Chili Sauce with Garlic 92
108. Hamburger Sauce Mix 92

PRESSURE CANNING RECIPES: MEAT, POULTRY AND SEAFOOD 93

109. Simple Canned Salmon 94
110. Chili Beef 94
111. Essential Chicken Soup 95
112. Easy Venison or Beef Stew 96
113. Sloppy Joes 96
114. Pressure Canned Venison 97
115. Ranch Chicken Pasta in a Jar 97
116. Pressure Canned Lamb 98
117. Beef Stroganoff with Mushroom 98
118. Pressure Canned Tilapia 99
119. Canned Chicken Pieces 99
120. Canned Turkey Meat 100
121. Canned Homemade Chili 100
122. Beef Paprikash 101
123. Chicken Jambalaya with Sausage 101
124. Pressure Canned Lamb Meat 102
125. Crumb Meatballs with Sauce 102
126. Pressure Canned Stewing Beef 103
127. Canned Mackerel 103
128. Canned Salmon 103
129. Canned Olive oil Tuna 104
130. Canned River Fish 104
131. Canned Shad 104
132. Raw-Pack Meat Can 104
133. Venison 105
134. Canned Pork 105
135. Beef Pot Roast 105
136. Moose 106
137. Canned Meatballs 106
138. Canned Chipotle Beef 106
139. Pot Roast in a Jar 107
140. Corned Beef and Potatoes 107
141. Roast Beef and Potatoes 108
142. Prawn, Rice, and Mango Salad 108
143. Canned Beef Stroganoff 109

- 144. Basic Pork and Beans 109
- 145. Canned Goulash 110
- 146. Chipotle Taco Beef 110
- 147. Pork Chops with Apple 110
- 148. Pork Goulash 111
- 149. Ginger Miso Salmon Salad 111

PRESSURE CANNING RECIPES: FRUITS, VEGETABLES AND LEGUMES 113

- 150. Coriander Carrots 114
- 151. Essential Mixed Vegetables 114
- 152. Tomato and Jalapeño Sauce 115
- 153. Singapore Pepper Sauce 116
- 154. Canned Spicy Garlic Pickled Carrots 116
- 155. Pickled Jalapenos 117
- 156. Canned Spicy Pickled Asparagus 117
- 157. Rainbow Beets 118
- 158. Simple Canned Tomatoes, Many Ways ... 118
- 159. End-of-Summer Bean and Tomato Stew ... 119
- 160. Sweet and Spicy Pickled Radishes 120
- 161. Baked Beans 120
- 162. Glazed Carrots 121
- 163. Green Beans 122
- 164. Tomatoes 122
- 165. Stewed Tomatoes 122
- 166. Herbed Peas 123
- 167. Herbed Tomatoes 123
- 168. Asparagus 124
- 169. Marinated Mushrooms 124
- 170. Dried Beans 124
- 171. Instant Hummus 125
- 172. Kidney Beans 125
- 173. Dilly Pickled Snap Peas 125
- 174. Black Eyed Peas 126
- 175. Chickpeas 126
- 176. Peas and Carrots with Chives 126
- 177. Lima Beans 127
- 178. Purple-hulled Field Peas 127
- 179. Pressure canned green peas 127
- 180. Canned Garlic Beans 128
- 181. Canned Garlic Garbanzo Beans 128
- 182. Canned Mustard Pork and Beans 129
- 183. Canned Pumpkin 129
- 184. Pressure Canned Hot peppers 130
- 185. Pressure Canned Sweet peppers 130
- 186. Pressure Canned Sweet Potatoes 131
- 187. Pressure Canned Broccoli 131
- 188. Canned Kale 132
- 189. Canning Turnips 132
- 190. Pressure Canned Caramelized Onions 133
- 191. Canned Fiddleheads 133
- 192. Pickled Garlic scrapes 134
- 193. Pineapple Zucchini 134
- 194. Sweet and Sour Pickled Zucchini Slices .. 134
- 195. Butternut Squash and Chickpea Hash 135
- 196. Spicy Green Beans 136
- 197. Simple Canned Sauerkraut 136
- 198. Fennel and Radish Slaw 137
- 199. Fig jam 137
- 200. Corn on the Cob 138
- 201. Canned Caramelized Onions 138
- 202. Garlic and Tomato Peach Sauce 138
- 203. Pressure Canned Spicy Corn 139
- 204. Canned Three-Bean Salad 139
- 205. Canned Potato with Onions and Mushroom 140
- 206. Cabbage and Carrot Coleslaw 141
- 207. Tomato Bell Pepper Salsa 141
- 208. Brandied Honey and Spice Pears 142
- 209. Squash and Pumpkin 142
- 210. Glazed Sweet Carrots 142
- 211. Apple Pie Filling with Maple and Cinnamon 143
- 212. Canned Pickled Small Beets 143

LOW-SODIUM AND LOW SUGAR CANNING AND PRESERVING RECIPES 145

- 213. Apple Butter 146
- 214. Applesauce 146
- 215. Pear Sauce 147
- 216. Blueberry Jam 147
- 217. Raspberry Jelly 148
- 218. Strawberry & Lemon Concentrate 148
- 219. Pickled Beets 149
- 220. Healthy Hot Sauce 149
- 221. BBQ Sauce 150
- 222. Canned Apple Slices 150
- 223. Light Turkey Tortilla Soup 151
- 224. Canned Chicken Stock 151
- 225. Potato and Chicken Stew 152
- 226. Pressure Canned Turkey Broth 152
- 227. Chicken Broth with Chile and Corn 153
- 228. Chicken Stew with Carrot 153
- 229. Bean and Tomato Chicken Soup 154
- 230. Texas Chili 154
- 231. Carrot, Coriander, and Ginger Soup 155
- 232. Mexican Chicken Soup 155
- 233. Five-Bean Medley 156
- 234. Chicken & Veggie Soup 156
- 235. Black Bean Chili with Potato 157
- 236. Onion Soup with Butter 157
- 237. Chicken Soup with Tomato 158
- 238. Venison & Tomato Chili 158
- 239. Pickled Kimchi Soup 158
- 240. Carrot Soup 159
- 241. Squash Soup with Chiles 160

242.	Black Bean Soup	160
243.	Pea Soup with Carrot	161
244.	Chicken Soup	161
245.	Bean and Bacon Soup	162
246.	Mexican Beef and Sweet Potato Soup	162
247.	Tomato Soup with Celery	163
248.	Green Lima Vegetable Soup	163
249.	Cabbage and Corned Beef Soup	164
250.	Split Pea Soup	164

OTHER WAYS TO PRESERVE YOUR FOOD 166

Freezing: What Is and How to Do It Right ... 167
    What Can Be Frozen? 167
    Frosty Facts 167
    Timing and Techniques for Blanching Vegetables
    168
    Fruit 169
    Packaging 169

CONCLUSION 171

INTRODUCTION

Canning and preserving is a wonderful way to store and eat fresh, healthy food throughout the year. Homemade preserves are a wonderful way to store and eat fresh, healthy food all year round. There's no better time than winter to pull out your preserves and the products of your summer garden and enjoy them. After all, what better way is there to use up those tomatoes that you didn't give away this time around?

Preserves can also make lovely homemade gifts for friends and family - it's great to give away something you've made yourself! There's no better feeling than opening up a jar of homemade jam at the height of winter and enjoying something so pleasurable in flavor, knowing that it's made right there in your own kitchen.

This book will give you all the useful information you need to better understand this delightful world and will provide you with many great recipes to try out and enjoy with your family and friends!

This journey will give you information on how canning can benefit you.

There are so many benefits of working with your own food that it's hard not to imagine yourself in the kitchen.

To be honest, making homemade preserves takes a lot of work and time. I like to say it's a wonderful pastime if you love being in a "kettle of water" during July. So why do I and so many others like me love to store food at home?

For one thing, consuming foods that have been stored indoors provides a pleasant feeling of accomplishment and independence, as well as the fact that the food tastes good.

Your home canning efforts will enable you to source food of the highest quality and taste.

You can avoid wasting your garden's bountiful crops or a good deal at the farmer's market.

Properly stored fresh fruit, the taste of jams, jellies, soups, vegetables, sauces, and so on, taste much better than most mass-produced, supermarket-sold alternatives.

This superior quality makes up for your work. After all, you get good food that money can't buy because you make it yourself with your own hands. Plus, when you can choose what you eat for yourself and your family, you can select the freshest food and treat it. This doesn't quite hold a candle to store-bought foods, bouncing off trucks on the way to processing plants.

When choosing your food, you are the judge of the quality.

Of course, the most satisfying way to eat is to grow your products, but you can also look for the best organic products when they are available or buy from a local producer, which allows you to buy "zero km" products, and to support the economy of your area.

The high quality of home-canned food makes it a huge added value, even if the investment of effort and equipment for home canning makes the food about the same price as that of the supermarket.

Good food creates a better quality of life. You will get so used to canned food that by the time you're done and have to buy something at the store, you will invariably be disappointed.

Besides good taste, there's another important reason to incorporate home canning into your diet as much as possible.

Commercial food cans are coated internally with an epoxy resin which most often contains a chemical called *Bisphenol A* (**BPA**). You may have heard of this toxic ingredient found in plastic food containers, from water bottles to baby bottles.

Eating canned food commercially could expose you to BPA, which is a harmful substance capable of altering the development of the reproductive, nervous, and immune systems, with more prognosed effects on children than on adults.

Studies on this substance are evolving and are leading to its gradual replacement with other harmless substances. In any case, by eating fresh or frozen foods and storing your food in glass containers, you will avoid BPA.

After completing a few homemade canning projects, you will taste the difference and probably won't even be ashamed to brag about your successes.

But there are several things you should know before diving into your next batch of jam or pickles.

Canning: a little bit of history

For centuries, canning has been used for a variety of purposes, such as making jams and pickles to feeding soldiers in wartime.

It was, however, the French Nicolas Appert who refined this method in 1809 to preserve food by cooking it and sealing it inside a jar. His invention led to what we know today as the process of canning.

The very first patent for a tin can was issued in England on January 2, 1810, to merchant Peter Durand. It is said that he got the idea from seeing food being preserved in glass jars in a store. He then began to experiment with different types of metal to see if they would be suitable for preserving food. He finally settled on tin-plated iron as the best choice of material.

His first successful experiment involved packing food into tin cans and then sealing them with a cork. He then placed them in boiling water to cook the food. The heat would cause the cork to contract and create a tight seal. Durand then took his creation from the kitchen to the docks, where he filled his new cans with fish and sold them.

It was the Englishman Bryan Donkin who understood what could be done with the invention and who commercialized it. He eventually brought uniformity into the production process. He also trained others in his trade. He opened a canning factory for this purpose and even obtained a patent for a tin can opener in 1855.

The Industrial Revolution was in full swing by then and new machines were being invented that could help speed up production. In 1858, John Hall and Bryan Dorkin established the world's first canning factory in England that operated on a commercial scale.

The new cans were much lighter than the ones used previously, which made transport over land easier. They were also waterproof and airtight, which prevented the food from spoiling.

However, we have to wait until 1858 when British inventor B.P. Allinson created the twist-on lid with a sealing compound that we know cans today.

Since its invention, canning has evolved in many ways and is now used to preserve an enormous variety of foods, including fruits, vegetables, meat, fish, and even dairy products. It is a safe and effective way to store food for long periods, making it a valuable tool for anyone who wants to keep their food costs down.

HOMEMADE PRESERVING AND CANNING: BASICS AND INGREDIENTS

Basics Of Preserving: What Is It and How It Works?

Why Preserve Food?

Storing food is one way to keep it from spoiling or drying out. Several processes can be used, the most common are the water bath, the pressure cooker, the jar method, and fermentation.

There are several rules on how to store food safely and how long it lasts. This chapter will give you an introduction to storing your food at home, so you can enjoy it all year round, without having to go shopping every week.

There are several reasons for choosing to store your food.

First of all, buying fresh produce and fruit at the grocery store (especially organic ones) is getting more and more expensive. We often end up buying frozen foods that have significantly lower prices, which are often quickly frozen after harvest to lock in their nutritional values. Other times we prefer to buy seasonal vegetables and fruit, which is when they can be bought much cheaper.

The downside is that fresh produce has a short shelf life, so unless we're going to use them immediately, we'll have to store them.

Another cheaper alternative, but certainly much more expensive in terms of time, to have good food available is to buy seeds and plants, grow them and store them. In this way, we will have genuine food for a longer time and we will be able to convert the surplus into preserves.

What are Preserves?

Preserves are preserved food products that have been subjected to heat treatments that enable them to keep for long periods at room temperature.

They are distinguished in acidic and non-acidic preserves, they can be preserved in glass or tinplate and can be treated with pickling, in a water bath canning, or pressure canning to guarantee their conservation stability.

Preserves must be subjected to one or more stabilization treatments, which are processes that block the activity of enzymes and microorganisms naturally present in food, which cause the food to deteriorate.

The main danger in homemade preserves is botulism, a disease caused by *Clostridium botulinum*.

This microorganism can be found in soil, sediments, and dust, it prefers foods characterized by low acidity (pH> 4.4) and high-water activity (aw> 0.93). It develops in the absence of air, at room temperature, and is capable of producing spores (dormant state of the bacterium, resistant to heating to 200°F).

Botulinum toxin is a neurotoxin capable of inducing muscle stiffening, paralysis, and in severe cases even death.

The symptoms of botulism poisoning can include blurred vision, difficulty swallowing, slurred speech and muscle weakness. If you experience any of these symptoms after eating homemade preserves, see your doctor immediately.

Although botulism is a rare disease, the consumption of contaminated food even in minimal quantities, associated with the difficulty of diagnosis, can lead to fatal outcomes.

Currently, the cases of botulism related to the consumption of domestic canned products are equal to about 90%, and only the remaining 10% concerns industrial products.

It is therefore important to always act safely and with the utmost care when preparing preserves, and throw away any jar that shows even the slightest signs of deterioration, such as mold, gas, turbidity, strange odors, or drainage.

Botulism is a very serious illness, and it can be fatal. So, if you are going to make your own preserves, be sure to take the necessary precautions to avoid botulism poisoning.

How to Prepare Preserves: Step-by-step Instructions

Choice of ingredients good preserves need raw materials always be fresh, made with seasonal products (rich in nutrients, mineral salts, and vitamins), and possibly organic crops. If fruit and vegetables come from your garden, they should be harvested no more than 12 hours in advance.

Selection, washing, and possible cooking of the products: food must be carefully selected, which means removing the pieces with dents, imperfections, and rotten parts. Once selected, the products must be washed carefully to eliminate any residual chemical products or soil on the skins, dried, and cut into regular pieces. You can now move on to the food's preparation and cooking. Keep in mind that you should always use high-quality raw ingredients, even for oil, vinegar, sugar, and salt.

Sanitizing the containers: jars and lids must be washed with detergent and hot water, rinsed, and dried carefully. They can be washed in the dishwasher at high temperatures and let dry completely inside, taking them out only at the time of use. However, it is preferable to sanitize the jars and all the tools used for preserves by boiling them in water for at least 10-20 minutes.

Filling of the containers: Each jar must be filled leaving at least 1/4-inch headspace, essential for the vacuum and therefore for the correct success of the preservation. Remember: the food inside must be submerged by the preservation liquid. To avoid any air bubbles you can use a spatula to press the food into the jar. In the case of hot filling, it is advisable to leave the containers in water until it is time to fill them, possibly at a temperature similar to that of the food to be inserted to avoid a possible thermal shock. In cold filling, the containers must be completely dry. Before closing the lid, the mouth of the jar should always be carefully cleaned, preferably with a clean cloth soaked in vinegar, for optimal closure. The lids must be tight but not too tightly, to allow the air to escape from the jars.

Stabilization of preserves (Pasteurization or Sterilization): Pasteurization and sterilization are processes that use heat to destroy or inactivate bacteria present in food or food preparation, which is also the main responsible for its deterioration. Inside pots full of water, the heat raises the temperature in the preserves jars to a level high enough to kill (or inactivate) molds, yeasts, bacteria, and spores found in food. As the heat inside grows, air bubbles are also formed which are pushed upwards. When the jars return to room temperature, the air pressure creates a vacuum, which prevents air and other organisms from entering the vessel, blocking its deterioration.

Inspection of the containers: When they are completely cooled, the jars must be sealed as a consequence of the creation of the vacuum inside them. The lids will be slightly concave and no sound will be heard by pressing them; if the jars are not sealed, however, the center of the lid will be convex and when you press it you will hear a clear click. In the latter case, there are two possibilities: consume the contents within a week or proceed with the pasteurization in a bain-marie again with a new lid.

Storage: Once we have checked the tightness of the jars, they can be stored, preferably in a cool and dark place, such as a cellar or pantry. Finally, always make sure, before eating it, that the contents of the jar show no signs of deterioration, such as mold, gas, turbidity, odors, or drainage.

Pickled and Fermented foods

In pickling as a method of stabilizing the product, instead of heat, anaerobic fermentation is used to transform the carbohydrates of foods into lactic acid by "good" microorganisms capable of surviving high saline concentrations, which develop inside the preserves.

The preserving liquid (called brine), consisting of water, salt, vinegar and oil in variable parts, contributes together with the lactic acid to lowering the pH of the solution and allows the preserves to stabilize, even without the intervention of heat, for a period of approximately six months.

Ingredients

Pectin

Pectin is a common ingredient in many canning recipes and is used as a thickener. This is a natural component present in fruit in varying quantities: some fruits have large quantities of it, such as oranges and apples, while others contain minimal quantities, such as cherries. This is why it is often necessary to add powdered pectin to make jams and marmalades. During the cooking process, pectin is released or added to the fruit, and with the right amounts of lemon juice and sweetener it thickens and becomes gelatinous.

Lemon juice

Lemon juice has a preservative effect due to its ascorbic acid content. Furthermore, in jams and marmalades, it prevents the sugar from crystallizing during cooking and helps the pectin to thicken. When it comes to fresh lemons, you can never tell exactly how acidic they are, because it depends a lot on many variables related to the growing conditions of lemons. Bottled lemon juice provides a perfectly regulated alternative with a constant pH (acid concentration). This is why you will find that most recipes call for bottled lemon juice, which is why you should stick with it for better and more consistent results.

Sweetener

Sweeteners, whether they are sugar or honey, play an important role in the preservation process for many reasons, first of all the reduction of available water (or "A_w") for microorganisms.

In sweet preserves, the added sweetness amplifies the flavor of the fruit and contrasts its sour taste. In savory preserves and pickles, it complements the acidity and adds some depth to the flavor. Sugar also helps make a tastier, brighter-looking jam, jelly, or preserve with a much better texture. That said, it is safe to cook jams and marmalades by reducing the sugar, but be sure to compensate with more lemon or vinegar in the preserves; in any case, you should never go below 700 g of sugar for every kg of fruit in order not to jeopardize its shelf life.

Vinegar

Adding wine or apple vinegar is essential for pickling. Always use high quality vinegar for pickling or to add a specific flavor to a preserve, use good vinegar and make sure it contains at least 5-6% acetic acid.

White wine vinegar can be used as a preserving liquid in pure form or mixed with the same amount of water; given the lower concentration of acetic acid, apple cider vinegar should only be used in pure form.

A little vinegar can be used to prevent your jars from becoming cloudy during packaging or for cleaning the mouths of the jars before closing to clean and sanitize them.

As already mentioned, acidity is an effective system for preserving food preservation from the action of microorganisms.

Spices

If you are going to play with fruits and vegetables, don't forget to experiment with the flavors. Spices can be that extra touch that adds flavor to the preserve when paired with the right fruit / vegetables. The only thing to remember is to add the spices in their whole form (seeds, sticks, leaves) without grinding and by treating them as the rest of the food placed in the jars.

The flavor spreads more evenly when the spices are added whole, and even if the flavor isn't as powerful, it will be consistent. You can simply adjust the amount as you wish.

Pickled salt

What sets this type of salt apart from others is that it has no added chemicals, such as iodine or other agents. Unlike table salt, pickle salt does not affect the color of the pickle water or the vegetables themselves. While other varieties of salt aren't bad, if the salt you're using has added chemicals, your liquid won't be as clear.

Main types of canned food

Jams, jellies and marmalades

The difference between jam and marmalades is the type of fruit used to make the preserve: the marmalade is a fruit preserve made from the juice and peel of citrus fruits; all the other fruits preserves are called jam or jelly.

Preparing jams and marmalades is simple: you have to wash, dry, and chop the fruits, add the sugar and any other ingredients and let everything boil according to the time of the recipe. Then you have to fill the sanitized jars with the hot mixture, close with the lids, and process them for 10-15 minutes. Let cool the preserves and enjoy.

The most important factors that affect the preservation of a marmalade/jam/jelly are acidity and sugar content.

The acidity of the fruit helps to preserve the fruit and prevents the crystallization of sugar during cooking. It is important not to overdo the quantities of sugar to prevent it from crystallizing during cooking, but also not to lack it, as it lowers the availability of free water, hindering the proliferation of pathogenic microorganisms within the preserves.

Pickled and fermented vegetables

The method of preserving food through the process of marinating in some form of brine is called pickling. In pickled vegetables, the preserving liquid, in which they are immersed, consists mainly of a mixture of water and salt, mixed with vinegar and oil. In this case, the jars of preserves in brine must be sanitized, but it is not necessary to subject the finished product to pasteurization or sterilization.

When vegetables are immersed in brine, their carbohydrates undergo a series of natural fermentation processes that transform them into lactic acid, by particular microorganisms capable of growing at high saline concentrations. The fermentation products make the preserves safe and give them their characteristic flavor. To be safe, the brine must contain at least 10% salt (100 g of salt per liter of water).

Pickled vegetables can be blanched briefly or left raw. Once placed in the jars, the vinegar is added and their pasteurization is carried out when required since safety in these preserves is guaranteed by the acidity of the vinegar. The preserving liquid can be composed of vinegar only or of a part of vinegar and one part of water (in this case it will be preferable to use white wine vinegar with an acidity of at least 6%. If you use apple cider vinegar, from the moment that its acidity is lower, it cannot be diluted, but it must be used alone.

The many varieties of pickled and fermented foods are classified by ingredients and method of preparation.

1) **Dill pickles and sauerkraut** are both fermented and cured for about 3-6 weeks.

2) **Refrigerator dills** are fermented for around 1 week. Colors and tastes change while they're curing, as well as acidity.

3) **Fresh-pack or quick-process pickles** are not fermented. They may be brined for a few hours or overnight, then drained and covered with vinegar and spices.

4) **Fruit pickles** are typically made by simmering fruit in a seasoned syrup that has been acidified with either lemon juice or vinegar.

5) **Relishes** are composed of diced fruits or vegetables that have been cooked with spices and vinegar.

Vegetables in oil

Vegetables preserved in oil must necessarily be blanched for a few minutes in water and wine vinegar in equal parts, to acidify the product. The wine vinegar must be white and have an acidity equal to or greater than 6%.

Aromatic herbs and spices added must also undergo the same treatment as vegetables. These must then be allowed to dry and cool completely, and when placed in the previously sanitized container, any empty spaces must be filled, covered with extra virgin olive oil, and removed any air trapped in the food.

We then proceed with the stabilization of the product through pasteurization or sterilization. If no other information is provided in the recipe, it is advisable to leave the preserves to rest for at least half a day before placing them in the pantry, because they could absorb the oil and therefore may need to be refilled. It is essential to consider that once the oil has been topped up, the preserves will have to be pasteurized again.

Other domestic preserves such as ***pestos, natural vegetable preserves, or sauces*** with fish or meat are preparations with little or no acidity and must be prepared by sterilization, a process that can only be obtained at home using a pressure food canner.

Alternatively, the only recommended storage method after preparation is freezing, which serves to block the growth of microorganisms and enzymatic activity.

Pressure Canning and Water Bath Canning

Over time, all foods are subject to natural degradation processes and the loss of their nutritional characteristics.

The need to stop or slow down these processes for shorter or longer times has led to the development of new ways of food stabilization which, through specific treatments, prevents or delays its alteration.

Among all the food stabilization techniques, only pasteurization, sterilization, and pickling can eliminate potentially pathogenic microorganisms for human health in the medium and long term.

Pasteurization and sterilization are procedures based on the use of heat to inactivate/eliminate microorganisms present in a food preparation, which are also the main culprits for its deterioration. Other valid methods are blanching, cooking, and frying, obviously with shorter storage times.

When choosing to make preserves at home and which recipes to try, there are several factors to keep in mind, one of which is the preparation method you want to use.

Home canning can be done in two ways:

- *__Pressure canning__*
- *__Water-Bath canning__*

1. Pressure Canning requires temperatures above 218°F, obtained through the combined use of heat and high pressures, which allows the preserves to be sterilized and therefore destroy all vital forms of microorganisms, including bacterial spores.

This process requires a domestic food canner, a special and elaborate pressure cooker equipped with internal pressure and temperature control and monitoring systems.

This type of pressure cooker can thus reach very high pressures: from 5 to 15 pounds per inch (PSI), equivalent to approximately 1.03 Bar (103.4 kPa). These autoclaves are sold and marketed only in the United States and Canada and are the USDA (US Department of Agriculture) recommended means of producing homemade canned food.

2. *Water-Bath Canning* is a pasteurization technique that uses temperatures of 214 °F for an extended amount of time to kill the majority of bacteria in foods, making them safe to eat.

Unlike sterilization, pasteurization has a limited effect on bacterial spores. Therefore, to increase the shelf life of the products treated with this method, it must be combined with other preservation systems such as acidification (by adding vinegar), reduction available water with salt or sugar, or refrigeration, to prevent the development of spore-forming microorganisms.

Water bath canning requires a deep pot to contain enough water to submerge the preserving jars at least 1-2-inch.

Canning and Preserving Food for Beginners

Water bath canning is the cheaper and most used way to make home canning. It's a good way to make and store hundreds of foods, including sauces, jams, jellies, fruit, and vegetables in oil.

This is an excellent canning method for beginners or avid conservatives.

Canning and Storage Supplies: What Do You Need to Get Started Safely?

Now that you've had a little introductory overview of canning and storage, it's time to introduce you to the supplies you'll need.

Tools for canning

For proper canning of food, you need canning tools that can easily be found in your kitchen. Before starting the food canning prep process, it's important to make sure you have all the necessary accessories.

The main tools that are part of the canning process are the following:

A pot - in water bath canning, the pot must have a flat bottom, made of stainless steel that does not release metals in contact with any leaks of food acids, and of a suitable size to contain the jars properly, because the level of the water must be at least 1-2 inch- above the caps of the jars.
A domestic food canner - used in pressurized preserves, is a special pressure cooker, more elaborate and equipped with internal pressure and temperature control and monitoring systems.
A jar lifter - this tool is like a plier and is used to lift jars from boiling water.
A blade spatula - the spatula can be rubber or plastic. The purpose of using a bladed spatula is to remove the bubble from the jars. If you don't have a bladed spatula, a pack of chopsticks is an inexpensive alternative. Using a knife or metal spatula should be avoided as it can change the color of the food.
A cutting board and knife - for cutting fruits and vegetables into small pieces so they can easily fit into a jar for further processing.
Measuring Cups and Spoons - to measure the exact amount of ingredients to add to the jars and spoons for mixing.
A kitchen timer - the correct preparation time is important for monitoring the boiling time of the water.
A jar holder - to protect hands from contact with hot surfaces and prevent spills.
Clean towels - After pasteurization or sterilization, place the jars on a towel and let them cool.
Jars and lids for canning – glass jars and metallic lids to seal the surface of the jars. They can be of two types: 2 or 3 pieces with metal or glass lids surrounded by a rubber ring.
Lid Checker - to make sure jar lids are properly secured and tightened.

Jars for canning

The jars to be used for preserves can be purchased today both online and in discount or food stores.

Recycled food jars can prove to be a viable option to use in the water bath canning process, but they may not withstand the pressure in the pressure canning process.

Using old jars that are not in good condition is not a good option for canning because they may break during processing.

They can be a good option if you want to store food for no more than two weeks.

As for the closure system of the jars, it is better to choose jars with metal capsule lids, but those that have a rubber seal and hinge are also fine.

Capsules and seals should be disposable to ensure they are airtight. If this is not possible, metal caps and lids that show deformation, dents, signs of rust, or corrosion should be discarded.

Another argument applies to the reuse of jars if they provide you with screw rings, flat jar lids with an intact rubber ring around them: in these cases, their recycling is completely safe, as long as they are checked and cleaned well after use.

The general rule is: use only intact, clean, and well-sealing lids to best protect the food from contamination. It is precisely the vacuum that occurs during the cooling of the jars after their processing, when the lids seal them correctly, which guarantees the stability and quality of our preserves.

Note: If you see a concave lid on the jars, this means the jar is well sealed.

Mason jars are the most famous and commonly used jars for food storage.

The reason for their popular use is the two-piece jar lid which is specially designed to produce the vacuum inside it. The jar lid has a flat part that rests on the mouth of the jar and has a rubber seal in the inner diameter and is held in place by a separate (reusable) metal ring.

With food safety as a major concern, only jars approved for home canning, made of tempered glass, should be used. Tempered glass has a high resistance to high temperatures under pressure and can prevent the jar from breaking during the pasteurization and sterilization process.

Home food storage canning jars come in different sizes.

Regular mouth jars can be used for frequent storage of foods such as condiments, jam, jelly, and other cooked items; wide-mouthed ones, on the other hand, are widely used for storing meat, pickles, and vegetables, because a wide mouth makes it easy to get the large pieces of food in and out of the jar.

If the jars are handled with care, they can be used multiple times for canning and food storage.

Proper use and cleaning of jars, lids, and seals keep them functional also reduce the likelihood of the jars breaking while processing the cans.

Jars Sanification

Starting to can and store, therefore, requires proper cleaning and preparation of jars and lids.

Before adding food, wash the jars and lids with detergent and hot water and rinse them thoroughly as even small traces of detergent can cause the development of unpleasant flavors and change the color of the food.

Before use, lids and jars must be completely dry.

To dry them, just let them drain and then use a clean cloth or absorbent paper that does not leave textile residues or lint. It is also possible to dry them in the oven at 113° F for a few minutes.

Another way to keep the jars clean is to use the dishwasher. Preheat the jars, let them wash and dry completely. Keep the jars in the dishwasher until the food to fill in the jars is ready.

Jars and other accessories needed for canning can be sanitized by boiling them in water for about ten minutes.

To keep them sanitized, avoid taking them out of the boiling water using your hands or anything that could contaminate them again. Keep the jars, lids, tongs, and other accessories in water until you prepare the food to be transferred into the jars, especially if the food is to be packaged hot: this will not only minimize the risk of contamination but will also reduce the thermic stress on the glass.

Water Bath Canning

You will need the following items to use the water bath canning:

- *Large pot for water-bath*
- *Glass storage jars with metal lids*
- *Removable perforated racks*
- *Kitchen utensils (such as a funnel, ladle, wooden spoon, spatula, kitchen gloves, dish towels)*

Pot made of porcelain-coated steel or aluminum are used in water-bath canning. They have removable perforated racks where you can safely store your bottles. If you don't have access to a canning pot, a large flat-bottomed, low-rim pot with a lid will be ok. Maintaining an adequate temperature for the right time inside the pot is essential for the correct success of pasteurization.

When proceeding with the water bath pasteurization, remember that the water boils at variable temperatures, based on the altitude. At higher altitudes, the pressure decreases and the water boils earlier than what occurs at sea level. Therefore, higher altitudes require longer processing times to reach the right temperature even in the heart of the preparations compared to the preparation times at sea level. You must therefore know the altitude at which you are working to avoid underestimating the pasteurization time of the preserves. Below you can see a simple table[1]

ALTITUDE	WATER BOILING TEMPERATURE	WATER BATH CANNING TIME
0 feet (sea level)	212°F	20-25 minutes (HOT) 25-30 minutes (RAW)
2,000 feet	208°F	25-30 minutes (HOT) 30-35 minutes (RAW)
4,000 feet	204°F	30-35 minutes (HOT) 35-40 minutes (RAW)
From 6,000 feet	201°F	35-40 minutes (HOT) 40-45 minutes (RAW)

Water Bath Canning method: a step-by-step guide

The following are step-by-step instructions for canning properly with the water bath method.

---

1 For others information's you can see the USDA website:
https://nchfp.uga.edu/how/general/selecting_correct_process_time.html

1. Prepare the jars and lids previously sanitized and the food to can.

2. Fill the pot halfway with cold water, inserting the rack inside it.

3. The amount of water should be adjusted in such a way that once immersed, the jars will be submerged. In the absence of the rack, place a clean cloth on the bottom to avoid direct contact between the jars and the canning.

4. Bring the water to a boil in the canning.

5. Fill the jars with the product to be stored, making sure to press the food well with a spatula to avoid leaving air bubbles inside. Cover the food with the preserving liquid if required by the recipe, always remembering to leave at least 1/4-inch headspace between the lid and the top of the jar contents, to allow the formation of the vacuum.

6. Before immersing the jars in the water bath canner, make sure they are tightly closed and free of air bubbles.

7. Place filled jars with suitable lids in the canning tin, lowering them onto the rack using jar tongs. Make sure jars are always kept upright, as tilting can cause food to spill, allowing air to enter and spoil the contents. You can insert a cloth between the various jars to prevent them from banging together during the treatment.

8. If necessary, add more boiling water to keep 1-inch of water above the jar lids.

9. Raise the heat and put the lid on the pot.

10. Starts a timer for the entire time required by the recipe for pasteurization. Make sure the pot is always covered. It is also essential to maintain a constant boiling throughout the water bath; if the water level drops and evaporates, add more boiling water.

11. Once the cooking time has elapsed, remove the pan from the heat. Remove the jars from the pot with tongs after waiting 5-10 minutes for the water to cool, and place them upside down on a towel.

12. Let the jars cool for 12-24 hours

13. Check the lids to verify the formation of the vacuum: make sure they are concave and do not make the classic click (or that the jar seal does not rise).

14. Store the jars in a cool, dark, and dry place.

Pressure Canning

When it comes to preserving food, you need to know the pressure canning process as well. This method is excellent for storing vegetables, poultry, pork, beef, shellfish, and in general all food that cannot be stored in a water bath due to its low acid ph.

The purpose of pressure canning is to sterilize and eradicate any pathogen within the food, such as mold, bacteria, and especially bacterial spores, which could cause rapid deterioration.

The basic structure of a domestic Pressure Canner

Most household pressure canners are lightweight, thin-walled kettles with openable lids fitted with gaskets. They also have removable racks, a steam vent tube on the lid, an automatic vent lock, a safety fuse, and a comparator (or a weighted manometer), to indicate and regulate the pressure.

Maintaining an adequate and regular internal pressure inside the pressure canner is essential for the correct success of the sterilization as it helps to maintain the temperature high enough to kill all types of microorganisms present, including spores.

To apply the right pressure it is necessary to know the altitude at which the processing is carried out, as this affects the boiling temperature of the water inside the pot.

Higher altitudes require higher pressures to keep the water at the right temperature. To adjust the internal pressure of the autoclaves, these are equipped with counterweights and pressure regulators.

Weighted gauges with counterweights are generally designed to "shake" several times per minute or to continue to rock smoothly when maintaining the correct pressure. Read the manufacturer's instructions to know how a particular weighted pressure gauge should oscillate to indicate that the correct pressure is being achieved and then maintained during processing.

Canners with a comparator usually have a counterweight or a pressure regulator, to seal the open vent tube and pressurize the autoclave. The pressure readings on an autoclave with a comparator are indicated by the dial on the lid. It is recommended that you always read the manufacturer's instruction manual for information on when and how to use the weighted indicator or dial.

Pressure canners are deep enough to process one layer of one-liter jars or two layers of smaller-sized jars. The USDA recommends that a canner be large enough to hold at least four 4-liter jars to be considered a pressure canner for approved processes.

Necessary tools for the production of canned goods with pressure canning

You will need the following items to successfully use the pressure canning technique:

- *Pressure canner (and related instructions for use)*
- *Glass preservation jars*
- *Metal lids in two parts: the lid and the closing ring*
- *Removable perforated racks*
- *Kitchen tools (such as a funnel, ladle, wooden spoon, spatula, kitchen gloves, dish towels)*

Pressure canning method: a step-by-step guide

The precise procedure to canning with the pressure canning technique is outlined below.

1. Prepare the jars and lids previously sanitized and the food to can.

2. Fill the pressure canner with 4-5 cm of hot water.

3. Fill the jars with the product to be stored, making sure to press the food well with a spatula to avoid leaving air bubbles inside. Cover the food with the preserving liquid if required by the recipe, always remembering to leave at least 1/4-inch headspace, to allow the formation of the vacuum.

4. Before immersing the cans in the canner, make sure they are tightly closed and free of air bubbles inside.

5. Arrange the filled jars on the rack, making sure they remain upright during treatment.

6. Securely fix the lid of the pressure cooker.

7. Remove the weight from the vent port of the pressure canner.

8. Light the fire and hold it up until the steam comes out of the vent hole. Let the steam escape freely from the vent hole for 10 minutes.

9. Put the counterweight back on and let the canner pressurize for the next 3-5 minutes.

10. The timing starts when the pressure canner gauge reaches the recommended pressure value.

11. Maintain constant pressure in the container, adjusting the flame, for all the time required in the recipe. Follow the manufacturer's instructions for using the weighted pressure gauge to maintain the necessary pressure.

12. Turn off the heat, let the canner cool to depressurize it. Never force the opening, otherwise, the sudden pressure surge could cause sealing problems of the cans.

13. Remove the weight from the lid only when the pot has depressurized and wait for 10 to 20 minutes before unfastening and removing the lid completely.

14. Move the jars onto cloth using the jar clamp. While cooling, leave the containers undisturbed for 12-24 hours at room temperature.

15. Check the lids to verify the formation of the vacuum: make sure they are concave and do not make the classic click (or that the jar seal does not rise).

16. Store the jars in a cool, dark, and dry place.

The jar lid retaining ring is required when processing products, however, it should be removed once the procedure is complete.

Save the rings to secure the lid if you are not using the entire contents of the jar the first time you open it for consumption.

Once the jar is open, store it in the refrigerator and use it within a week.

Canning and Preserving Food for Beginners

How do choose the right canning method for different foods?

When working with foods that have a high acid content, the water bath procedure is ideal.

This is the method to use if you want to can box fruit juices, sauces, tomatoes, vegetables in oil, chutneys, sauces, fruit creams, jams, jams, jellies, and various condiments.

In these preparations, the shelf life of food is guaranteed by the acidity of the food and the added ingredients, which create an unfavorable environment for microbial growth, such as vinegar, oil, sugar, or salt, as mentioned above.

The pressure canning method, on the other hand, is recommended for foods such as meat, fish, beans, some types of vegetable broth, and in general for all those foods with low acidity, for which it is not safe to use the canning method. water bath.

Below is a summary table of the foods with the relative recommended preparation technique.

LOW ACID FOODS – PRESSURE CANNER	HIGH ACID FOODS – WATER BATH CANNER
BEANS	PICKLES
CARROTS	TOMATOES (WITH AN ACID)
CORN	JAMS, JELLIES, MARMALADES
POTATOES	APPLES, PEACHES, PEARS
MEAT OR POULTRY	FRUIT BUTTERS
SEAFOOD	APPLESAUCE
STOCKS AND STEWS	MEATLESS SPAGHETTI SAUCE
LOW ACID VEGETABLES	KETCHUP

PRESERVES RECIPES: JAMS, MARMALADES AND JELLIES

1. Cinnamon Blueberry Jam

Preparation Time: 5 minutes

Cooking Time: 10 minutes.

Servings: 2-3 8oz jars

INGREDIENTS

- 1 pound (about 1 quarter) fresh or frozen bloom berry.
- 3 ½ cups sugar
- 1 tbsp bottled lemon juice
- ¼ tsp ground cinnamon
- ⅛ tsp ground cloves
- 1 pouch (3 oz.) liquid fruit pectin

DIRECTIONS

1. Wash, dry and add the blueberries to a large pot along with the sugar, lemon juice, cinnamon and cloves. Bring to a boil, stirring often, over high heat. Quickly incorporate the pectin.
2. Return to a high rolling boil, stirring frequently for 1 minute.
3. Remove the pan from the heat and skim off the froth.
4. Ladle heated mixture into hot half-pint jars with a 1/4-inch headspace.
5. Remove any air bubbles, clean the rims, and adjust the lids as needed.
6. Place the jars upside down on a table covered with a tea towel.
7. Leave them to cool and check the seal of the vacuum before placing them in the pantry.

2. Apricot Habanero Jam

Preparation Time: 10 minutes

Cooking Time: 10 minutes.

Servings: 3-5 8oz jars

INGREDIENTS

- 3 pounds fresh apricots
- 6 tbsp bottled lemon juice
- 2 to 4 habanero peppers, seeded
- 1 package (1 ¾ oz.) powdered fruit pectin
- 7 ½ cups sugar

DIRECTIONS

1. Wash, pit and cut the apricots into chunks.
2. Put in a saucepan, add the lemon juice and mix well.
3. In a blender, mix the habaneros and a little portion of the apricot mixture. Process till smooth, covered.
4. Put the saucepan to the stove. Add the pectin and mix well. Bring a complete rolling boil over high heat, stirring frequently.
5. Bring to a full boil for a couple of minutes after adding the sugar.
6. Remove from heat and skim off any excess foam.
7. Fill the hot sterilized jars with the heated mixture, allowing a 1/4-inch headspace. Remove air bubbles and, if necessary, correct headspace by adding heated mixture. Clean the rims. Screw on bands until fingertip tight; center lids on jars.
8. Place the jars upside down on a table covered with a tea towel.
9. Leave them to cool and check the seal of the vacuum before placing them in the pantry.

3. *Over-The-Top Cherry Jam*

Preparation Time: 10 minutes

Cooking Time: 5 minutes.

Servings: 5-6 8oz jars

INGREDIENTS

- 2-½ pounds fresh tart cherries, pitted
- 1 package (1-¾ oz.) powdered fruit pectin
- ½ tsp butter
- ½ tsp ginger powder
- 4 ¾ cups sugar

DIRECTIONS

1. Melt the butter in a saucepan over low heat. In the meantime, wash, dry, blend the cherries and add them to the butter. Turn up the heat, mix well and add the ginger powder.
2. After a couple of minutes, add the pectin and bring it to a complete boil over high heat, stirring often.
3. After about 2 minutes, add the sugar and bring it back to the boil for about 1 minute, stirring constantly
4. Remove from heat and skim off excess foam.
5. Fill the sanitized jars with the hot jam, leaving a 1/4-inch headspace. Remove air bubbles and, if necessary, correct the headspace by adding more jam. Clean the edges of the jars and screw the caps tightly.
6. Turn the jars upside down and set them aside to cool.
7. Allow them to cool and check the vacuum before placing them in the pantry.
8. Leave to rest for two weeks at room temperature for an optimal result.

4. *Raspberry and Mint Jam*

Preparation Time: 5 minutes

Cooking Time: 60 minutes

Servings: 5-6 8oz jars

INGREDIENTS

- 5 cups crushed raspberries
- 3 cups sugar
- 20 peppermint leaves

DIRECTIONS

1. Wash and dry the raspberries and mint leaves well. Finely chop the mint.
2. Mix the raspberries, mint and sugar in a saucepan. Place the pot on the stove, bring to a boil and cook, stirring periodically, until the sugar has dissolved and the liquid begins to foam: it will take about 15 minutes.
3. Cook over low heat, stirring occasionally, for about 45 minutes. When cooked, after checking that the temperature of the jam has reached 220°F, turn off the heat and remove the foam. Pour the heated mixture into the sanitized hot jars and leave a 1/4-inch headspace. Remove any air bubbles, clean the edges and close tightly, tightening the lids as needed.
4. Place the jars in a pot with plenty of boiling water and boil vigorously for at least 15-20 minutes.
5. Carefully remove the jars from the pot and place them upside down on a table.
6. Let them cool and place them in the pantry until ready for use.

5. *Flavorful Strawberry-Rhubarb Jam*

Preparation Time: 30 minutes

Cooking Time: 5 minutes

Servings: 4-5 16oz jars

INGREDIENTS

- 4 cups fresh strawberries, crushed
- 2 cups chopped fresh rhubarb
- ¼ cup bottled lemon juice
- 1 package (1-¾ oz.) powdered fruit pectin
- 5-½ cups sugar

DIRECTIONS

1. Mix the strawberries, rhubarb and lemon juice in a saucepan. Add the pectin and mix. Bring to a boil over high heat, stirring constantly. Add the sugar and bring to a complete boil, stirring constantly. Let everything boil briskly for at least 15 minutes.
2. Remove the pot from the heat and remove the foam. Fill the previously sanitized hot jars, leaving a 1/4-inch headspace. Remove any air bubbles and, if necessary, correct the headspace with more jam.
3. Clean the edges of the jars and tightly close the lids on the jars
4. Place the jars in a pot with plenty of boiling water and boil vigorously for at least 10-15 minutes.
5. Carefully remove the jars from the pot and place them upside down on a table and let them to cool.
6. Check the seal of the vacuum before placing them in the pantry.
7. Leave to rest for two weeks for the jam to harden at room temperature for an optimal result.

6. *Pineapple-Rhubarb Jam*

Preparation Time: 35 minutes

Cooking Time: 10 minutes

Servings: 4-5 16oz jars

INGREDIENTS

- 5 cups sliced fresh or frozen rhubarb (about 12 stalks)
- 5 cups sugar
- 1 can (20 oz.) unsweetened crushed pineapple, undrained
- ½ cup water
- • 1 tsp powdered ginger
- • 1 packet (50 g) powdered fruit pectin

DIRECTIONS

1. Clean, wash and slice the rhubarb and pineapple and put the slices in a pot.
2. Add the sugar, water and ginger to the pot and put on the stove, bringing to a boil, stirring constantly.
3. Once it has boiled, cover and cook for about 20 minutes, until the rhubarb is soft, stirring periodically.
4. Add the pectin and let it dissolve completely. Remove the foam that forms, if necessary, using a skimmer.
5. When cooked, fill the jars that have already been sanitized, leaving a 1/4-inch headspace.
6. Remove air bubbles and, if necessary, correct the headspace by adding the jam. Clean the edges of the jars and screw the lids on.
7. Place the jars in a pot with plenty of boiling water and boil vigorously for at least 10-15 minutes.
8. Carefully remove the jars from the pot and place them upside down on a table.
9. Allow them to cool and check the vacuum before placing them in the pantry.

7. *Roasted Beet Jam*

Preparation Time: 15 minutes (+3 hours of cooking fresh beets)

Cooking Time: 80 minutes

Servings: 4-5 16oz jars

INGREDIENTS

- 2-½ pounds fresh or pre-cooked beets (about 10 small)
- 2 tsp lemon juice
- 1 cinnamon stick (3 inches)
- 8 whole cloves
- 3 cups sugar
- 1/3 cup of maple syrup
- 2 tbsp finely chopped crystallized ginger
- ⅛ tsp salt

DIRECTIONS

1. Boil 6 cups of lightly salted water. Wash and peel the beets, put them in the water, and cook for about 3 hours. Alternatively, you can use pre-cooked beets that are available on the market.
2. Allow to cool slightly and cut the beets into small pieces. In the meantime, sanitize the jars and lids.

3. Place cinnamon and cloves inside a spice bag and close it again.

4. In a saucepan, add the beets, sugar, maple syrup, ginger, salt, lemon juice, and the bag of spices and bring to a boil. Cook over low heat, uncovered, for about 50-60 minutes, or until the sauce has thickened. Remove the spice bag and allow it to cool slightly.

5. Fill the sanitized hot jars, leaving a 1/4-inch headspace. Remove any air bubbles and, if necessary, correct the headspace with more jam.

6. Clean the edges of the jars and tightly close the lids on the jars

7. Place the jars in a pot with plenty of boiling water and boil vigorously for at least 15 minutes.

8. Carefully remove the jars from the pot and place them upside down on a table. Let them cool for 4 hours and put them in the pantry.

8. *Ginger Pears Jam*

Preparation Time: 30 minutes

Cooking Time: 10 minutes

Servings: 4-5 16oz jars

INGREDIENTS

- 5-½ cups fresh pears (about 10 medium)
- 1 package (1-¾ oz.) powdered fruit pectin
- 2 tbsp lemon juice
- 1 grated lemon zest
- 1 tsp minced fresh ginger root
- 4 cups sugar
- 1 tsp vanilla extract

DIRECTIONS

1. Wash, peel and finely chop the pears in a bowl. Add the pectin, lemon juice, lemon zest and ginger

2. Transfer the ingredients to a saucepan and bring to a full boil over high heat, stirring often. After boiling for a couple of minutes, add the sugar and vanilla extract, mixing well.

3. Remove any excess foam and boil for another 3-4 minutes.

4. When cooked, turn off the heat and fill all the previously sanitized containers, leaving a 1/4-inch headspace.

5. Clean the top edges of the containers, then immediately cover them with the lids. Let it sit upside down on a table for about 4 hours at room temperature.

6. The jam is now available for use or can be stored in the pantry.

9. *Rhubarb Jelly*

Preparation Time: 30 minutes

Cooking Time: 10 minutes

Servings: 4-5 8oz jars

INGREDIENTS

- 5 pounds rhubarb (4-½ to 5 quarts), cut into 1-inch pieces
- 7 cups of sugar
- Red food coloring 1 to 2 drops, optional
- 2 pouches (3 oz.) liquid fruit pectin

DIRECTIONS

1. In a food processor, finely chop the rhubarb.

2. Place a sieve covered with a clean cloth on a basin, add the rhubarb on top, and cover. Leave to rest for

30 minutes and squeeze the contents of the dishcloth well into the bowl to recover the juice.

3. Fill a saucepan halfway with juice, sugar, and food coloring, if desired. Bring to a boil, stirring over high heat for a couple of minutes; then add the pectin.
4. Cook and stir for 1 minute.
5. Turn off the heat and allow it to cool for a few minutes after removing it from the heat. Remove the foam and carefully pour the heated mixture into the sanitized jars, leaving a 1/4-inch headspace. Air bubbles must be removed and the edges must be cleaned.
6. Tightly screw the lids onto the jars. Fill a saucepan halfway with boiling water and place the jars in the canning, making sure they are completely submerged. After bringing to a boil, cook for 15 minutes.
7. Remove the jars from the oven and set them aside to cool upside down.
8. Let sit upside down on a table for about 4 hours at room temperature. The jelly is now available for use or can be put in the pantry.

10. *Rhubarb Raisin Marmalade*

Preparation Time: 25 minutes

Cooking Time: 10 minutes

Servings: 4-5 8oz jars

INGREDIENTS

- 2 medium oranges
- 1 medium lemon
- 6 cups of sugar
- 6 cups of diced fresh or frozen rhubarb
- 1-½ cups of fresh or frozen strawberries
- Pinch salt
- 1 cup raisins

DIRECTIONS

1. Finely grate the peels of oranges and lemons; squeeze the juices and set them aside.
2. Put the peels, juices, sugar, rhubarb, strawberries, and salt in a saucepan and mix well. Cook until the sugar has dissolved, stirring often; wait 10 minutes and add the raisins.
3. Bring back to a full boil, then reduce to low heat and simmer for 4-5 minutes, or until the jam has thickened. Remove the saucepan from the heat and skim the foam that has formed.
4. Carefully pour the heated mixture into sanitized jars, leaving a 1/4-inch headspace. Remove air bubbles and clean the edges of the jars.
5. Close jars tightly and immerse them in a pot of boiling water. Leave to boil for 15 minutes.
6. Remove the jars from the pot and let them sit upside down on a table for about 4 hours at room temperature.
7. The marmalade is now available for use or can be put in the pantry.

11. *Blackberry Apple Jelly*

Preparation Time: 45 minutes

Cooking Time: 15 minutes

Servings: 4-5 8oz jars

INGREDIENTS

- 3 pounds blackberries
- 4 cups water
- 7 - 8 medium apples
- Bottled apple juice, optional
- 1/4 cup bottled lemon juice
- 8 cups sugar
- 2 pouches (3 oz. every) liquid fruit pectin

DIRECTIONS

1. Bring the blackberries and 2 cups of water to a boil in a large pot. Lower the heat and cook over low heat for 5 minutes.
2. Place a sieve covered with a clean cotton mat on a basin, and pour the contents of the pot over it. Cover and let the blackberry juice filter for 30

minutes, keeping the juice and discarding the pulp.

3. Remove the stalks and trimmings from the apples and discard them. Cut the apples into pieces and put them in a pot with 2 cups of water. Bring the water to a boil. Reduce heat to low and cook for 20 minutes or until apples are soft.

4. Drain the apple juice in the bowl with the blackberry juice, discarding the pulp. Put the blackberry and apple juices back into the pot after measuring them. Add water or bottled apple juice to reach 4 cups if needed. After that, add the lemon juice and sugar. Over high heat, bring to a full boil, stirring often.

5. Add the pectin and mix well. Boil for another minute, stirring often. Remove the excess foam from the heat and turn off the heat.

6. Fill the hot sterilized jars with the heated mix, leaving a 1/4-inch headspace. Clean the edges. Tightly screw the lids onto the jars.

7. Place the jars in boiling water in a saucepan, and let them boil for 15 minutes.

8. Remove from the pot and allow the jars to cool.

12. Strawberry Jam and Balsamic Vinegar

Preparation Time: 25 minutes
Cooking Time: 15 minutes
Servings: 3-4 8oz jars

INGREDIENTS

- 4 cups fresh strawberries
- 1 package (1-¾ oz.) powdered fruit pectin
- 4 Tbsps. Balsamic Vinegar
- 5 cups sugar

DIRECTIONS

1. Wash, dry, and slice the strawberries.

2. Mix the strawberries and pectin in a large saucepan; bring to a boil over high heat, stirring often.

3. Add the sugar and bring it back to a boil, stirring. When the sugar has dissolved completely, add the balsamic vinegar and mix well.

4. Remove the pan from the heat and remove any excess foam if necessary.

5. Fill the jars, leaving a 1/4-inch headspace, wipe the sides and immediately cover them with lids.

6. Place the jars in boiling water in a saucepan, and let them boil for 15 minutes.

7. Remove from the pot and allow the jars to cool. Let stand upside down for 24 hours at room temperature.

The jam is now ready for use or for storing in the pantry.

13. Luscious Blueberry Jam

Preparation Time: 20 minutes
Cooking Time: 10 minutes
Servings: 3-4 8oz jars

INGREDIENTS

- 8 cups fresh blueberries, mashed
- 2 tbsps. lemon juice
- 1 package (1-¾ oz.) powdered fruit pectin
- 7 cups sugar

DIRECTIONS

1. To make blueberry jam, let boil the jars and lids in boiling water for 15 minutes. Thoroughly dry the rinsed items.

2. Then, transfer mashed blueberries into a saucepan and mix them with lemon juice and pectin. Bring to a full rolling boil over high heat, stirring frequently.

3. Add the sugar and bring to a full rolling boil again for 1 minute while continually stirring.

4. Remove from heat and skim off foam.

5. Pour the jam into sanitized jars leaving a 1/4-inch headspace.
6. Place the jars in boiling water in a saucepan, and let them boil for 15 minutes.
7. Remove from the pot and allow the jars to cool.
8. The jam is now ready for use or for storing in the pantry.

14. Lemon-Rosemary Marmalade

Preparation Time: 10 minutes
Cooking Time: 130 minutes
Servings: 3-4 8oz jars

INGREDIENTS

- 7 medium lemons (about 2 pounds)
- ½ tsp baking soda, divided
- 9 cups water
- 4 cups sugar
- 4 tsp minced fresh rosemary
- 2 drops yellow food coloring, optional

DIRECTIONS

1. Peel the lemons into wide strips with a vegetable peeler. Remove the white stone from the skins with a sharp knife. Cut the peels into a 2 cm strip. Set the fruit aside.
2. In a small bowl, put the lemon strips, add the baking soda, and 2 cups of boiling water. Leave the skins to infuse for 10 minutes, then drain, rinse and set the skins aside.
3. Cut the top and bottom of the lemons, remove the excess white part, and cut them into thin slices. Meanwhile, bring a saucepan with 2 cups of water to a boil and add the sliced lemons.
4. Reduce over medium heat for 10 minutes, then strain the remaining liquid and pour it into a saucepan, squeezing the lemons and removing the solid parts.
5. Add 5 cups of water and lemon zests and bring the pot to a boil.
6. Simmer over low heat, uncovered, for about 5 minutes. Then add the sugar and bring it back to the boil.
7. Continue cooking, stirring periodically, for about 40-50 minutes or until the jam has thickened.
8. Remove from the heat, add the rosemary and food coloring and pour into the previously sanitized jars, leaving a 1/4-inch headspace. Clean the edges of the jars and screw the lids tight.
9. Immerse the jars in a pot full of boiling water, making sure they are completely covered. Bring to a boil for 10-15 minutes.
10. Remove the jars from the pot and let them sit upside down on a table for about 4 hours at room temperature.
11. The marmalade is now ready to be used or to be stored in the pantry.

15. Red Onion Apricot Jelly

Preparation Time: 5 minutes (+4 hours to rest)
Cooking Time: 10 minutes
Servings: 3-4 4oz jars

INGREDIENTS

- 1 ½ cups white vinegar 5% acidity
- 1 cup finely chopped dried apricots
- 3 cups sugar
- ½ cup finely chopped red bell pepper
- ½ cup finely chopped red onion
- 3 oz Ball Liquid Pectin

DIRECTIONS

1. In a medium bowl, mix the apricots and vinegar. Cover and set aside for at least 4 hours in the refrigerator.
2. In a saucepan, combine the apricot mixture, sugar, pepper, and red onion. Bring to a boil over high heat, and stir regularly.
3. Add the pectin, boil for 1 minute, stirring constantly.

4. Remove the pot from the heat. If necessary, remove any foam that may have formed.
5. Fill the sanitized jars with the hot gelatin, leaving a 1/4-inch headspace. Clean the rim of the jars and close the lids tightly.
6. In a pot of boiling water, immerse the jars and let them boil over high heat for 10-15 minutes.
7. Remove the jars from the heat, carefully check the tightness of the lids, and set them aside for 5 hours, upside down.
8. The jam is now ready to be used or to be stored in the pantry.

16. *Easy Blood Orange Marmalade*
Preparation Time: 20 minutes
Cooking Time: 10 minutes
Servings: 3-4 8oz jars
INGREDIENTS

- 4 cups blood oranges, diced (6-10 medium oranges)
- 2 ¼ cups sugar
- ¾ cup water
- 1.75-oz. powdered fruit pectin
- 2 tbsps. fresh lemon juice
- 2 tsps. fresh ginger, grated, optional

DIRECTIONS
1. Wash the oranges thoroughly before drying them with a clean cloth. Using a tiny zester, remove the colorful zest from 6 oranges.
2. The peel should next be sliced into tiny slivers or coarsely chopped. Every orange should have the top and bottom cut off.
3. Then, take out all the white pith that's left.
4. Remove the white core from the center of every orange by cutting it in half.
5. Chop the remaining fruit coarsely, retaining any juice and tossing out any seeds.
6. In a large mixing bowl, measure out 4 cups of oranges. Mix the zest, diced oranges, juice, ginger, and sugar in a big saucepan on the stove.
7. Stir the mixture well. Cook for another 2 minutes if it's still grainy. Stir everything together thoroughly. At this stage, most of the sugar should have dissolved. Bring the liquid to a full boil for 1 minute and put it aside.
8. In a medium saucepan, mix the water and pectin. On high heat, bring to a full rolling boil, stirring for 1 minute.
9. Toss the fruit mixture with the heated pectin and lemon juice and whisk for 3 minutes.
10. Fill the sanitized jars with the hot marmalade, leaving 1/4-inch headspace. Clean the rim of the jars and close the lids tightly.
11. Place the jars in boiling water in a saucepan, and let them boil for 15 minutes.
12. Remove from the pot and allow the jars to cool.
13. Allow them to stand for 24 hours at room temperature.
14. Now the marmalade is ready to use.

17. *Pink Grapefruit Marmalade*
Preparation Time: 10 minutes
Cooking Time: 20 minutes
Servings: 4-5 8oz jars
INGREDIENTS

- 2 pounds pink grapefruits
- 2 ½ cups sugar
- 2 ½ cups brown sugar
- 2 tbsps. fresh lemon juice
- ¾ cup water
- 1.75-oz. powdered fruit pectin

DIRECTIONS
1. Wash the pink grapefruits thoroughly before drying them with a clean cloth. Using a tiny zester, remove the colorful zest from 6 oranges.

2. The peel should next be sliced into tiny slivers or coarsely chopped. Every grapefruit should have the top and bottom cut off.
3. Then, take out all the white pith that's left.
4. Remove the white core from the center of every pink grapefruit by cutting it in half.
5. Chop the remaining fruit coarsely, retaining any juice and tossing out any seeds.
6. In a large mixing bowl, add the pink grapefruits with their juices, the zest, the lemon juice and sugar in a big saucepan on the stove.
7. Stir the mixture well. Cook for another 2 minutes if it's still grainy. Stir everything together thoroughly. At this stage, most of the sugar should have dissolved. Bring the liquid to a full boil for 1 minute and put it aside.
8. In a medium saucepan, mix water and pectin. On high heat, bring to a full rolling boil, stirring for 1 minute.
9. Toss the fruit mixture with the heated pectin and whisk for 3 minutes.
10. Fill the sanitized jars with the hot marmalade, leaving 1/4-inch headspace. Clean the rim of the jars and close the lids tightly.
11. Place the jars in boiling water in a saucepan, and let them boil for 15 minutes.
12. Remove from the pot and allow the jars to cool. Allow them to stand for 24 hours at room temperature.
13. Now the marmalade is ready to use.

18. Apricot Amaretto Jam
Preparation Time: 15 minutes
Cooking Time: 10 minutes
Servings: 6-8 8oz jars

INGREDIENTS

- 4 ¼ cups peeled, crushed apricots
- ¼ cup lemon juice
- 6¼ cups sugar, divided
- 1 package powdered fruit pectin
- ½ tsp. unsalted butter
- 1/3 cup amaretto

DIRECTIONS

1. Mix in a saucepan the lemon juice and the apricots. Add pectin and ¼ cup sugar.
2. Bring to a boil over high heat, and stir regularly.
3. Add butter and bring again to a full boil over medium-high heat, stirring constantly.
4. Mix in the remaining sugar and let boil 1-2 minutes, stirring constantly.
5. Remove from heat and wish in amaretto.
6. Let the jam sit for 5 minutes, stirring occasionally.
7. Divide the hot mixture between the jars, leaving a ¼-inch headspace. Wipe the rims carefully. Place tops on jars and screw on bands until fingertip tight.
8. Place the jars in boiling water in a saucepan, and let them boil for 15 minutes.
9. Remove from the pot and allow the jars to cool upside down for 24 hours at room temperature.
10. The jam is now ready for use or for storing in the pantry.

19. Raspberry Peach Jam
Preparation Time: 5 minutes
Cooking Time: 15 minutes
Servings: 3-4 8oz jars
INGREDIENTS

- 2 2/3 cups peeled, chopped peaches
- 1½ cups crushed raspberries
- 4 cups sugar
- 1½ tsp lemon juice

DIRECTIONS

1. In a saucepan, combine peaches, raspberries, lemon juice and sugar.
2. Let cook over medium-low heat, stirring until the sugar has dissolved and the mixture is bubbly, about 10 minutes.
3. Bring to a full boil for 35-40 minutes, stirring constantly, until mixture thickens.
4. Remove from heat and skim off foam.
5. Carefully scoop the hot mixture into hot sterilized jars, leaving ¼-inch headspace. Remove air bubbles. Wipe the rims carefully. Place tops on jars and screw on bands until fingertip tight.
6. Place jars into canner with boiling water, ensuring that they are completely covered with water. Let boil for 15 minutes.
7. Remove jars and cool upside down.
8. Now the jam is ready for use or to be put into place.

20. *Blueberry Cinnamon Jam*

Preparation Time: 15 minutes

Cooking Time: 10 minutes

Servings: 6-8 8oz jars

INGREDIENTS

- 8 cups fresh blueberries
- 6 cups sugar
- 3 tbsp lemon juice
- 2 tsp ground cinnamon
- 2 tsp grated lemon zest
- ½ tsp ground nutmeg
- 2 (3 oz) pouches liquid fruit pectin

DIRECTIONS

1. Crush the blueberries in a food processor and transfer them into a casserole.
2. Stir in the lemon juice, sugar, cinnamon, nutmeg, and lemon zest.
3. Bring to a rolling boil over high heat, stirring constantly.
4. Add in pectin. Boil for 3 minute, stirring constantly.
5. Remove from the heat, skim off foam.
6. Scoop the hot mixture in hot sterilized half-pint jars, leaving ¼-inch space of the top. Remove air bubbles. Wipe the rims carefully. Place tops on jars and screw on bands until fingertip tight.
7. Place jars into canner with boiling water, ensuring that they are completely covered with water. Let boil for 10 minutes.
8. Remove jars and let them cool upside down.
9. Now the jam is ready for use or to be put into place.

21. *Carrot Pineapple Pearl Jam*

Preparation Time: 45 minutes

Cooking Time: 5 minutes

Servings: 7-8 8oz jars

INGREDIENTS

- 20 oz crushed pineapple, undrained
- 1½ cups peeled, shredded carrots
- 1½ cups ripe, peeled, chopped pears
- 3 tbsps. lemon juice
- 1 tsp ground cinnamon
- ¼ tsp ground cloves
- ¼ tsp ground nutmeg
- 1 package powdered fruit pectin
- 6½ cups sugar

DIRECTIONS

1. Wash, dry and chop pineapples, carrots and pears and combine them in a saucepan.
2. Bring to a boil, stirring constantly.
3. Reduce heat and simmer, covered, until pears are tender, 15-20 minutes, stirring occasionally.
4. Add pectin. Bring to a full boil, stirring constantly.
5. Stir in sugar. Boil and stir for 1 minute.
6. Remove from heat and skim off foam.
7. Scoop the hot mixture in hot sterilized half-pint jars, leaving ¼-inch space of the top. Remove air bubbles and if necessary, adjust headspace by adding hot mixture.

8. Wipe the rims carefully. Place tops on jars and screw on bands until fingertip tight.
9. Place jars into canner with boiling water, ensuring that they are completely covered with water. Let boil for 10-15 minutes. Remove jars and let them cool upside down.
10. Now the jam is ready for use or to be put into place.

22. Green Tomato Jam

Preparation Time: 5 minutes
Cooking Time: 30 minutes
Servings: 3-4 8oz jars
INGREDIENTS

- 3 cups pureed green tomatoes
- 2 cups sugar
- ½ tsp cinnamon grounded, optional
- 3 Tbsps. lemon juice
- Salt to taste

DIRECTIONS

1. In a large saucepan, bring sugar and tomatoes to a boil.
2. Reduce heat and let simmer, uncovered, for 20 minutes, then add cinnamon, salt and lemon juice, stirring constantly, for 10 minutes. Use a jelly thermometer and boil until mixture reaches the 220°F.
3. Remove from the heat and skim off any foam.
4. Scoop the hot mixture in hot sterilized half-pint jars, leaving ¼-inch space of the top. Remove air bubbles and if necessary, adjust headspace by adding hot mixture. Wipe the rims carefully.
5. Place jars into canner with boiling water, ensuring that they are completely covered with water.
6. Let boil for 10-15 minutes.
7. Let cool upside down for 24 hour
8. The jam is now ready for use or for storing in the pantry.

23. Pineapple Rhubarb Jam

Preparation Time: 15 minutes
Cooking Time: 30 minutes
Servings: 7-8 8oz jars
INGREDIENTS

- 5 cups sliced fresh rhubarb
- 5 cups sugar
- 1 can (20 oz) unsweetened crushed pineapple, undrained
- ¼ cup water
- 1 (6 oz) package unflavored gelatin

DIRECTIONS

1. In saucepan combine pineapple, rhubarb, sugar, and water. Bring to a boil.
2. Reduce heat and simmer, uncovered, for 20 minutes or until rhubarb is broken down, stirring occasionally.
3. Add gelatin and stir until dissolved and bring to a boil again. Use a jelly thermometer and boil until mixture reaches the 220°F.
4. Remove from heat and skim off foam.
5. Scoop the hot mixture in hot sterilized half-pint jars, leaving ¼-inch space of the top. Remove air bubbles and if necessary, adjust headspace by adding hot mixture. Wipe the rims carefully. Place tops on jars and screw on bands until fingertip tight.
6. Place jars into canner with boiling water, ensuring that they are completely covered with water.
7. Let boil for 10-15 minutes.
8. Let cool upside down for 24 hour
9. The jam is now ready for use or for storing in the pantry.

24. Plum Orange Jam

Preparation Time: 30 minutes
Cooking Time: 5 minutes
Servings: 8-10 8oz jars

INGREDIENTS

- 10 cups chopped plums, skinless
- 1 cup orange juice
- 1 package (1,5 oz) powdered fruit pectin
- 3 cups sugar
- 3 tbsp grated orange zest
- 1½ tsp ground cinnamon

DIRECTIONS

1. Add orange juice and plums in a saucepan and bring to a boil.
2. Reduce heat and simmer, covered, 5-7 minutes or until softened, stirring occasionally.
3. Stir in pectin. Bring to a rolling boil, stirring constantly.
4. Add cinnamon, sugar, and orange zest. Let boil for 2 minutes, stirring until sugar completely dissolves. Use a jelly thermometer and boil until mixture reaches the 220°F.
5. Remove from heat and skim off foam.
6. Scoop the hot mixture in hot sanitized half-pint jars, leaving ¼-inch space of the top. Remove air bubbles and if necessary, adjust headspace by adding hot mixture. Wipe the rims carefully. Place tops on jars and screw on bands until fingertip tight.
7. Place jars into canner with boiling water, ensuring that they are completely covered with water. Let boil for 15 minutes.
8. Let cool upside down for 24 hour
9. The jam is now ready for use or for storing in the pantry.

25. Pina Colada Zucchini Jam

Preparation Time: 15 minutes
Cooking Time: 20 minutes
Servings: 6-7 8oz jars

INGREDIENTS

- 6 cups peeled, shredded zucchini
- 1 can (8oz) crushed pineapple, undrained
- 6 cups sugar
- ¼ cup lime juice
- 2 packages (3 oz) pineapple gelatin
- 1 tsp rum extract

DIRECTIONS

1. In a saucepan, combine zucchini, pineapple, lime juice, and sugar. Bring to a boil and cook for 10 minutes, stirring constantly.
2. Remove from heat and stir in rum extract and gelatin until gelatin is dissolved. Bring to a boil and cook 2 minutes, then wait until mixture reaches the 220°F.
3. Remove from heat and skim off foam.
4. Scoop the hot mixture in hot sterilized half-pint jars, leaving ¼-inch space of the top. Remove air bubbles and if necessary, adjust headspace by adding hot mixture.
5. Wipe the rims carefully and place tops on jars and screw on bands until fingertip tight.
6. Place jars into canner with boiling water, ensuring that they are completely covered with water. Let boil for 10 minutes.

7. Let cool upside down for 24 hour
8. The jam is now ready for use or for storing in the pantry.

26. Strawberry Mint Jam

Preparation Time: 30 minutes

Cooking Time: 10 minutes

Servings: 5-6 8oz jars

INGREDIENTS

- 4 cups fresh, washed, mashed strawberries
- 5½ cups sugar
- 1 cup light corn syrup
- ¼ cup lemon juice
- ¾ cup lukewarm water
- 1 tsp. mint, minced
- 1 package powdered fruit pectin

DIRECTIONS

1. Place strawberries in a large saucepan. Add lemon juice, sugar, and corn syrup. Bring to a rolling boil for 10 minutes.
2. Put in a pan pectin and water, and mix well. Combine to strawberries mixture and bring to a rolling boil and boil for 2 minutes, stirring constantly, until mixture reaches the 220°F.
3. Remove from heat and skim off foam.
4. Pour into sterilized jars, leaving ¼-inch headspace. Wipe the rims carefully and place tops on jars and screw on bands until fingertip tight.
5. Place jars into canner with boiling water, ensuring that they are completely covered with water. Let boil for 10-15 minutes.
6. Let cool upside down for 24 hour
7. The jam is now ready for use or for storing in the pantry.

27. Caramel Apple Jam

Preparation Time: 30 minutes

Cooking Time: 10 minutes

Servings: 7-8 8oz jars

INGREDIENTS

- 6 cups fresh, peeled, diced apples
- ½ cup water
- ½ tsp butter
- ½ tsp ground cinnamon
- ¼ tsp ground nutmeg
- 1 package powdered fruit pectin
- 3 cups sugar
- 2 cups brown sugar

DIRECTIONS

1. In a saucepan, combine the apples, butter, water, nutmeg, and cinnamon. Cook, stirring, over low heat for 30 minutes, or until apples are tender.
2. Stir in pectin and sugars and bring to a rolling boil for 3 minutes.
3. Remove from heat when the mixture will reach the 220°F, and skim off foam.
4. Scoop the hot mixture in hot sterilized half-pint jars, leaving ¼-inch space of the top. Remove air bubbles and if necessary, adjust headspace by adding hot mixture. Wipe the rims carefully. Place tops on jars and screw on bands until fingertip tight
5. Place jars into canner with boiling water, ensuring that they are completely covered with water.
6. Let boil for 10-15 minutes.
7. Let cool upside down for 24 hour
8. The jam is now ready for use or for storing in the pantry.

28. Christmas Raspberries Jam

Preparation Time: 25 minutes

Cooking Time: 10 minutes

Servings: 7-8 16oz jars

INGREDIENTS

- 2½ lbs. frozen unsweetened raspberries, thawed or fresh raspberries, hulled
- 1 lb. fresh or frozen cranberries, thawed
- 1 1/4 tsps. ground cinnamon
- 5 lbs. sugar
- 2 (3 oz) pouches liquid fruit pectin

DIRECTIONS

1. Blend cranberries and raspberries in a food processor until smooth, then pour into a casserole.
2. Add sugar and bring to a boil. Let boil for 1 minute.
3. Stir in pectin and return to a boil. Boil for 1 minute, stirring constantly.
4. Remove from heat when the mixture will reach the 220°F, and skim off foam.
5. Scoop the hot mixture in hot sterilized half-pint jars, leaving ¼-inch space of the top. Remove air bubbles and if necessary, adjust headspace by adding hot mixture. Wipe the rims carefully. Place tops on jars and screw on bands until fingertip tight
6. Place jars into canner with boiling water, ensuring that they are completely covered with water. Let boil for 15 minutes.
7. Remove jars and let cool upside down.
8. The jam is now ready for use or for storing in the pantry.

29. Candy Apple Jelly

Preparation Time: 10 minutes

Cooking Time: 5 minutes

Servings: 6-7 8oz jars

INGREDIENTS

- 4 cups apple juice
- ½ cup Red Hots candy
- 1 package powdered fruit pectin
- 4½ cups sugar

DIRECTIONS

1. In a large saucepan, combine candies, apple juice, and pectin. Bring to a rolling boil, stirring constantly.
2. Stir in sugar and let boil, stirring, for 1 minute.
3. Remove from heat when the mixture will reach the 220°F, and skim off foam.
4. Scoop the hot mixture in hot sterilized half-pint jars, leaving ¼-inch space of the top. Remove air bubbles and if necessary, adjust headspace by adding hot mixture. Wipe the rims carefully. Place tops on jars and screw on bands until fingertip tight.
5. Place jars into canner with boiling water, ensuring that they are completely covered with water. Let boil for 15 minutes.
6. Remove jars and let cool upside down.
7. The jelly is now ready for use or for storing in the pantry

30. Lime Mint Jelly

Preparation Time: 10 minutes

Cooking Time: 10 minutes

Servings: 5-6 8oz jars

INGREDIENTS

- 4 cups sugar
- 1¾ cups water
- ¾ cup lime juice
- 3 drops green food coloring
- 3 oz liquid fruit pectin
- 3 tbsp chopped fresh mint leaves
- ¼ cup grated lime zest

DIRECTIONS

1. In a large saucepan, mix lime juice, sugar, water, and food coloring. Bring to a rolling boil, stirring constantly.
2. Stir in lime zest, pectin, and mint. Continue boiling for 2 minutes, stirring constantly.

Canning and Preserving Food for Beginners

3. Remove from heat when the mixture will reach the 220°F, and skim off foam.
4. Scoop the hot mixture in hot sterilized half-pint jars, leaving ¼-inch space of the top. Remove air bubbles and if necessary, adjust headspace by adding hot mixture. Wipe the rims carefully. Place tops on jars and screw on bands until fingertip tight.
5. Place jars into canner with boiling water, ensuring that they are completely covered with water. Let boil for 15 minutes.
6. Remove jars and let cool upside down.
7. The jelly is now ready for use or for storing in the pantry.

31. Watermelon Jelly

Preparation Time: 25 minutes
Cooking Time: 10 minutes
Servings: 5-6 8oz jars
INGREDIENTS

- 6 cups chopped, seeded watermelon
- 5 cups sugar
- 1/2 cup lemon juice
- 2 drops red food coloring
- 3 oz liquid fruit pectin

DIRECTIONS

1. Blend watermelon in a food processor until pureed. Place pureed watermelon in a cheesecloth-lined strainer, with a bowl underneath to capture liquid. Let stand 10 minutes until liquid measures 2 cups.
2. Discard watermelon pulp from cheesecloth and place the liquid in a large saucepan.
3. Stir in sugar, lemon juice, and food coloring. Bring to a boil, stirring constantly.
4. Add pectin. Continue boiling for 1 minute, stirring constantly.
5. Remove from heat when the mixture will reach the 220°F, and skim off foam
6. Scoop the hot mixture in hot sterilized half-pint jars, leaving ¼-inch space of the top. Remove air bubbles and if necessary, adjust headspace by adding hot mixture. Wipe the rims carefully. Place tops on jars and screw on bands until fingertip tight
7. Place jars into canner with boiling water, ensuring that they are completely covered with water. Let boil for 15 minute.
8. Remove jars and cool.

32. Cucumber Jelly

Preparation Time: 15 minutes
Cooking Time: 10 minutes
Servings: 7-8 8oz jars
INGREDIENTS

- 2 ½ cups cucumber juice, strained
- 6 cups sugar
- 1 cup vinegar
- Seeds scraped from one vanilla bean
- 3 oz. liquid fruit pectin

DIRECTIONS

1. Mix cucumber juice, sugar and vanilla seeds in a pot and bring to a rolling boil, stirring constantly for 2 minutes, then remove from heat.
2. Stir in the vinegar and pectin, then return to a boil. Boil and stir for 1-2 minutes.
3. Remove from heat when the mixture will reach the 220°F, and skim off foam
4. Scoop jelly into hot sterilized half-pint jars, leaving ¼ inch headspace. Remove air bubbles and if necessary, adjust headspace by adding hot mixture. Wipe the rims carefully. Place tops on jars and screw on bands until fingertip tight.
5. Place jars into canner with boiling water, ensuring that they are completely covered with water. Let boil for 15 minutes.

6. Remove jars and let cool upside down.
7. The jelly is now ready for use or for storing in the pantry.

33. Three-Fruit Marmalade
Preparation Time: 15 Minutes

Cooking Time: 15 Minutes

Servings: 7-8 8oz jars

INGREDIENTS

- 2 cups fresh peaches
- 2 cups fresh pears
- 5 cups sugar
- 1 Medium orange
- 1 ¾ oz. powdered fruit pectin

DIRECTIONS

1. Wash, dry and chop the peaches and the pears and set them aside.
2. Wash, dry and grate the orange zest. Peel and slice the orange fruit. Put the orange slices and zest in a casserole.
3. Add peaches, pears and add the pectin; bring it to a full boil on high heat.
4. Stir often and add the sugar. Return to a complete rolling boil, and stir for 2 minutes.
5. Remove from heat when the mixture will reach the 220°F, and skim off foam.
6. Ladle the hot marmalade into the sterilized half-pint jars with ¼- inch headspace. Remove the air bubbles, adjusting headspace by pouring the hot mixture if needed.
7. Wipe the rims with cloth, center the lids on the jars and screw on band up to fingertip tight.
8. Place the jars in the canner with enough simmering water to cover the entire jars.
9. Bring water to a full rolling boil and process for 15 minutes.
10. Remove the jars from the canner and let it cool.
11. Serve or store in the pantry!

34. Orange Pineapple Marmalade
Preparation Time: 15 Minutes

Cooking Time: 20 Minutes

Servings: 2-3 8oz jars

INGREDIENTS

- 4 cups drained crushed pineapple
- 2 Medium oranges
- 1 tsp ground ginger
- 2 Tablespoons lemon juice
- 4 cups sugar

DIRECTIONS

1. Wash the jars and lids and sterilize them with boiling water. Dry and set them aside.
2. Scrape the orange zest and set it aside. Peel off the orange, discarding the white membrane, slice the flesh and remove the seeds.
3. Combine in a food processor the orange slices and zest. Cover and pulse until the orange turns into small bits.
4. Place lemon juice, orange mixture, sugar, and pineapple in a casserole and bring it to the rolling boil for 2 minutes.
5. Stir and heat until bubbly, add ginger and cook for another 4 minutes.
6. Remove from heat when the mixture will reach the 220°F, and skim off foam.
7. Ladle the hot marmalade into the jars, leaving a ¼-inch headspace.
8. Place jars into canner with boiling water, ensuring that they are completely covered with water. Let boil for 15 minutes.
9. Remove jars and let cool upside down.
10. The jelly is now ready for use or for storing in the pantry.

35. Pear Pineapple Jam

Preparation Time: 15 Minutes
Cooking Time: 10 Minutes
Servings: 2-3 8oz jars
INGREDIENTS

- 1 cup undrained unsweetened crushed pineapple
- 4-5 medium pears
- 2 Tbsps. lemon juice
- 5 ½ cups sugar
- ½ cup orange juice
- 1 ¾ oz. powdered fruit pectin
- 1 Tbsp. grated orange zest

DIRECTIONS

1. Wash, dry and chop pears. Place them in a food processor in batches, and cover and pulse until smooth.
2. Measure out the pears to come up with 1 ½ cups, set aside.
3. Place in a casserole lemon juice, pear puree, orange zest, orange juice and pineapple.
4. Add pectin to the fruit mixture and bring it to a complete rolling boil on high heat. Stir often and add the sugar. Bring all to rolling boil for 1 minute, stirring frequently.
5. Remove from heat when the mixture will reach the 220°F, and skim off foam.
6. Ladle the hot jam into the jars, leaving a ¼-inch headspace.
7. Place jars into canner with boiling water, ensuring that they are completely covered with water. Let boil for 15 minutes.
8. Remove jars and let cool upside down.
9. The jam is now ready for use or for storing in the pantry!

36. Tomato Lemon Marmalade

Preparation Time: 40 Minutes
Cooking Time: 60 Minutes
Servings: 8-9 8oz jars
INGREDIENTS

- 4 cups tart apples, chopped and peeled
- 5 medium ripe tomatoes
- 6 cups sugar
- 2 medium lemons, seeded and finely chopped
- 8 Whole cloves
- 2 ¼ tsps. ground ginger

DIRECTIONS

1. Wash, dry, peel and chop tomatoes.
2. Place tomatoes in a colander to drain for 30 minutes before placing them in a saucepan.
3. Add the lemons and apples, cook for 15 minutes on moderate heat, stirring often.
4. Stir in ginger and sugar. Place cloves in cheesecloth bag and tie; add to the mixture.
5. Bring the mixture to a complete rolling boil; stirring often and cook until the sugar has melted. Simmer on low for 40 minutes, stirring frequently. After that, remove from heat when the mixture will reach the 220°F, and skim off foam.
6. Discard the spice bag and ladle the hot marmalade into the sterilized hot half-pint jars with a 1/4-inch headspace.

7. Remove the air bubbles with a plastic knife, adjusting the headspace and wipe the rims, center the lids on the jars and screw them on the bands.
8. Place the jars into the canner with simmering water, just enough to cover it; bring to a full boil and process it for 15 minutes.
9. Remove the jars and place them upside down on a padded work surface. Let it cool.
10. Enjoy!

37. Mixed Citrus Marmalade

Preparation Time: 15 Minutes
Cooking Time: 60 Minutes (+overnight Chilling)
Servings: 8-10 8oz jars
INGREDIENTS

- 1 lb. fresh oranges,
- 1 lb. fresh grapefruits
- 1 lb. fresh lemons
- 8 cups sugar
- 2 Quarts water

DIRECTIONS

1. Wash, dry, and peel oranges, grapefruits and lemons, then slice them and remove their seeds.
2. Combine all fruits in a large mixing bowl with water; cover and chill overnight.
3. Place the fruit mixture in a casserole, and bring to a complete rolling boil and cook on low heat for about 10-15 minutes, or until they will be tender.
4. Add the sugar, stir, and boil. Cook for 45 minutes, stirring often until thickened. Remove from heat when the mixture will reach the 220°F, and skim off foam.
5. Slowly ladle the hot marmalade into sterilized half-pint jars with a ¼- inch headspace.
6. Remove the air bubbles using a plastic spoon, wipe the rims, and adjust the lids.
7. Process for 15 minutes in a canner filled with boiling water.
8. Remove jars and let cool upside down.
9. The marmalade is now ready for use or for storing in the pantry.

38. Blackberries Orange Marmalade

Preparation Time: 15 Minutes
Cooking Time: 30 Minutes
Servings: 8-10 8oz jars
INGREDIENTS

- 2 medium lemons
- 2 medium oranges
- ⅛ tsp. baking soda
- 6 oz. liquid fruit pectin
- ½ cup water
- 7 cups sugar
- 1 quart crushed ripe blackberries

DIRECTIONS

1. Wash, dry and remove the zest of lemons and oranges. Remove the fruits' white membrane and discard them.
2. Chop the fruit zest and put them in a saucepan. Pour ½ cup of water and add the baking soda. Cover and boil, reduce the heat and simmer for 10 minutes.

3. Slice the lemons and oranges, reserve the juice and add it to the saucepan. Cover and simmer on low heat for 20 minutes. Stir in blackberries and let cook for 5 minutes.
4. Measure out the fruit to come up with 4 cups and place it in the pan, discarding the excess.
5. Stir in sugar and boil it uncovered, for 5 minutes. Add pectin and boil it for 1 minute, stirring frequently.
6. Remove from heat when the mixture will reach the 220°F, and skim off foam.
7. Cautiously ladle the hot marmalade into the jars, leaving an allowance of ¼-inch headspace.
8. Remove any air bubbles with a plastic knife, adjusting the headspace.
9. Wipe the rims, center the lids on the jars, and screw on the bands.
10. Place the jars in boiling water in the canner, boil, and process for 15 minutes.
11. Remove the jars and let cool.

39. *Jalapeño Pepper Jelly*

Preparation Time: 10 Minutes
Cooking Time: 20 Minutes
Servings: 5-6 8oz jars

INGREDIENTS

- 2 cups green bell peppers
- 1/3 cup jalapeño peppers
- 4 cups sugar
- 1 cup cider vinegar
- 6 oz. powder fruit pectin

DIRECTIONS

1. Wash, dry and chop finely the green bell and jalapeño peppers.
2. Mix all the ingredients together, except pectin, in a large saucepan, and let it boil for about 5 minutes.
3. Add pectin and bring to rolling boil for 1 minute, stirring frequently.
4. Remove from heat when the mixture will reach the 220°F, and skim off foam.
5. Slowly ladle the hot jelly into sterilized half-pint jars with a ¼- inch headspace.
6. Remove the air bubbles using a plastic spoon, wipe the rims, and adjust the lids.
7. Process for 15 minutes in a canner filled with boiling water.
8. Remove jars and let cool upside down.
9. The jelly is now ready for use or for storing in the pantry.

40. *Just Jalapeño Blackberry Jelly*

Preparation Time: 10 minutes
Cooking Time: 40 minutes
Servings: 5-6 8oz jars

INGREDIENTS

- 4 cups blackberry juice
- 1 red jalapeño pepper, minced
- 1 Green jalapeño pepper, minced
- 4 cups white sugar
- 1.75 oz. powdered pectin

DIRECTIONS

1. In a bowl, mix in the sugar (½ cup) and pectin crystals.
2. To make the jelly, take a heavy saucepan; mix in the jalapeño (both), pectin mixture and blackberry juice.
3. Keep the heat on a medium setting; let the mixture heat for 5 minutes.
4. Then mix in the rest of sugar (3 ½ cups) and continue heating for 5 minutes, or until it dissolves completely.
5. Remove from heat when the mixture will reach the 220°F, and skim off foam.

6. using a spoon.
7. Then take the pre-sterilized jars; place the blackberry jelly mixture into the jars.
8. Keep a ¼- inch headspace from the top.
9. Use a damp cloth to clean jar rims, then close them with the lid and band.
10. Afterwards, place the jars in the canning pot filled with boiling water.
11. Set the canning timer at 10- 15 minutes; adjust the canning time based on your altitude level.
12. After the canning time is over, take out the hot jars, wipe them and take off the bands.
13. Store in a dry, cool place and enjoy the delicious jelly!

41. *Savory Ruby Port Vinegar Jelly*
Preparation Time: 10 Minutes
Cooking Time: 30 Minutes
Servings: 3-4 8oz jars
INGREDIENTS

- ¼ cup orange zest, shredded
- 1/3 cup balsamic vinegar
- 3 cups sugar
- 3 oz. liquid fruit pectin
- 2 cups ruby port

DIRECTIONS

1. To make the jelly, take a heavy saucepan; mix in the orange zest and vinegar.
2. Keep the heat on a medium setting; let the mixture boil for about 4-5 minutes.
3. Remove the zest from the hot mixture.
4. Place the vinegar mixture back in the saucepan and add the port and sugar.
5. Keep the heat on a high setting and bring to rolling boil; then add in the pectin and let continue boiling for about 1-2 more minutes.
6. Remove from heat when the mixture will reach the 220°F, and skim off foam.
7. using a spoon.
8. After that, slowly ladle the hot jelly into the sanitized jars.
9. Keep a ¼- inch margin from the top.
10. Use a damp cloth to clean jar rims; then close them with the lid and band.
11. Afterwards, place the jars in the canning pot filled with water.
12. Set the canning timer at 10-15 minutes; adjust the canning time based on your altitude level.
13. After the canning time is over, take out the hot jars, wipe them and let cool upside down.
14. Store in a dry, cool area and enjoy the delicious jelly.

42. *Rosy Jelly Retreat*
Preparation Time: 10 Minutes
Cooking Time: 25 Minutes
Servings: 3-4 8oz jars
INGREDIENTS

- 2 cups white sugar
- ¾ cup grape juice
- 2 cups cranberry juice
- 2 oz. dry pectin

DIRECTIONS

1. To make the jelly, take a heavy cooking pot; mix in the pectin and both grape and cranberry juices in it.
2. Keep the heat on a medium setting; bring to rolling boil for 5 minutes.
3. Mix in the sugar, stir the mixture and let it dissolve completely.
4. Remove from heat when the mixture will reach the 220°F, and skim off foam, using a spoon.
5. After that, slowly ladle the hot jelly into the sanitized jars.

6. Keep a ¼- inch margin from the top.
7. Use a damp cloth to clean jar rims; then close them with the lid and band.
8. Afterwards, place the jars in the canning pot filled with water.
9. Set the canning timer at 10-15 minutes; adjust the canning time based on your altitude level.
10. After the canning time is over, remove jars and let cool upside down.
11. The jelly is now ready for use or for storing in the pantry.
12. Store in a dry, cool area and enjoy the delicious grape jelly!

WATER BATH CANNING RECIPES: VEGETABLE PICKLES

43. Bread and Butter Pickles

Preparation Time: 30 minutes

Cooking Time: 20 minutes

Servings: 8-9 16 oz. jars

INGREDIENTS

- 15 cups sliced pickling cucumbers - about 6 lbs.
- 7 cups onions sliced thinly
- ¼ cup pickling salt
- 4 cups cider vinegar
- 4 ½ cups sugar
- ¾ tsp. turmeric
- ½ tsp. celery seed
- 1 Tbsp. mustard seeds

DIRECTIONS

1. Mix the onions, salt, and cucumbers together in a bowl. Cover with 2-inch crushed or cubed ice.

2. Place a plate on top of the bowl with a gallon of water or something heavy on the plate. This serves as a weight. Let it stand for about 4 hours in the fridge.

3. After 4 hours, rinse, and drain the cucumbers very well.

4. Mix the sugar, vinegar, celery seed, mustard seed, and turmeric together in a large pot. Let boil for 10 minutes.

5. Add the drained cucumbers and slowly reheat to boiling.

6. Right at boiling, remove from heat, and fill the sanitized jars with slices and cooking syrup, leaving 1/2-inch headspace.

7. Adjust lids and process the jars in a hot water bath for 10 minutes.

8. Heat the water enough to maintain 180 to 185°F water temperature for 30 minutes. Check with a jelly thermometer to be certain that the water temperature is at least 180°F during the entire 30 minutes.

9. Let cool completely before storing jars.

10. After processing and cooling, jars should be stored 4 to 5 weeks to develop ideal flavor.

44. Roasted Beet Pickles

Preparation Time: 10 minutes

Cooking Time: 30 minutes

Servings: 1 pint

INGREDIENTS

- 2 medium beets, roasted and peeled (2 cups)
- ½ cup white wine vinegar (5% acidity)
- ½ cup water
- ½ cup raw cane sugar or granulated sugar
- 2 tsp. s Morton pickling salt
- 1 tsp. black peppercorns
- 4 (2-inch) strips orange peel

DIRECTIONS

1. In a small saucepan, bring the vinegar, water, sugar, salt, peppercorns, and orange zest to a simmer, stirring until the sugar dissolves.

2. Meanwhile, using a mandolin or very sharp knife, cut the cooked beets into ¼-inch or thinner slices.

3. Add the beets to the simmering brine, remove the pan from the heat, and let sit for at least 30 minutes, until they have cooled to room temperature.

4. Strain the beets from the brine, collecting the brine in a small measuring cup.

5. Eat immediately or pack the beets into a clean pint jar and pour in the brine, ensuring the slices are submerged.

6. Screw on a nonreactive lid and store in the refrigerator for up to 2 weeks.

*Try It With: Beets, especially red ones, are messy if eaten directly with your fingers. Slice these beets as thin as possible, and you can serve them on crackers or pita bread with cheese and fresh basil.

45. *Orange and Golden Beets with Roasted Garlic*

Preparation Time: 10 minutes

Cooking Time: 30 minutes

Servings: 1 pint

INGREDIENTS

- 1-pound small golden beets, roasted and peeled (2 cups)
- 4 roasted garlic cloves
- 2 tablespoons freshly squeezed orange juice
- 1 tablespoon balsamic vinegar (6% acidity)
- 2 slices red onion, minced (1 tsp.)
- Pickling or sea salt
- Freshly ground black pepper
- 1 tablespoon extra-virgin olive oil (optional)

DIRECTIONS

1. Cut the beets into ¼-inch-thick slices and put them in a shallow bowl or container.

2. Into a small measuring cup, squeeze the roasted garlic, then mash it with a fork.

3. Add the orange juice, vinegar, and onion, whisking with the fork until the mixture is combined.

4. Pour the liquid over the beets, tossing gently to coat; add salt and pepper to taste.

5. Refrigerate for at least 30 minutes. If desired, drizzle the beets with oil just before serving. These beets are best eaten within a few hours.

*Ingredient Tip: A gourmet grocery store may sell roasted garlic in its antipasti segment, but it's easy to roast at home. Set a whole, unpeeled head on a baking tray, drizzle it with a little olive oil, and bake at 350°F for 30 to 45 minutes, depending on the size and age of the head, until the paper around the cloves begins to brown and the cloves are slightly soft to the touch.

46. *Eight-Hour Cortado (Cabbage Slaw)*

Preparation Time: 20 minutes, (+2 hours salting time)

Cooking time: 6 hours

Servings: 1 quart

INGREDIENTS

- ¼ medium green or white cabbage, shredded (3½ cups)
- 2 medium purple carrots, grated (1 cup)
- 1 small red onion, thinly sliced (1 cup)
- 2 tsp. s Diamond Crystal kosher salt
- 1 tablespoon minced fresh oregano, or 1 tsp. crumbled dried oregano
- 1 serrano Chile, thinly sliced (1½ tablespoons)
- ½ cup apple cider vinegar (5% acidity)
- ½ cup water
- ½ tsp. brown sugar

DIRECTIONS

1. In a large bowl, combine the cabbage, carrots, and onion. Sprinkle with the salt and toss to combine.

2. Cover the bowl with a dish towel and let sit for about 2 hours, occasionally massaging the vegetables to release more liquid.

3. Uncover the bowl and sprinkle the vegetables with the oregano and Chile slices before tossing to combine.

4. Pack the vegetables loosely into a clean wide-mouth quart jar.

5. In a medium measuring cup, whisk the vinegar, water, and sugar until the sugar dissolves.

6. Pour the brine over the vegetables, pressing them down under the liquid until they are submerged.

7. Screw on a nonreactive lid and store in the refrigerator for at least 6 hours before eating.

8. If the vegetables stay submerged, the cortado will keep for weeks in the refrigerator.

Don't Forget: Many tools, including a food processor with a slicer attachment, work for the vegetable prep, but I prefer a sharp knife for shredding cabbage, a large-holed cheese grater for grating carrots, and a mandolin for thinly slicing onions.

47. *Carrot and Daikon Radish*

Preparation Time: 10 minutes, (+ 20 minutes salting time)

Cooking Time: 1 -2 hours

Servings: 1 pint

INGREDIENTS

- 2 medium carrots (1 cup)
- 1 (2½-inch) piece daikon radish (1 cup)
- 1½ tsp. s Diamond Crystal kosher salt
- ¼ cup unseasoned rice vinegar (4.3% acidity)
- 1 tablespoon sugar
- ¼ tsp. minced fresh ginger

DIRECTIONS

1. Using a mandolin with a fine julienne or coarse grating blade, shred the carrots and radish; alternatively, use a very sharp knife to cut the vegetables into thin matchsticks.

2. Transfer the carrot and radish to a colander set over a bowl, toss with the salt, and let sit for 20 minutes.

3. In a small measuring cup, combine the vinegar and sugar. Stir until the sugar dissolves, then stir in the ginger.

4. Rinse the salt from the vegetables under cool water, then gently squeeze out the water.

5. Transfer the carrot and radish to a clean lidded container, pour the brine over the vegetables, and toss to mix well.

6. Refrigerate for 1 to 2 hours before straining and serving chilled. Leftover pickles can be stored, submerged in their brine, in the refrigerator for a couple of weeks.

Switch Things Up: You can use just carrots, just radish, or different proportions of each, depending on what you have on hand. If you don't have a mandolin, a good knife is better than a food processor, which tends to shred too finely.

48. *Ginger-Spiked Carrot and Apple Pickle*

Preparation Time: 15 minutes

Cooking Time: 35 minutes

Servings: 1-2 pints

INGREDIENTS

- 2 medium carrots (1 cup)
- 1 medium crisp apple, like Fuji or Braeburn, quartered (1 cup)
- 1 (2-inch) piece peeled fresh ginger
- Splash of freshly squeezed lemon juice or vinegar
- 2 tsp. s Diamond Crystal kosher salt
- ½ cup unseasoned rice vinegar (4.3% acidity)
- ¼ cup sherry
- 1½ tsp. s sugar
- 1 tablespoon coriander seeds, crushed

DIRECTIONS

1. Cut the carrots, apple quarters, and ginger crosswise into paper-thin pieces with a similar diameter, using a mandolin or very sharp knife.

2. Transfer the vegetables to a colander set over a bowl, toss with the lemon juice and then the salt, and let sit for 30 minutes.

3. Combine the vinegar, sherry, and sugar in a small cup. Stir until the sugar dissolves, then add the coriander seeds.

4. Rinse the salt from the vegetables under cool water, then gently squeeze out the water.

5. Transfer the vegetables to a bowl, pour in the brine, and toss to mix well before serving.

6. These pickles will keep for at least 1 week in a clean lidded container in the refrigerator submerged in their brine.

49. Rainbow Chard Stems

Preparation Time: 10 minutes

Cooking Time: 30 minutes

Servings: 1 pint

INGREDIENTS

- ½ cup apple cider vinegar (5% acidity)
- ½ cup water
- 2 tablespoons sugar
- 1 tsp. Morton pickling salt
- 1 garlic clove, smashed
- ⅛ tsp. fennel seeds
- ⅛ tsp. celery seeds
- 3 rainbow chard stems, cut into ¼-inch slices (1 cup)

DIRECTIONS

1. Add the vinegar, water, sugar, salt, and garlic in a small saucepan and bring to a boil, stirring to dissolve the sugar and salt.

2. Add the fennel seeds, celery seeds, and chard stems. Simmer for 30 seconds to blanch the stems, then remove from the heat.

3. Let sit for about 30 minutes, until cooled to room temperature.

4. Drain and use immediately or transfer the chard stems and brine to a clean lidded container and store submerged in their brine in the refrigerator for up to a week.

Try It With: Besides pizza, pickled rainbow chard is delicious in sushi rolls, as a relish with grilled halibut or snapper, or tossed in a mixed bean or cabbage salad.

50. Corn and Chile Pickle

Preparation Time: 20 minutes

Cooking Time: 30 minutes

Servings: 2-3 12 oz. jars

INGREDIENTS

- 1½ cups corn kernels (cut from 2 ears)
- 1 medium onion, minced (½ cup)
- 1 Anaheim pepper or another mild Chile, minced (¼ cup)
- 1 jalapeño pepper or serrano Chile, minced (1½ tablespoons)
- ½ tsp. coriander seeds, crushed
- ¼ tsp. yellow mustard seeds, crushed
- ½ cup white wine vinegar (5% acidity)
- ½ cup water
- ¼ cup bottled lime juice (5% acidity)
- 1 tsp. Diamond Crystal kosher salt

DIRECTIONS

1. In a medium bowl, combine the corn, onion, peppers, and coriander and mustard seeds, and toss to mix.

2. Divide the vegetables between 2-3 clean jars.

3. In a small cup, combine the vinegar, water, lime juice, and salt. Stir until the salt dissolves.

4. Pour the brine over the vegetables in each jar, ensuring they are submerged.

5. Screw a nonreactive lid on each and let sit for at least 30 minutes before eating. For longer storage, refrigerate submerged in brine for up to 1 month.

51. *Russian-Inspired Pickled Mushrooms*

Preparation Time: 15 minutes

Cooking Time: 2 hours

Servings: 1 pint

INGREDIENTS

- 8 oz. mushrooms (2½ cups) like chestnut boletes, king oysters, blue oysters, or humble cremini
- ¼ cup white wine vinegar (5% acidity)
- ¼ cup boiling water
- 1 tsp. Morton pickling salt
- 1 tsp. sugar
- 1 tsp. Sweet-Savory Spice Blend
- 1 bay leaf
- ¼ tsp. dill seeds
- 1 tablespoon extra-virgin olive oil, for serving (optional)

DIRECTIONS

1. Cut the mushrooms into slices or pieces less than 1¼ inch in diameter and put them in a clean lidded container.

2. In a small cup, whisk together the vinegar, boiling water, salt, and sugar, stirring until the salt and sugar dissolve.

3. Pour the brine over the mushrooms, then add the spice blend, bay leaf, and dill seeds; stir to combine.

4. Let sit at room temperature for 2 hours, stirring occasionally so that all the mushrooms are exposed to the brine.

5. To serve, strain the mushrooms, tossing them with olive oil, if desired. Leftover mushrooms can be stored in the refrigerator submerged in their brine, without oil; the brine should cover the mushrooms now that they've released their liquid. They are best eaten within 2 weeks.

Ingredient Tip: Wild and substrate-cultivated mushrooms can hold dirt or sawdust. If brushing them with a dry or damp cloth doesn't remove these particles, drop them in a bowl of cold salted water, agitate them briefly, drain them through a colander, and let them dry completely on a dish towel.

52. *Mushrooms Pickled in White Wine*

Preparation Time: 15 minutes

Cooking Time: 2 hours

Servings: 1 pint

INGREDIENTS

- 8 oz. chestnut bolete mushrooms or king oysters caps slices (2½ cups), cut lengthwise down their caps and stems into ½-inch sticks,
- ¼ medium onion, finely chopped (2 tablespoons)
- ¼ cup white wine, such as sauvignon Blanc or pinot grigio
- ¼ cup boiling water
- 1 tablespoon white wine vinegar (5% acidity)
- 1 tsp. Morton pickling salt
- 1 tablespoon finely chopped fresh dill or 1 tsp. dried dill
- 1 tsp. black peppercorns, crushed
- ½ tsp. prepared stone-ground mustard or German-Inspired Spicy Mustard
- 2 tablespoons extra-virgin olive oil, for serving

DIRECTIONS

1. In a clean lidded container, combine the mushrooms and onion.

2. In a small measuring cup, whisk together the wine, boiling water, vinegar, and salt, stirring until the salt dissolves.

3. Pour the liquid over the mushrooms, tossing to combine.

4. Let sit at room temperature for 2 hours, stirring occasionally, so that all the mushrooms are exposed to the liquid.

5. Stir the dill, peppercorns, and mustard into the mushrooms and refrigerate them for at least 1 hour, until completely chilled, and up to 24 hours before serving.

6. To serve, strain most of the liquid from the mushrooms and toss them with the olive oil; eat immediately.

7. Leftover mushrooms can be stored in the refrigerator submerged in their brine, without oil; they are best eaten within 2 weeks.

53. *Kosher-NYC Style Dill Pickles*

Preparation Time: 20 minutes, (+ 8 hours salting time)

Cooking Time: 20 minutes

Servings: 7-8 quarts

INGREDIENTS

- 9 pounds (4-inch or smaller) fresh pickling cucumbers
- 1¼ cups Morton pickling salt, divided
- 2½ gallons water, divided
- 6 cups apple cider vinegar (5% acidity)
- 2 tablespoons sugar
- 14 slices peeled horseradish root
- 14 garlic cloves
- 7 tablespoons Basic Dilly Spice Blend

DIRECTIONS

1. Cut a thin slice from the blossom end of each cucumber (see Tip).

2. Cut the cucumbers into spears.

3. In a large bowl, dissolve ¾ cup of salt by stirring it into 2 gallons of water.

4. Add the cucumbers, cover the bowl with a dish towel, and let the cucumbers sit in the salt brine overnight.

5. Drain the cucumbers, rinse them under cool running water, then drain again.

6. In a stockpot, combine the vinegar, the remaining 8 cups of water, the remaining ½ cup of salt, and the sugar.

7. Bring the mixture to a boil, stirring to dissolve the salt and sugar.

8. Lower the heat to just below a simmer and keep the brine hot.

9. Place 2 horseradish slices, 2 garlic cloves, and 1 tablespoon of spice blend in the bottom of each of seven clean, hot wide-mouth quart jars.

10. Fill each jar with the cucumbers, packing them firmly but without bruising.

11. 5.Ladle in the hot brine, submerging the cucumbers; leave ½ inch of headspace. Remove any air bubbles with a bamboo or wooden chopstick and wipe each jar's rim.

12. Cap each jar with a two-piece canning lid. Add the jars to a boiling-water bath.

13. Process the jars in the boiling-water bath for 15-20 minutes.

14. Store the jars in a dry, dark, cool place for at least 2 weeks before eating. The pickles are best eaten within a year.

Ingredient Tip: Cutting the blossom end off cucumbers removes enzymes that can make them mushy. If you can't tell the stem end and blossom end apart, slice off both. For the crispest pickles, use just-picked pickling cucumbers; you can also add horseradish or grape leaves.

**Switch Things Up: For even more flavorful pickles, use the same amount of Ultra Pickling Spice Blend or replace the dry spices with 1 fresh dill head, 1 Chile, 1 bay leaf, and 1 tsp. of mustard seeds per jar.*

54. *Smoky Full-Sour Pickles*
Preparation Time: 30 minutes

Cooking Time: 1- 4 weeks

Servings: 1 half-gallon

INGREDIENTS

- 2 pounds 3- to 6-inch pickling cucumbers
- 1-quart unchlorinated water
- 6 tablespoons Diamond Crystal kosher salt
- 1 to 2 fresh horseradish or grape leaves (optional)
- 1 garlic head, separated into cloves
- 1 tablespoon coriander seeds
- 2 tsp. s smoky tea leaves, such as Russian Caravan or Lapsang souchong
- ½ tsp. mustard seeds
- 1 tsp. Szechuan peppercorns
- 1 dried chipotle pepper or another smoked Chile, crumbled (optional)

DIRECTIONS

1. Cut off a thin slice from the blossom end of each cucumber (see Tip), and then thoroughly chill the cucumbers in the refrigerator.

2. In a large measuring cup, whisk together the water and salt, stirring until the salt dissolves.

3. Line the bottom of a clean ½ gallon jar or crock with the horseradish leaves (optional).

4. Add the peeled garlic cloves, coriander seeds, tea leaves, mustard seeds, peppercorns, and Chile (optional).

5. Add the cucumbers, packing them vertically and firmly but without bruising, up to the shoulder of the container.

6. Pour in the brine, submerging the cucumbers, store extra brine in a small, lidded jar.

7. Top the cucumbers with a weight if needed and cover the fermenting vessel, preferably with an air lock.

8. Let sit in a dark, cool place to cure.

9. After 24 hours, start to check the fermentation daily, ensuring the pickles are submerged and skimming off any filmy surface layer. If they're

exposed, add enough brine with a 5% concentration to submerge the cucumbers.

10. Taste after 1 week of curing; continue fermenting for an additional 3 weeks as needed, until the pickles reach your preferred flavor.

11. Store the finished pickles in a glass container with a nonreactive lid in the refrigerator. If they stay submerged in their brine, they will keep for months.

Ingredient Tip: Cutting the blossom end off cucumbers, chilling, and adding tannin-laden horseradish or grape leaves all improve cucumber pickle. But the best way to get crunchy pickles is to start with ultra-fresh pickling cucumbers.

**Switch Things Up: Dried chipotle chiles may be harder to find than powdered smoked paprika, but specialty stores and spice shops often carry them. For a substitution, choose non-smoked red pepper flakes instead of a smoked powder.*

55. *Half-Sour Dill Pickles*

Preparation Time: 15 minutes

Cooking Time: 1- 4 weeks

Servings: 1 half-gallon

INGREDIENTS

- 2 pounds 3- to 6-inch pickling cucumbers
- 4 cups unchlorinated water
- ¼ cup Diamond Crystal kosher salt
- 1 or more fresh horseradish or grape leaves (optional)
- 4 garlic cloves
- 1 red jalapeño pepper, halved lengthwise (optional)
- 1 fresh dill head (optional)
- 1 tablespoon Basic Dilly Spice Blend

DIRECTIONS

1. Cut off a thin slice from the blossom end of each cucumber (see Tip), and then thoroughly chill the cucumbers in the refrigerator.

2. In a large measuring cup, whisk together the water and salt, stirring until the salt dissolves.

3. Line the bottom of a clean ½-gallon jar or crock with the horseradish leaves (optional).

4. Add the garlic, pepper, dill head (optional), and spice blend.

5. Add the cucumbers, packing them vertically and firmly but without bruising, up to the shoulder of the container. Pour in the brine, submerging the cucumbers, store extra brine in a small, lidded jar.

6. Top the cucumbers with a weight if needed and cover the fermenting vessel, preferably with an air lock.

7. Let sit in a dark, cool place to cure.

8. After 24 hours, start to check the fermentation daily, ensuring the pickles are submerged and skimming off any filmy surface layer. If they're exposed, add enough brine with a 3.5% concentration to submerge the cucumbers.

9. Taste after 1 week of curing; continue fermenting for an additional 3 weeks as needed, until the pickles reach your preferred flavor.

10. Store the finished pickles in a glass container with a nonreactive lid in the refrigerator. If they stay submerged in their brine, they will keep for at least 6 months.

Don't Forget: The brine prevents spoilage, so the cucumbers must remain submerged throughout the fermentation process. If they start to float, add a weight.

**Tips: Less salty than full sours, half-sour pickles are infused with the classic dill flavor. For extra heat and flavor, add a fresh Chile and a dill head. The longer these pickles ferment, the better they taste. To check for full fermentation, slice into a pickle; it should be uniform in color, crunchy, and full of flavor.*

56. *Dilly and Mustardy Kohlrabi Pickles*

Preparation Time: 25 minutes

Cooking Time: 1 - 2 weeks

Servings: 1 half-gallon

INGREDIENTS

- 2½ pounds kohlrabi
- 4 cups unchlorinated water
- 6 tablespoons Diamond Crystal kosher salt
- 2 tablespoons peeled and coarsely chopped horseradish root
- 4 tsp. s yellow mustard seeds
- 1½ tsp. s celery seeds
- 2 fresh dill heads or 4 tsp. s dill seeds
- 1 small onion, thinly sliced (1 cup)

DIRECTIONS

1. Cut off the kohlrabi leaves, reserving them for another use, then cut the remaining stalks into 3-inch lengths. Peel the bulbs, then cut them into 3-inch-long, ½-inch-wide spears.

2. In a large measuring cup, whisk together the water and salt, stirring until the salt dissolves.

3. In the bottom of a clean ½-gallon jar or crock, place the horseradish root, mustard seeds, celery seeds, and dill heads.

4. Add the kohlrabi stalks and spears and onion slices, packing them firmly but without bruising, up to the shoulder of the container.

5. Pour in the brine, submerging the pieces, store extra brine in a small, lidded jar.

6. Cover the surface with a whole kohlrabi leaf, top with a weight if needed, and cover the fermenting vessel, preferably with an air lock.

7. Let sit in a dark, cool place to cure.

8. 4.After 24 hours, start to check the fermentation daily, ensuring the pickles are submerged and skimming off any filmy surface layer. If they're exposed, add enough brine with a 5% concentration to submerge the kohlrabi.

9. Taste after 1 week of curing; continue fermenting for an additional week as needed, until the pickles reach your preferred flavor.

10. Store the finished pickles in a glass container with a nonreactive lid in the refrigerator. If they stay submerged in their brine, they will keep for months.

Ingredient Tip: Look for full, unwilted leaves when buying kohlrabi; they indicate it was freshly picked and are delicious in salads and stir-fries. Young, small kohlrabi bulbs may be easy to peel with a vegetable peeler, but larger ones may have thick skin that requires a knife. Older kohlrabi may have tough stalks that will be woody when fermented; replace these with extra bulbs.

57. *Pickled Cherry Tomatoes*

Preparation Time: 30 minutes

Cooking Time: 15 minutes

Servings: 7-8 12 oz. Jars

INGREDIENTS

- 8 cups cherry tomatoes
- 2 cups coarsely chopped celery

- 4 cups coarsely chopped onion
- 2 cups coarsely chopped sweet pepper
- 4-½ cups water
- 4-1/2 cups white vinegar (5%)
- 1 cup sugar
- 6 tbsp canning salt
- Optional: 1 cup Cuca melon
- 6-7 garlic cloves
- 6-7 heads of dill

DIRECTIONS

1. Mix water, vinegar, salt, and sugar in a saucepot, large, then boil for 5 minutes.

2. Add to each hot sanitized jar 1 garlic clove and 1 head of dill. Pack the vegetable and leave 1-inch headspace.

3. Scoop hot liquid into the hot jars and leave 1/4-inch headspace. Remove air bubbles, checking headspace.

4. Wipe jar rims with a clean damp cloth and apply 2-piece caps.

5. Process in a pressure canner for about 15 minutes following the manufacturer's guide and according to the altitude.

6. Store the finished pickles in the refrigerator.

58. *Canned Garlic Dill Pickles*

Preparation Time: 45 minutes

Cooking Time: 15 minutes

Servings: 15 Quart jars

INGREDIENTS

- 3 lbs. onions
- 20 lbs. sliced pickling cucumbers, whole or speared
- 10 cups water
- 10 cups white vinegar
- 1-1/3 cup pickling salt
- 45 garlic cloves, peeled
- 15 sprig fresh dill

DIRECTIONS

1. Layer onions and cucumber in a bowl, large, then cover with salt. Top them with ice cubes then cover and refrigerate for about 4 hours.

2. Use a colander to rinse and drain them very well.

3. In the meantime, combine water, vinegar, and pickling salt in a pot and bring to boil for 5 minutes.

4. Add 3 garlic cloves and 1 fresh dill sprig to each hot quart jar, then fill with onions and cucumbers.

5. Ladle hot vinegar mixture to the hot jar and leave ½-inch headspace.

6. Release any air bubbles then wipe jar rims. Place lids and rings on.

7. Place jars in a canner filled half way with warm (140°F) water. Then, add hot water to a level 1 inch above jars.

8. Heat the water enough to maintain 180°F water temperature for 30 minutes for pint or quart jars. Check with a candy or jelly thermometer to be certain that the water temperature is at least 180°F during the entire 30 minutes.

9. Let cool, for 12-24 hours.

10. Store the finished pickles. For best results, use them after 4 weeks

59. *Pickled Cauliflower*

Preparation Time: 30 minutes

Cooking Time: 10 minutes

Servings: 6-7 12 oz. Jars

INGREDIENTS

- 2-½ lbs. cauliflower florets
- 2 cups white wine vinegar
- 2 onions, medium, thinly sliced
- ½ tbsp red pepper flakes, hot
- 2 cups sugar
- 1/4 cup pickling salt
- 2 cups water

DIRECTIONS

1. Boil a pot with water over high heat then add some salt to taste.

2. Add the florets and bring to a boil for 3 minutes, then drain.

3. Combine salt, vinegar, onions, pepper flakes, and sugar in a medium pot, bring to a boil, stirring, until sugar is dissolved.

4. Let boil over low-medium heat, gently, for about 5 minutes; then remove from heat.

5. Pack florets into hot jars then cover with the vinegar solution. Make sure pepper flakes are evenly distributed. Leave ½-inch headspace.

6. Wipe the rims of the jars then set lids and rings ensuring fingertip tightness.

7. Place the jars in a pressure canner and process for about 10 minutes following manufacturers guide and according to altitude.

8. Control the vacuum of the jars, turn them upside down and let them flavor for about 3 weeks before consuming.

This is a healthy canning recipe that you must come across. Pickled cauliflower is easy to make and can in a pressure canner that your family will be left yearning for more. Enjoy it.

60. *Pickled Red Grapes*

Preparation Time: 30 minutes

Cooking Time: 10 minutes

Servings: 3-4 8 oz. jars

INGREDIENTS

- 2 lb. red grapes
- 2 cups red wine vinegar
- 2 cups water
- 2 cups sugar
- 12 black peppercorns
- 3-4 ginger slices

DIRECTIONS

1. Wash and dry grapes, remove from the stem and set aside.

2. Combine vinegar, water and sugar in a small saucepan, over low heat, stirring until sugar dissolves.

3. Increase heat and bring to a boil for 5 minutes, then remove from heat.

4. Put 4 peppercorns and 1 ginger slice into each hot jar.

5. Now pack the grapes carefully and tightly into the jars.

6. Add vinegar solution to each jar leaving ½-inch headspace, and remove air bubbles if any.

7. Wipe the jar rims using a clean damp cloth and place lids and rings making its fingertip tight.

8. Process the jars in a pressure canner for about 15 minutes following the manufacturer's guide and according to altitude.

9. Control the vacuum of the jars, turn them upside down and let cool them

10. Put the jars in the pantry and let flavor for about 4 weeks before consuming.

These pickled grapes are great and goes well with cheese, topped on baked ricotta, makes an addition to roasted meat dishes and as an addition to salads.

61. Mustard Pickled Vegetables

Preparation Time: -10 minutes (+8 hours to marinate)

Cooking Time: 35 minutes

Servings: 4 pints

INGREDIENTS

- 1 head cauliflower
- 20 small green tomatoes
- 3 green bell peppers
- 4 cups pickling onions
- 2 pickling cucumbers
- 1 cup sugar
- ¾ cup flour
- ½ cup dry mustard 1 tbsp. turmeric
- 7 cups apple cider vinegar
- 7 cups water
- 1 cup pickling salt

DIRECTIONS

1. Wash all the veggies and chop them.

2. Toss the vegetables in a large non-reactive bowl or pot with salt.

3. Pour a quart of water over all of them and let this stand overnight.

4. Drain, cover with boiling water, and let it stand for ten minutes. Drain.

5. Combine sugar, flour, spices, vinegar, and 3 cups of water, then cook until thick.

6. Mix in the veggies and cook for 4 minutes, or until tender-crisp.

7. Pack into pint jars, dividing liquid evenly and leaving ½-inch of headspace.

8. Wipe rims; screw on lids and rings.

9. Finish the canning process in a boiling water bath for 15 minutes.

10. Control the vacuum of the jars, turn them upside down and let them flavor for about 5 weeks before consuming.

62. Pickled Snap Pea with Carrot

Preparation Time: 10 minutes

Cooking Time: 5 minutes

Servings: 2 pints

INGREDIENTS

- 1½ lbs. sugar snap peas
- 1 julienned carrot
- 2 sliced jalapeño peppers
- 4 chopped garlic cloves
- 2 cups distilled white vinegar
- 1 cup water
- 2 tsps. canning salt

DIRECTIONS

1. Wash the pea pods, trim off the ends, and remove the stringy portion. Cut the pea pods into thirds, making bite-sized pieces.

2. Mix the chopped-up peas, carrots, jalapeños, and garlic.

3. In a medium-sized, nonreactive saucepan, boil water, vinegar and salt for 3 minutes.

4. Fill the prepared jars with the vegetables and transfer the hot brine into the jars, leaving ½ inch headspace.

5. Rinse the rims of the jars with a dampened, clean, lint-free cloth or paper towel and again with a dry towel, then tighten the lids.

6. Transfer the covered jars to the water bath.

7. Finish the canning process in the water bath for 10 minutes.

8. Control the vacuum of the jars, turn them upside down and let cool them

9. Put the jars in the pantry and let flavor for about 2 weeks before consuming.

63. *Pickled Onions*

Preparation Time: 10 minutes

Cooking Time: 20 minutes

Servings: 6 12 oz. jars

INGREDIENTS

- 2 cups vinegar
- 4 cups water
- 7 tbsp. salt
- 2/3 cup sugar
- 3½ tsp. salt
- 4 lbs. red onions
- 6 bay leaves
- 3 tsps. peppercorns

DIRECTIONS

1. Wash, dry and trim the onions. Slice them thinly into strips.

2. Toss the onions with 1¾ tsp. of salt. Allow to set for ½ hour. Rinse.

3. Meantime, to create the brine, combine the water, salt, vinegar, and sugar in a sauce pot. Simmer on low heat.

4. Stir often until the sugar and salt dissolve. Set the pan aside.

5. Distribute bay leaves and peppercorns evenly into your jars.

6. Add roughly ½ pound of onions to each of your six jars. Press with tongs and pack loosely.

7. Cover onions with brine and leave ½ inch of space at the top.

8. Rinse rims of jars with a clean towel. Place lids on jars. Seal with bands, using fingertips only.

9. Process for 8-10 minutes the jars in hot water boiling. When the timer goes off, remove the jars from the hot water bath with a jar lifter. Place them on towels. Allow to cool upside down for about 24 hours.

10. After a day, remove bands and test the seals. The jars that have good seals are fine to keep in a cool, dark place for up to one year. In cases where the seal was broken, store in your fridge and use within two weeks.

64. *Lime Jalapeño Pickles*

Preparation Time: 5 minutes (+19 hours to rest)

Cooking Time: 5 minutes

Servings: 6 12 oz. jars

INGREDIENTS

- 3 lbs. jalapeño peppers
- 1½ gallons water
- 1½ cups pickling lime
- 7½ cups apple cider vinegar
- 1¾ cups water
- 2½ tbsps. canning salt
- 6 tbsps. yellow mustard seed, divided
- 3 tbsps. celery seed, divided

DIRECTIONS

1. Fill a large bowl with the water and carefully stir in the pickling lime. Add the peppers, cover and refrigerate for 18 hours.

2. In a colander, drain and rinse the peppers under cold running water. Rinse the bowl, return the peppers to it, and cover with cold water. Refrigerate for 1 hour.

3. Meantime, sanitize the jars and the lids in a hot water bath, placing the jars in it to keep warm. Wash the lids and rings in hot, soapy water, and set everything aside.

4. In a large saucepot set over high heat, combine the cider vinegar, and canning salt. Bring to a boil for 5 minutes.

5. In each jar, add 1 tablespoon of mustard seed and 1½ tsp. s of celery seed. Fill the jars with the peppers, leaving 1- inch of headspace.

6. Ladle the hot vinegar brine over this, leaving ½ inch of headspace. Use a non-metallic spatula to release any air bubbles.

7. Rinse the rims clean and seal with the lids and rings.

8. Process the jars in a hot water bath for 30-35 minutes.

9. When the timer goes off, remove the jars from the hot water bath with a jar lifter. Place them on towels.

10. Allow to cool upside down for about 24 hours.

11. After a day, remove bands and test the seals. The jars that have good seals are fine to keep in a cool, dark place for up to one year. In cases where the seal was broken, store in your fridge and use within two weeks.

WATER BATH CANNING RECIPES: SALSAS AND SAUCES

65. Zesty Salsa

Preparation Time: 20 Minutes

Cooking Time: 10 Minutes

Servings: 12 8 oz. jars

INGREDIENTS

- 10 cups tomatoes
- 4 bell peppers, seeded
- 6-8 red onions, medium
- 2 ½ cups hot jalapeno peppers, seeded
- 1 ½ cups cider vinegar
- 3 minced garlic cloves
- 2 tablespoons minced cilantro
- 3 tsp. s salt

DIRECTIONS

1. Wash, dry and chop onions, tomatoes, bell peppers and jalapeno peppers and set aside.

2. Put all the ingredients into a large pot. Let boil, stirring constantly, for about 8-10 minutes or until thick.

3. Ladle the hot salsa into jars, leaving about ¼- head space.

4. Let the jars sit in a water bath for about 15 minutes.

5. Let cool completely before storing.

66. Homemade Pizza Sauce

Preparation Time: 20 minutes

Cooking Time: 80 minutes

Servings: 4 pints

INGREDIENTS

- 25-28 red and ripe tomatoes, medium-sized
- 2 large yellow onions, peeled
- 4 large garlic cloves, peeled
- 3 tablespoons of olive oil
- 2 tablespoons of lemon juice
- 1 tsp. freshly ground black pepper
- 1 tablespoon of white sugar
- 2 tablespoons of chopped parsley
- 1 tablespoon of oregano
- 1 tablespoon of dry basil
- 1 tsp. of dry rosemary
- 1 tsp. of celery seed
- 2 tsp. s of kosher salt

DIRECTIONS

1. Peel the tomatoes. Blanch them for 2-3 minutes in boiling water.

2. Puree them in a blender or food processor.

3. Mince the onions and garlic cloves.

4. Sauté the onions and garlic in a large saucepan with the olive oil for about 3-4 minutes until tender and fragrant.

5. Add the tomato puree. Bring to a boil on medium-high heat. Reduce heat to low, and let simmer for 45 minutes

6. Once the sauce thickens, put it into jars

7. Let the jars sit in a water bath for about 25 minutes.

8. Let cool completely before storing.

67. Red Tomato Ketchup

Preparation Time: 25 minutes

Cooking Time: 80 minutes

Servings: 7 pints

INGREDIENTS

- 3 tablespoons celery seeds
- 4 tsp. whole cloves
- 2 cinnamon sticks
- 1 ½ tsps. whole allspice
- 3 cups cider vinegar
- 24 pounds red tomatoes, cored and quartered
- 3 cups chopped onions
- 1 tsp. cayenne pepper
- 1 ½ cups granulated sugar
- ½ cup pickling salt such as Ball salt and preserving

DIRECTIONS

1. Create a spice bag with the first four Ingredients by wrapping them in a piece of cheesecloth.
2. Mix the vinegar and spice bag in a saucepan, bring to a boil on high heat, remove, and let sit for 25 minutes. Throw away spice bag.
3. Put together the tomatoes, cayenne, and onions in a large saucepan, bring to a boil on high heat, then let sit for 20 minutes on reduced heat.
4. Add the infused vinegar, and boil until the vegetables are soft, and it begins to thicken. This will take about another 30 minutes.
5. Add sugar and salt and bring to a boil over medium heat. Reduce the heat, and let it sit for about 45 minutes. Do not puree it.
6. Put the ketchup into the jars, and let the jars sit in a water bath for about 15 minutes.
7. Let cool completely before storing.

68. Unripe Tomato Salsa

Preparation Time: 30 minutes

Cooking Time: 60 minutes

Servings: 8 pints

INGREDIENTS

- 5 pounds of unpeeled green tomatoes, finely chopped
- 6 yellow onions, chopped small
- 3 jalapeños, chopped with the seeds
- 4 large green bell peppers, chopped
- 6 garlic cloves, minced
- 1 cup of fresh cilantro, chopped
- 1 cup of lime juice
- 1 tablespoon of salt
- ½ tablespoon of cumin
- 1 tablespoon of dried oregano leaves
- 2 tablespoons of pepper

DIRECTIONS

1. Combine all the ingredients together in a large pot and bring to a boil, mixing for the next 30 to 40 minutes.
2. After the time is up, and it's at a boil again, put the salsa into the sterilized jars.
3. Let the jars sit in a water bath for about 15 minutes.
4. Let them sit at room temperature for about 24 hours before refrigerating or storing.

69. Cucumber Relish

Preparation Time: 45 minutes

Cooking Time: 4 hours and 20 minutes

Servings: 5 pints

INGREDIENTS

- 4 unpeeled and diced cucumbers
- 2 diced green peppers
- 1 diced red pepper
- 1 tablespoon of celery seed
- 3 cups of ground onions
- 3 cups of finely diced celery
- ¼ cup of salt
- 2 cups of white vinegar
- 1 tablespoon of mustard seeds
- 3 ½ cups of sugar

DIRECTIONS

1. Place all the ingredients in a food processor and pulse until the cucumber are finely chopped.

2. Place the relish in a large bowl and cover with cold water, letting it sit for about 4 hours.

3. Drain the mixture and combine with sugar

4. . Bring to a boil. As it heats up, liquids will come out. Stir until the sugar is dissolved.

5. Pack into jars and let sit in water bath for about 15 minutes.

6. Let cool completely before storing.

70. Hot Pepper Mustard Butter

Preparation Time: 15 minutes

Cooking Time: 5 minutes

Servings: 8-9 pints

INGREDIENTS

- 36 large hot peppers (or 50 small ones), washed and trimmed
- 1 yellow bell pepper, seeded, chop in a few pieces
- 1 red onion, trimmed and quartered
- 1 quart of prepared yellow mustard
- 1 quart of cider vinegar
- 6 cups of sugar
- 1 ¼ cup of flour
- 1 ½ cups of water
- 1 tsp. of salt

DIRECTIONS

1. Wash, dry and place hot peppers, bell pepper and onion in the food processor and pulse until finely minced.

2. Mix all the ingredients together in a large saucepan.

3. Bring to a boil while stirring continuously. Reduce heat to low and let simmer for 15 minutes, stirring a few times.

4. Put into hot sterilized jars, put the lids on, and let them sit in a water bath for about 15 minutes.

5. Let cool completely before storing.

71. Asian Plum Sauce

Preparation Time: 15 minutes

Cooking Time: 60 minutes

Servings: 6 half-pint jars

INGREDIENTS

- 4 cloves of garlic, minced
- ¼ cup of fresh ginger, grated
- 1 yellow onion, diced finely
- 1 cup of brown sugar
- 2 cups of water
- ⅛ cup of teriyaki sauce
- 1 tsp. of sesame oil
- ⅛ cup of soy sauce
- ½ tsp. of crushed and dried chili
- 3 pounds of chopped and pitted plums

- 1 tablespoon of cornstarch
- 1 lemon, squeezed for the juice

DIRECTIONS

1. Mix all the ingredients together and bring to a boil in a large pot for about 30 minutes.

2. Simmer for around 5-8 minutes or until it is thick, and then put into jars.

3. Let the jars sit in a water bath for about 15 minutes.

4. Let cool completely before storing. Store in a cool and dark place.

72. *Peaches and Vanilla Syrup*

Preparation Time: 10 minutes

Cooking Time: 30 minutes

Servings: 4-pint jars

INGREDIENTS

- 5 cups of peaches, pureed
- 2 cups of sugar
- 2 tablespoons of lemon juice
- 2 tsp. s of vanilla

DIRECTIONS

1. Mix peach puree with sugar and lemon juice in a medium-sized sauce pot and bring to a boil.

2. Let it simmer for about 5 minutes, and then add the vanilla.

3. Pour the mixture into jars and seal them.

4. Let the jars sit in a water bath for about 20 minutes before storing.

5. Let cool completely before storing.

73. *Corn Relish*

Preparation Time: 20 minutes

Cooking Time: 50 minutes

Servings: 3-4 pints

INGREDIENTS

- 1 large cucumber, peeled, seeded, roughly chopped
- 2 cups of chopped onions
- 1 red bell peppers, seeded and chopped
- 4 cups corn kernels (cut from 4-6 ears, depending on how big the ears are)
- 2 plum or Roma tomatoes, diced the size of a corn kernel
- 1 red or green serrano chili peppers, seeded and minced
- 1 1/4 cups sugar
- 2 tablespoons kosher salt
- ½ tsp. black pepper
- 1 ½ cups apple cider vinegar (5% acidity)
- ½ tsp. turmeric
- 2 tsp. s mustard seeds
- ½ tsp. ground cumin

DIRECTIONS

1. Pulse cucumbers, onions, bell peppers: Working in batches, if necessary, pulse the cucumbers, onions, and bell peppers in a food processor just 3 or 4 pulses, so they are still distinguishable from each other, not puréed.

2. Combine with remaining ingredients, simmer 25 minutes:

3. Place mixture in a medium pot. Add the corn, tomatoes, serrano chiles, sugar, salt, pepper, vinegar, turmeric, mustard seed, and ground cumin.

4. Bring to a boil. Reduce heat to a simmer. Cover and cook for 25 minutes.

5. Scoop into jars: Spoon the corn relish into clean jars and seal,

6. will last for 4-6 weeks refrigerated.

7. If you would like to store your pickles outside of the refrigerator, sterilize canning jars before canning, and process the relish-filled jars in a hot water bath for 15 minutes after canning.

74. Green Salsa

Preparation Time: 20 minutes

Cooking Time: 10 minutes

Servings: 3 pints

INGREDIENTS

- 12 medium green tomatoes, cored, peeled, and diced
- 6 to 8 jalapenos, seeded and minced
- 2 large red onions, diced
- 1 tsp. of minced garlic
- ½ cup of fresh lime juice
- ½ cup of fresh chopped cilantro
- 1 ½ tsp. s ground cumin
- 1 tsp. dried oregano
- Salt and pepper to taste

DIRECTIONS

1. Prepare your water bath canner as well as your lids and bands.

2. Combine the tomatoes, jalapenos, onion, garlic, and lime juice in a large saucepan.

3. Cover and bring to a boil then stir in the remaining ingredients.

4. Reduce heat and simmer for 5 minutes then spoon the mixture into your jars, leaving about ½-inch of headspace.

5. Clean the rims add the lid and seal with a metal band then place the jars in the water bath canner and bring the water to boil.

6. Process the jars for 20 minutes then remove the jars and wipe them dry.

7. Place the jars on a canning rack and cool for 24 hours before storing it.

75. Simple Salsa

Preparation Time: 15 minutes

Cooking Time: 15 minutes

Servings: 3 pints

INGREDIENTS

- 4 cups slicing tomatoes (peeled, cored and chopped)
- 2 cups green chilies (seeded and chopped)
- ¾ cup onions (chopped)
- ½ cup of jalapeno peppers (seeded and chopped)
- 4 garlic cloves (chopped finely)
- 1 tsp. ground cumin
- 1 tablespoon cilantro
- 1 tablespoon basil dried
- 2 cups distilled white vinegar
- 1 ½ tsp. table salt

DIRECTIONS

1. Place all the ingredients above in a large pot. Place the pot on the stove and bring to a rolling boil while stirring constantly to prevent burning.

2. Reduce the heat a bit and let the mixture simmer for about 20 minutes. Stir frequently.

3. Divide the salsa among 4 jars.

4. Make sure to leave about ½-inch of space at the top of each jar.

5. Place the lids on the jars and process using the water bath canning method for 20- 25 minutes.

6. Remove the jars and wipe them dry.

7. Place the jars on a canning rack and cool for 24 hours before storing it.

76. Mango Salsa

Preparation Time: 20 minutes

Cooking Time: 10 minutes

Servings: 3 pints

INGREDIENTS

- ½ water cup
- 1 ¼ cup cider vinegar, 5%
- 2 tsp. s ginger, chopped finely
- 1 ½ cup red bell pepper, diced
- ½ tsp. red pepper flakes, crushed
- 6 cups mango, unripe, diced
- ½ cup yellow onion, chopped finely
- 2 tsp. s of garlic, chopped finely
- 1 cup of brown sugar, light

DIRECTIONS

1. Wash and dry the mangoes, ginger, peppers, onions and garlic.
2. Peel the mangoes before chopping in half-inch cubes.
3. Chop the yellow onion into fine bits and dice the red bell pepper in half-inch strips.
4. Place all the ingredients in a stockpot, stir to combine, and heat over high heat for 5 minutes.
5. Once the mixture is boiling, cook and stir for 5-10 minutes to dissolve the sugar.
6. Turn the heat down to medium and allow the mixture to simmer for about 5 minutes.
7. Pour the hot salsa into clean and hot Mason jars, leaving 1/2- inch of headspace in each jar.
8. Take out any air bubbles before securing the jar lids.
9. Place in the water bath pot with boiling water and process for 15 minutes.
10. Remove the jars and wipe them dry.
11. Place the jars on a canning rack and cool for 24 hours before storing it.

77. Pineapple Chipotle

Preparation Time: 20 minutes

Cooking Time: 10 minutes

Servings: 3 pints

INGREDIENTS

- 4 cups seeded papaya
- 2 cups chopped or cubed pineapples
- 1 cup raisins
- 1 cup lemon juice
- ½ cup lime juice
- ½ cup pineapple juice
- ½ cup Anaheim peppers
- 2 Tsp. s chopped onions
- 2 Tsp. s chopped cilantro
- 2 Tsp. s of brown sugar

DIRECTIONS

1. Add all the ingredients together in a saucepan and bring to a boil, stirring constantly.
2. Reduce to a steady simmer and let thicken for 20 minutes
3. Add to the canning jars and seal.
4. Place in the water bath pot with boiling water and process for 15 minutes.
5. Remove the jars and wipe them dry.
6. Place the jars on a canning rack and cool for 24 hours before storing it.

78. Hot Green Sauce

Preparation Time: 10 minutes

Cooking Time: 20 minutes

Servings: 3 pints

INGREDIENTS

- 7 cups chopped green tomatoes
- 3 cups chopped jalapenos
- 2 cups chopped red onions
- 2 tsp. s minced garlic
- ½ cup of lime juice
- ½ cup of finely packed chopped cilantro
- 2 Tsp. ground cumin

DIRECTIONS

1. Combine all the vegetables and the garlic and lime in a saucepan and boil then simmer for 5 minutes,
2. Once the mixture is boiling, cook and stir for 5-10 minutes
3. Pour the hot salsa into clean and hot jars, leaving 1/2- inch of headspace in each jar.
4. Take out any air bubbles before securing the jar lids.
5. Place in the water bath pot with boiling water and process for 15 minutes.
6. Remove the jars and wipe them dry.
7. Place the jars on a canning rack and cool for 24 hours before storing it.

79. *Corn & Cherry Tomato Salsa*

Preparation Time: 20 minutes

Cooking Time: 10 minutes

Servings: 6 pints

INGREDIENTS

- 5 pounds cherry tomatoes, roughly chopped
- 2 cups corn kernels (about 2 large ears fresh, but frozen-thawed is fine)
- 1 cup red onion, finely chopped
- 2 tsp. s salt
- ½ cup fresh lime juice (about 3 large or 4 medium limes)
- 2 jalapeño peppers, seeded and minced
- 1 tsp. chipotle chili powder, optional
- ½ cup chopped fresh cilantro

DIRECTIONS

1. Prepare the boiling water canner. Heat the jars in simmering water until they're ready for use. Do not boil.
2. Wash the lids in warm soapy water and set them aside with the bands.
3. Bring all the ingredients to a boil in a large stainless-steel or enameled saucepan.
4. Reduce the heat and simmer for 5 to 10 minutes, stirring occasionally.
5. Ladle the hot salsa into a hot jar, leaving ½-inch of headspace.
6. Remove the air bubbles. Wipe the jar rim clean. Center the lid on the jar. Apply the band and adjust to fingertip tight.
7. Place the jar in the boiling water canner. Repeat until all the jars are filled.
8. Process the jars for 15 minutes, adjusting for altitude. Turn off the heat; remove the lid, and let the jars stand for 5 minutes. Remove the jars and let them cool.

80. *Italian Tomatoes Pepper Spread*

Preparation Time: 60 min

Cooking Time: 20 Min

Servings: 5-6 8 oz. jars

INGREDIENTS

- 6 lb. red bell peppers
- 1 lb. Italian tomatoes
- 2 large, unpeeled cloves garlic
- 1 small onion (white)
- ½ cup red wine vinegar

- 2 tsp. s thinly sliced fresh basil
- 1 tsp. granulated sugar
- 1 tsp. salt

DIRECTIONS

1. Prepare the canning jars following the direction.

2. Roast tomatoes, red pepper, onion, and garlic on a grill or under a broiler at 425°F. Keep roasting for about 15 minutes or until peppers and tomatoes are scorched blackened and softened, and onion and garlic are blackened in spots.

3. Take them out of the heat. Leave onion and garlic to cool.

4. Put tomatoes and peppers in paper bags. Secure openings and leave for about 15 minutes for it cool enough.

5. Peel dried skin off onion and garlic.

6. Thinly cut onion, measure ¼ cup and set aside. Thinly cut garlic and put it to one side.

7. Peel and seed the tomatoes and peppers. Working in batches, put tomatoes and peppers in a food processor or blender and mash until smooth.

8. Combine pepper and tomato purée, onion, garlic, basil, vinegar, salt, and sugar in a large saucepot.

9. Place over medium-high heat. Bring to a boil, reduce heat, and cook slowly, stirring frequently to avoid sticking.

10. Boil it for about 20 minutes or until the mixture becomes thickened and mounds on a spoon.

11. Ladle hot spread into each canning jar. Remember to leave 1-inch headspace. Use spatula to remove air bubbles, then use a clean cloth to wipe jar rims, after that, adjust lids, and screw band.

12. Set the filled jars in a pressure canner at 11 pounds pressure for dial-gauge or 10 pounds for the weighted-gauge canner.

13. Process heat jars for 15 minutes, adjusting for altitude. Switch off the heat and let pressure drop naturally.

14. Remove the lid and cool the jars in canner for 5 minutes.

15. Take out the jars and cool. Inspect lids seal after 24 hours.

81. *Roasted Tomato Chipotle Sauce*

Preparation Time: 60 min

Cooking Time: 20 Min

Servings: 4-5 16 oz. jars.

INGREDIENTS

- 2 oz. chipotle chilies, seeded and roasted (about 12)
- 3 lb. Italian plum tomatoes, roasted, peeled, and chopped
- ½ lb. small size onions, roasted, peeled, and chopped
- 1 lb. sweet green peppers, roasted, peeled, and chopped
- 1 head garlic, roasted, peeled, and chopped
- 2 tsp. s granulated sugar
- 1 cup vinegar
- 1 tsp. salt

DIRECTIONS

1. Prepare the canning jars following the directions to sanitize them.

2. In the meantime, add in a medium bowl, put roasted chilies and add 2 cups of boiling water. Place a weight on top of chilies to submerge them, and set them aside.

3. Combine onions, tomatoes, garlic cloves, and peppers in a large saucepot and place over medium heat.

4. Purée chilies with soaking water and pour it to the roasted veggies mixed with vinegar, salt, and sugar.

5. Stirring frequently, allow it to boil and keep cooking for 20 minutes. Remove from heat and let it cool.

6. Ladle hot sauce into each canning jar. Remember to leave 1/2-inch headspace. Use spatula to remove air bubbles, then use a clean cloth to wipe jar rims, after that, adjust lids, and screw band.

7. Set the filled jars in a pressure canner at 11 pounds pressure for dial-gauge or 10 pounds for the weighted-gauge canner.

8. Process heat jars for 20-25 minutes, adjusting for altitude.

9. Switch off the heat and let pressure drop naturally.

10. Remove the lid and cool the jars in canner for 5 minutes.

11. Take out the jars and cool. Inspect lids seal after 24 hours.

82. *Fiesta Tomatoes Sauce*

Preparation Time: 15 min

Cooking Time: 75 Min

Servings: 7-8 16 oz. jars

INGREDIENTS

- 18 cups thinly chopped fresh tomatoes
- ¾ cup vinegar (5% acidity)
- 189 g (1 can) Fiesta Salsa Mix

DIRECTIONS

1. Prepare the canning jars following the direction.

2. In a large saucepot, combine tomatoes, Fiesta Salsa mix and vinegar, and place over medium-high heat.

3. Allow the mixture to boil with frequent stirring. Reduce heat and leave to boil for 5 minutes.

4. Ladle the hot salsa into each canning jar. Remember to leave 1-inch headspace. Use spatula to remove air bubbles, then use a clean cloth to wipe jar rims, after that, adjust lids, and screw band.

5. Set the filled jars in a pressure canner at 11 pounds pressure for dial-gauge or 10 pounds for the weighted-gauge canner.

6. Process heat jars for 75 minutes, adjusting for altitude. Then, switch off the heat and let pressure drop naturally.

7. Remove the lid and cool the jars in canner for 5 minutes.

8. Take out the jars and cool. Inspect lids seal after 24 hours.

Using salsa mixture to transform your garden's fresh produce to fiesta sauce is the easiest thing. It is ideal for the amateur in the homemade canning settings. Be it beginners or intermediate, this mixture cuts down the number of required ingredients as well as preparing and cooking time. They're very useful when you have many visitors

83. *Spicy Corn Sauce*

Preparation Time: 60 min

Cooking Time: 15 Min

Servings: 6-7 16 oz. jars

INGREDIENTS

- 8 cups whole kernel corn
- 12 cups thickly chopped tomatoes approx. 20 media
- 1¾ cup cider vinegar
- 1 cup Fiesta Salsa Mix

DIRECTIONS

1. Prepare the canning jars following the direction.

2. Rinse, seed, and cut tomatoes.

3. Draw off excess liquid and measure twelve cups. Blanch ears of fresh corn in boiling water for a minute prior to cutting off kernel. Measure 8 cups and set aside.

4. Combine Fiesta salsa mix and vinegar in a large saucepot and place over medium-high heat.

5. Add corn and tomatoes. Allow mixture to boil while stirring constantly. Reduce heat and cook slowly, stirring frequently until mixture is heated through.

6. Ladle hot sauce into each canning jar. Remember to leave 1-inch headspace. Use spatula to remove air bubbles, then use a clean cloth to wipe jar rims, after that, adjust lids, and screw band.

7. Set the filled jars in a pressure canner at 11 pounds pressure for dial-gauge or 10 pounds for the weighted-gauge canner. Process heat jars for 15 minutes, adjusting for altitude.

8. Switch off the heat and let pressure drop naturally.

9. Remove the lid and cool the jars in canner for 5 minutes.

10. Take out the jars and cool. Inspect lids seal after 24 hours.

Stir in a can of black beans to an opened jar for a great savoring sauce! Add one to two tsp. s of red pepper flakes, or one tsp. cayenne pepper or hot pepper to this recipe if you desire a spicier sauce.

84. *Spicy Tomato Sauce*

Preparation Time: 60 min

Cooking Time: 15 Min

Servings: 6-7 16 oz. jars

INGREDIENTS

- 12 cups peeled and cubed tomatoes
- 9 chili peppers, dried
- 3 cups sliced red onions
- 15 cloves garlic, thinly sliced
- 1½ cups tightly packed thinly sliced cilantro
- ¾ cup red wine vinegar
- 6 jalapeño peppers, seeded and sliced
- ¾ tsp. hot pepper flakes
- 1 tablespoon salt
- Hot water

DIRECTIONS

1. Prepare the canning jars following the direction.

2. Place rinsed dried chilies in a large bowl and pour hot water to cover. Submerge chilies in water for 15 minutes or until softened.

3. Draw off half of the water. Purée the chilies with remaining water in a blender until smooth.

4. Combine tomatoes, chili purée, cilantro, onions, jalapeño peppers, garlic, hot pepper flakes, vinegar, and salt in a large saucepot.

5. Place over medium-high heat, bring to a boil, stirring frequently.

6. Reduce heat and cook slowly, stirring constantly, for about ten minutes or until slightly thickened.

7. Ladle hot sauce into each canning jar. Remember to leave 1-inch headspace. Use spatula to remove air bubbles, then use a clean cloth to wipe jar rims, after that, adjust lids, and screw band.

8. Set the filled jars in a pressure canner at 11 pounds pressure for dial-gauge or 10 pounds for the weighted-gauge canner.

9. Process heat jars for fifteen minutes, adjusting for altitude.

10. Switch off the heat and let pressure drop naturally.

11. Remove the lid and cool the jars in canner for 5 minutes.

12. Take out the jars and cool.

13. Inspect lids seal after 24 hours.

85. Pears and Peaches Salsa

Preparation Time: 60 Min

Cooking Time: 15 Min

Servings: 4-5 16 oz. jars

INGREDIENTS

- 7 medium cored pears, peeled and chopped (5 cups)
- 14 medium peaches, peeled and chopped (10 cups)
- 1 cup Fiesta Salsa Mix
- 4 tablespoon honeys
- ½ cup grated zest, lime juice,

DIRECTIONS

1. Sanitize lids and jars

2. In a large saucepot pot, combine pears and peaches; add salsa mix, honey, and lime juice to fruit. Place the mixture over medium-high heat and bring it to boil.

3. Reduce heat and let boil, stirring frequently), until the mixture is well cooked.

4. Ladle the hot salsa into each canning jar. Remember to leave 1-inch headspace. Use spatula to remove air bubbles, then use a clean cloth to wipe jar rims, after that, adjust lids, and screw band.

5. Set the filled jars in a pressure canner at 11 pounds pressure for dial-gauge or 10 pounds for the weighted-gauge canner. Process heat jars for fifteen minutes, adjusting for altitude.

6. Switch off the heat and let pressure drop naturally.

7. Remove the lid and cool the jars in canner for 5 minutes.

8. Take out the jars and cool. Inspect lids seal after 24 hours.

Pears and peaches plus salsa mix create a snappy condiment to liven up menus year-round. Whether garnished, served as a dip or stirring into recipes, this easy-to-get ready salsa will surely become your family favorite.

86. Zesty Yellow Tomato Spread

Preparation Time: 60 Min

Cooking Time: 20 Min

Servings: 6-7 8 oz. jars

INGREDIENTS

- 35-40 medium yellow tomatoes
- 4 cups granulated sugar
- 2 cups honey
- 2 pieces of ginger root, peeled
- 2 tablespoon whole allspice
- 2 (8-inch) cinnamon sticks

Canning and Preserving Food for Beginners

DIRECTIONS

1. Prepare the canning jars following the direction.

2. Wash and chop tomatoes. Put a large saucepot over medium-high heat, add tomatoes and bring to a boil, stirring frequently.

3. Reduce heat; simmer for about 10 minutes so tomatoes are tender, stirring intermittently.

4. Press through a food mill or sieve. Measure 18 cups of tomato mash.

5. Combine tomato mash, honey, and sugar in a large saucepot.

6. Tie allspice, cinnamon, and ginger root in a large square of cheesecloth, making a spice bag.

7. Combine it with the tomato mix.

8. Stirring frequently. Boil mixture slowly for about 30 minutes or until it's thickened enough to be mounted on a spoon

9. Ladle hot butter into each canning jar. Remember to leave 1-inch headspace. Use spatula to remove air bubbles, then use a clean cloth to wipe jar rims, after that, adjust lids, and screw band.

10. Set the filled jars in a pressure canner at 11 pounds pressure for dial-gauge or 10 pounds for the weighted-gauge canner. Process heat jars for 20 minutes, adjusting for altitude. Switch off the heat and let pressure drop naturally.

11. Remove the lid and cool the jars in canner for 5 minutes.

12. Take out the jars and cool. Inspect lids seal after 24 hours.

87. *Horseradish Tomato Sauce*

Preparation Time: 90 min

Cooking Time: 25 Min

Servings: 9-10 16 oz. jars

INGREDIENTS

- 3 cups peeled and grated horseradish
- 13 cups seeded and chopped tomatoes
- 2 lemons, zest, and juice
- 3 cloves garlic, crushed
- 1 cup white vinegar
- 1½ cup granulated sugar
- 2 tablespoons Worcestershire Sauce
- 2 tablespoons pickling salt
- 2 tsp. dry mustard
- 1 tsp. onion powder
- 1 tsp. cayenne pepper
- ½ tsp. black pepper

DIRECTIONS

1. Place a large saucepot over medium-high heat. Add tomatoes and bring to rolling boil.

2. Reduce heat and simmer lightly for about 45 minutes.

3. Add lemon peel, lemon juice, Worcestershire sauce, vinegar, garlic, onion powder, black pepper, cayenne pepper, sugar, and mustard to tomato paste. Stir it constantly.

4. Allow to boil, take it out of heat source and then stir in horseradish.

5. Ladle sauce into each canning jar. Remember to leave 1-inch headspace. Use spatula to remove air bubbles, then use a clean cloth to wipe jar rims, after that, adjust lids, and screw band.

6. Set the filled jars in a pressure canner at 11 pounds pressure for dial-gauge or 10 pounds for the weighted-gauge canner. Process heat jars for 25 minutes, adjusting for altitude.

7. Switch off the heat and let pressure drop naturally.

8. Remove the lid and cool the jars in canner for 5 minutes.

9. Take out the jars and cool. Inspect lids seal after 24 hours.

Tomatoes, lemon, and horseradish make the wonderful sauce for shrimp cocktail. Do not limit the use to just shrimp, use it as an addition to any choice of seafood.

88. Cherry Chutney

Preparation Time: 10 minutes

Cooking Time: 60 minutes

Servings: 2-3 8 oz. jars

INGREDIENTS

- 16 oz. pitted cherries
- 8 oz. cider vinegar
- 4 oz. rice vinegar
- 1 large, chopped onion
- 1 peeled and cored Granny Smith apple, chopped
- 2 oz. white sugar
- 2 oz. brown sugar
- 1-oz. fresh ginger, minced
- 1 oz. Chinese five-spice powder
- 1 tsp. salt
- 1/4 tsp. nutmeg, ground

DIRECTIONS

1. Put all Ingredients in a big saucepan and then bring to a simmer on medium high heat.

2. Reduce heat to medium low and simmer, cover the pan and simmer for 60 minutes. Stir often.

3. Remove lid and keep simmering until you have the desired consistency.

4. Add to the canning jars leaving ½-inch headspace, and seal.

5. Place in the water bath pot with boiling water and process for 15-20 minutes.

6. Remove the jars and wipe them dry.

7. Place the jars on a canning rack and cool for 24 hours before storing it.

Try to serve this chutney with some goat cheese and buttery crackers as an appetizer for holiday gatherings. This recipe tastes amazing with some grilled pork loin as well.

89. Mint Chutney

Preparation Time:10 minutes

Cooking Time: -

Servings: 2 8oz. jars

INGREDIENTS

- 1 bunch fresh cilantro
- 12 oz. fresh mint leaves
- 1 green Chile pepper
- ½ tsp. salt
- ½ oz. lemon juice
- 1 medium onion, cut into chunks
- 2 oz. water

DIRECTIONS

1. Combine all ingredients except for water in a food processor and purée until a fine paste forms.

2. Add enough water to reach desired thickness.

3. Add to the canning jars leaving ½-inch headspace, and seal.

4. Refrigerate and consume in a week or two.

5. If you want to can this recipes, add the mixture to the canning jars leaving ½-inch headspace, and seal.

6. Place in the water bath pot with boiling water and process for 15-20 minutes.

7. Remove the jars and wipe them dry.

8. Place the jars on a canning rack and cool for 24 hours before storing it

This mint chutney works well as a delicious dip for samosas when you are having guests over. You can also add some yogurt to the chutney for a creamier texture.

90. *Christmas Chutney*

Preparation Time: 15minutes

Cooking Time: 20 minutes

Servings: 2-3 8z. jars

INGREDIENTS

- 32 oz. fresh cranberries
- 8 oz. raisins
- 4 oz. white sugar
- 6 oz. brown sugar, packed
- 1/3-oz. cinnamon, ground
- 1 tsp. fresh ginger root, minced
- 1/4 tsp. cloves, ground
- 8 oz. water
- 4 oz. onion, minced
- 4 oz. Granny Smith apple, chopped
- 4 oz. celery, finely chopped

DIRECTIONS

1. Mix cranberries, raisins, sugar, ginger, cinnamon, ginger root, cloves, and water in a large pan and bring to a boil on medium high.

2. Reduce heat to low and simmer for 5 minutes until berries burst.

3. Stir in onion, apple and celery and cook for 5-10 minutes until mixture thickens.

4. Pour into a sealable container and chill overnight. Use it or transfer into hot sanitized jars and close the lids.

5. Place in the water bath pot with boiling water and process for 20-25 minutes.

6. Remove the jars and wipe them dry.

7. Place the jars on a canning rack and cool for 24 hours before storing it.

This recipe is a holiday favorite at my house for Thanksgiving and Christmas. You can use frozen cranberries, but I prefer the taste of the fresh for this dish.

91. *Spiced Apple Chutney*

Preparation Time: 15 minutes

Cooking Time: 50 minutes

Servings: 2-3 8 oz. jars

INGREDIENTS

- 12 oz. white vinegar
- 12 oz. white sugar
- 4 peeled and cored tart apples, cubed
- 2 oz. dried apricots, diced
- 2 oz. golden raisins

- 2 oz. shallots, diced
- 1/4 tsp. Aleppo pepper flakes
- 5 thick slices fresh ginger
- 1 whole star anise
- ½ tsp. yellow mustard seed
- 2 minced garlic cloves
- 1 tsp. kosher salt

DIRECTIONS

1. Place vinegar and sugar in a large saucepan and whisk until well combined.
2. Add apples, apricots, raisins, shallots, pepper flakes, ginger, and star anise.
3. Bring mixture to boil on medium high heat.
4. Reduce heat to medium low and stir in the rest of the ingredients.
5. Simmer for 45 minutes until liquid has reduced and fruit is tender.
6. Remove pan from heat and take out ginger and star anise.
7. Season with salt and pepper and transfer into hot sanitized jars.
8. Place in the water bath pot with boiling water and process for 20-25 minutes.
9. Remove the jars and wipe them dry.
10. Place the jars on a canning rack and cool for 24 hours before storing it.

Try to offer this chutney at Thanksgiving as a garnish for turkey or a spread for fresh dinner rolls. It is also ideas for ham and chicken when you want to spice up your meal.

92. *Spiced Cranberry Apple Chutney*

Preparation Time: 15 minutes

Cooking Time: -60 minutes

Servings: 4-5 8 oz. jars

INGREDIENTS

- 16 oz. fresh cranberries
- 16 oz. white sugar
- 1 ½ oz. water
- 1 large peeled and cored Granny Smith apple, chopped
- 2 finely chopped stalks celery
- ½ oz. orange zest, grated
- 8 oz. fresh orange juice
- 2 oz. pecans
- 8 oz. golden raisins
- ½ tsp. ginger, ground
- 1/4 tsp. cloves, ground
- a pinch salt

DIRECTIONS

1. Bring cranberries, white sugar, and water to a boil in a large pan on medium high heat.
2. Reduce heat to medium and cook for 8-10 minutes until berries have burst.
3. Stir in the rest of the ingredients and cook for 35 minutes until liquid is reduced and celery is softened.
4. Remove pan from heat and let mixture stand for 15-20 minutes until thickened.
5. Use it or transfer into sanitized jars and close the lids.
6. Place in the water bath pot with boiling water and process for 20-25 minutes.
7. Remove the jars and wipe them dry.
8. Place the jars on a canning rack and cool for 24 hours before storing it.

This recipe is delicious with some cheese, crackers or spread on fresh crusty bread. I like to serve this chutney even with turkey, ham, and chicken.

93. Spiced Cranberry Chutney

Preparation Time: 30 minutes

Cooking Time: -15 minutes

Servings: 4-5 8 oz. Jars

INGREDIENTS

- 2 oz. finely chopped dried apricots
- 4 oz. brown sugar
- 4 oz. raisins
- 8 oz. water
- 24 oz. fresh cranberries
- 1 peeled and cored Granny Smith apple, chopped
- 1 tsp. lemon zest, grated
- 2 oz. fresh lemon juice
- 2 oz. crystallized ginger, chopped
- ½ tsp. red pepper flakes

DIRECTIONS

1. Mix apricots, sugar, water, and raisins in a large saucepan. Bring to a boil on the medium high heat.
2. Reduce the heat to medium-to-low and then simmer for 5 minutes.
3. Stir in berries, apple and zest and simmer for 10 more minutes.
4. Add the rest of the ingredients, stir, and remove pan from heat. Chill overnight and pour into jars to store or serve.
5. Use the chutney or transfer into sanitized jars and close the lids.
6. Place in the water bath pot with boiling water and process for 20-25 minutes.
7. Remove the jars and wipe them dry.
8. Place the jars on a canning rack and cool for 24 hours before storing it.

Try this cranberry chutney for Thanksgiving as an alternative to the traditional cranberry sauce. The spicy flavor is unique and a refreshing change from the norm.

94. Mango-Pineapple Chutney

Preparation Time: 5 minutes

Cooking Time: 30 minutes

Servings: 4-5 16 oz. Jars

INGREDIENTS

- 1 oz. vegetable oil
- 1 tsp. red pepper flakes, crushed
- 1 large minced sweet onion
- 4" peeled piece ginger root, minced
- 1 large diced yellow bell pepper
- 3 large peeled and pitted ripened mangoes, diced
- 1 small peeled and diced pineapple
- 4 oz. brown sugar
- ¾ oz. curry powder
- 4 oz. apple cider vinegar

DIRECTIONS

1. Heat oil in a large pan on medium heat and sauté the pepper flakes in the oil until they sizzle. Add onion to the pepper flakes and stir.
2. Reduce heat to low and cover the pan. Cook for 20 minutes until onions have softened. Stir frequently.
3. Uncover the pan and turn heat up to medium. Add ginger and bell pepper and stir well. Cook for 2-3 minutes until fragrant.
4. Stir in the rest of the ingredients and increase heat to a simmer. Cook for 30 minutes while stirring frequently.
5. Remove pan from heat and cool before storing in a sealable container and placing in the refrigerator.

I love to pile this chutney on top of grilled chicken with some mashed potatoes and green beans. The tangy taste of the fruit makes any meat come alive with flavor.

95. Tomato And Peach Chutney

Preparation Time: 15 minutes

Cooking Time: 25 minutes

Servings: 7-8 16 oz. jars

INGREDIENTS

- 15 peeled tomatoes, chopped
- 5 peeled and pitted fresh peaches, chopped
- 5 peeled and cored red apples, diced
- 4 diced medium onions
- 4 diced stalks celery
- 12 oz. distilled white vinegar
- ½ oz. salt
- 8 oz. pickling spice, wrapped in cheesecloth

DIRECTIONS

1. Mix all Ingredients in a large pot and bring to a boil on medium heat.

2. Reduce the heat to low and then simmer for 2 hours until desired thickness is achieved. Remove from heat and cool.

3. Transfer to jars and store in the refrigerator or in plastic containers in the freezer.

I never considered pairing tomato and peach when making chutney until I tried this recipe. You will yield a large batch of this preserve so I would recommend using a canner to preserve this delicious garnish.

96. Sweet Tamarind Chutney

Preparation Time: 15 minutes

Cooking Time: 30 minutes

Servings: 2-3 8 oz. jars

INGREDIENTS

- ½ oz. canola oil
- 1 tsp. cumin seeds
- 1 tsp. ginger, ground
- ½ tsp. garam masala
- ½ tsp. cayenne pepper
- ½ tsp. asafetida powder
- ½ tsp. fennel seeds
- 10 oz. white sugar
- 16 oz. water
- 1 ½ oz. tamarind paste

DIRECTIONS

1. Heat canola oil in a pan on medium heat and sauté cumin, ginger, pepper, garam masala, asafetida powder and fennel in the oil for 2 minutes.

2. Add water, sugar and tamarind paste to the mixture and stir. Bring to a boil on medium high heat.

3. Reduce heat to low and simmer for 20-30 minutes until mixture turns deep brown and is thick enough to coat the back of a spoon.

4. Remove pan from heat and cool mixture until it reaches desired thickness.

5. Transfer into hot sanitized jars.

6. Place in the water bath pot with boiling water and process for 20-25 minutes.

7. Remove the jars and wipe them dry.

8. Place the jars on a canning rack and cool for 24 hours before storing it.

This chutney has a unique and mouth-watering flavor that is addictive. I like to use this recipe when I make lamb and serve it as a garnish.

97. Cilantro Chutney

Preparation Time: 20 minutes

Cooking Time: 30 minutes

Servings: 2-3 8 oz. jars

INGREDIENTS

- 2 bunches fresh cilantro, leaves picked from stems
- 1-oz. fresh ginger root, minced

- 1 tsp. cumin seeds
- 2 green Chile peppers
- 1 oz. lemon juice
- 1 oz. tomato sauce
- ½ oz. water

DIRECTIONS

1. Place all Ingredients in a blender and process until finely ground.
2. Stir water into the mixture until a sauce of the desired consistency is made.
3. Transfer into hot sanitized jars.
4. Place in the water bath pot with boiling water and process for 20-25 minutes.
5. Remove the jars and wipe them dry.
6. Place the jars on a canning rack and cool for 24 hours before storing it.

This chutney tastes amazing with everything! I have used it as a dip for pita crackers, bread, and spread it on my turkey at holiday dinners.

98. *Lemon Strawberry Sauce*

Preparation Time: 35 minutes

Cooking Time: 15 minutes

Servings: 2 pints

INGREDIENTS

- 2 lbs. strawberries
- 4 cups granulated sugar
- ¼ cup lemon juice

DIRECTIONS

1. In a sizable bowl, use a potato masher to crush the strawberries in batches until you have 3 cups of mashed berries. Leave strawberries more intact if you prefer more chunkiness.
2. In a heavy-bottomed, nonreactive pot, mix the strawberries, sugar, and lemon juice. Stir over low heat until the sugar is dissolved, then increase the heat to high and boil for 15 minutes as you stir occasionally.
3. Ladle the sauce into a prepared jar. Use a funnel to safely transfer the sauce, leaving some headspace.
4. Rinse the rims of the jars with a dampened, clean, lint-free cloth or paper towel and once again with a dry towel to remove any sauce or liquid from the rim of the jar.
5. Arrange the canning lid on the jar and twist the canning ring on until it's just-snug on the jar. Carefully transfer the jars into the water bath using the canning tongs and place the lid on the canning pot.
6. Start the timer and process in the water bath for 10 minutes.

99. *Peach Chili Sauce*

Preparation Time 35 minutes

Cooking Time: 20 minutes

Servings: 5 pints

INGREDIENTS

- 5 lbs. tomatoes
- 1½ lbs. chopped peaches
- 3 chopped sweet onions
- 3 chopped pears
- 2 chopped green peppers
- 2 stripped jalapeno peppers
- 2 chopped celery ribs
- 1 tsp mixed pickling spices
- 3 cups sugar
- 3 tsps. salt
- 2 cups white vinegar

DIRECTIONS

1. In a Dutch oven, bring 2 quarts of water to a boil.
2. Place 1-2 tomatoes in the boiling water for 30-60 seconds. Remove and plunge into ice water. Peel and finely chop the tomatoes.
3. Tie pickling spices in a cheesecloth bag.

4. Place all ingredients in the pot and bring to a boil.
5. Reduce the heat and simmer, uncovered, 2-2½ hours until thickened, stirring occasionally. Discard the spice bag.
6. Carefully scoop the hot mixture into hot, sterilized 1-pint jars, leaving a ½-inch headspace.
7. Rinse the rims carefully. Place the tops on the jars and screw on the bands until fingertip tight.
8. Place the jars into the canner with boiling water, ensuring that they are completely covered with water.
9. Let them boil for 20 minutes.
10. Remove the jars and cool.

100. *Pear Barbecue Sauce*

Preparation Time: 35 minutes

Cooking Time: 5 minutes

Servings: 4 pints

INGREDIENTS

- 3 cups soy sauce
- 3 cups brown sugar
- 1 cup plus ¼ cup water, divided
- 1 cup's sake
- ½ cup gochujang
- ½ cup mild honey
- 1/3 cup rice wine vinegar
- ¼ cup plus 2 tbsps. minced garlic
- ¼ cup grated fresh ginger root
- 4 sliced scallions
- 1 grated pear
- 1 tsp. black pepper
- 1 tsp. crushed red pepper flakes
- 3 tbsps. canning starch

DIRECTIONS

1. Place the 1 cup of water, ginger root, sake, light brown sugar, vinegar, gochujang, honey, rice wine soy sauce, garlic, black pepper, sliced scallions, grated pear, and chili powder or crushed red pepper flakes in a sizable stainless-steel stockpot.
2. Boil for 5 minutes as you stir occasionally.
3. In another bowl, place the ¼ cup water and canning starch, and mix evenly.
4. Add the water mixture to the sauce then return the barbecue sauce to a boil and boil for another minute.
5. Fill into sterilized pint jars, leaving some headspace.
6. Rinse the rims of the jars clean and tighten the lids.
7. Arrange the jars in a canner full of boiling water and process for 15 minutes.
8. Remove the jars and cool.

101. *Honey Mustard*

Preparation Time: 35 minutes

Cooking Time: 14 minutes

Servings: 5 jars

INGREDIENTS

- 1 cup mustard powder
- 6 tbsps. yellow mustard seeds
- 1 cup honey
- 1½ cups cold water

- 2/3 cups white wine vinegar

DIRECTIONS

1. Place all ingredients together in a sizable bowl covered with plastic wrap and set aside at room temperature for 72 hours.
2. Blend the contents in the bowl until smooth, then pour into a stainless-steel saucepan to boil as you stir over medium heat.
3. Fill the hot mustard into the jars, leaving some headspace.
4. Rinse the rims carefully and tighten the lids.
5. Arrange the jars in a canner full of boiling water and process for 10 minutes.

102. *Pickled Pullet Eggs*

Preparation Time: 30 minutes (+ 2-3 weeks to seasoning)

Cooking Time: 15-20 minutes

Servings: 2-3 Quart Jars

INGREDIENTS

- 1 white onion, sliced
- 2 Vidalia onions, sliced
- 4-6 fresh garlic cloves, diced
- 2 tbsp pickling salt
- 1 tbsp mustard seed
- 1 tbsp celery seed
- 1 tbsp pickling spice
- 4-7 chili peppers, fresh
- 3 cups white vinegar
- 1 cup cider vinegar
- 1 cup water
- 24 hard-boiled eggs, peeled

DIRECTIONS

1. Put onions and garlic in a saucepan.
2. Add the remaining ingredients except eggs and bring them to boil for 5 minutes.
3. Place 12 peeled eggs into each hot jar, glass, then pour in hot sauce.
4. Wipe the jar rims with clean damp cloth. Place lids immediately.
5. Process in boiling water in a pressure canner for about 15 minutes.
6. Cool to seal.
7. Store the finished pickles in a glass container with a nonreactive lid. The eggs may require 2 to 4 weeks to become well-seasoned. For best results, use them after 3-4 months.

103. *Spaghetti Sauce*

Preparation Time: -35 minutes

Cooking Time: 40 minutes

Servings: 9 quarts

INGREDIENTS

- 25 lbs. tomatoes
- 4 green peppers
- 4 chopped onions
- 2 cans tomato paste
- 8 minced garlic cloves
- 4 tsps. dried oregano
- 2 tsps. dried parsley flakes
- 2 tsps. dried basil
- 2 tsps. crushed red pepper flakes
- 2 tsps. Worcestershire sauce
- ¼ cup canola oil
- 2/3 cup sugar
- ¼ cup salt
- 1 cup + 2 tbsp bottled lemon juice
- 2 bay leaves

DIRECTIONS

1. In a Dutch oven, bring 2 quarts of water to a boil.
2. Place 1-2 tomatoes in boiling water for 30-60 seconds. Remove each tomato and plunge them

into ice water. Peel and quarter tomatoes, then place in a stockpot.

3. Pulse onions and green peppers in batches in a food processor until finely chopped, then transfer to the stockpot.
4. Stir in the next 11 ingredients.
5. Add water to cover. Bring to a boil.
6. Reduce the heat and let this simmer for 4-5 hours, stirring occasionally while uncovered.
7. Discard the bay leaves.
8. Add 2 tbsp lemon juice to each of the nine shots, sterilized 1-quart jars.
9. Scoop hot mixture into the jars, leaving a ½-inch headspace.
10. Rinse the rims carefully. Place the tops on the jars and screw on the bands until fingertip tight.
11. Place the jars into the canner with boiling water, ensuring that they are completely covered with the water.
12. Let them boil for 40 minutes. Remove the jars and cool.

104. *Pepper Sauce with Tomato*

Preparation Time: 35 minutes

Cooking Time: 30 minutes

Servings: 5 half pints

INGREDIENTS

- 3 oz. dried chipotle peppers
- 1 dried ancho chili
- 3 cups boiling water
- 4 cups tomato purée
- 1 cup cider vinegar
- 1 cup diced onion
- ¾ cup brown sugar
- 8 minced garlic cloves
- 1 tsp. kosher salt
- 1 tsp. ground cumin
- 1 tsp. ground cinnamon

DIRECTIONS

1. Remove any stems and caps from the chipotle and ancho peppers.
2. Place the peppers into a heatproof bowl, pour in the boiling water, and cover the bowl tightly with plastic wrap.
3. Leave the peppers to rehydrate for 30 minutes.
4. Use tongs to move the ancho chiles into a blender. Ladle some of the soaking liquid into the blender, fix the lid in place, and blend on high.
5. Pour the smooth mixture into a stainless-steel stockpot. Use tongs to transfer the soaked chipotle peppers into the pot.
6. Pour the soaking water through a fine mesh sieve into the pot to filter out any particles that fell to the bottom.
7. Place the remaining ingredients in the pot and boil, stirring frequently.
8. Reduce the heat to medium-low and simmer for at least 30 minutes, stirring very frequently to prevent scorching, or until the sauce is reduced by more than half and is as thick as ketchup.
9. Ladle into jars, leaving some headspace.
10. Rinse the rims and tighten the lids.
11. Arrange the jars to a canner filled with boiling water and process for 15 minutes.
12. Let them boil for 40 minutes.
13. Remove the jars and cool.

105. Homestyle Spaghetti Sauce

Preparation Time: 30 minutes

Cooking Time: 20 minutes

Servings: 4-pint jars

INGREDIENTS

- 2 lbs. ground beef
- 4 cups chopped onion
- 16 oz. tomato sauce
- 24 oz. tomato paste
- 4 tsps. pepper
- 4 tsps. dried parsley
- 4 tsps. dried basil
- 4 tbsps. brown sugar
- 4 tsps. salt
- 8 cups water
- 2 bay leaves

DIRECTIONS

1. Place a large saucepot over medium-high heat. Boil the ground beef with the onion until all pink disappears.
2. Reduce the heat and add tomato paste, tomato sauce, pepper, and every other ingredient. Stirring frequently, boil for 45 minutes.
3. Ladle the hot sauce into each canning jar. Remember to leave a 1-inch headspace. Use a spatula to remove any air bubbles, then use a clean cloth to wipe the jar rims. After that, adjust the lids and screw bands.
4. Set the filled jars in a pressure canner at 11 pounds of pressure for dial-gauge or 10 pounds for the weighted-gauge canner.
5. Process hot jars for 20 minutes, adjusting for altitude.
6. Switch off the heat and let the pressure drop naturally.
7. Remove the lid and cool the jars in the canner for 5 minutes.
8. Take out the jars and cool further.
9. Inspect lid seals after 24 hours.

106. Roasted Garlic Pasta Sauce

Preparation Time: -35 minutes

Cooking Time: 50 minutes

Servings: 6 pints

INGREDIENTS

- 6 roasted and chopped garlic cloves
- 3 tbsps. olive oil
- 4 roasted green sweet peppers
- 2 tbsps. kosher salt
- 3 tbsps. packed brown sugar
- 12 lbs. ripe tomatoes
- 1 tbsp. balsamic vinegar
- 2 cups fresh basil leaves
- 1 tsp. black pepper
- 6 tbsps. lemon juice
- 1 cup assorted fresh herbs

DIRECTIONS

1. In a large pot, mix the garlic, tomatoes, brown sugar, salt, vinegar, and pepper, and boil for 50 minutes.
2. Add the peppers and boil for 10 minutes.

3. Move away from the heat and stir in the basil and the assorted herbs.
4. Fill 1 tablespoon of the lemon juice into each of the sterile jars. Pour the sauce into the jars with the lemon juice, leaving a ½ inch head space.
5. Rinse the jar rims clean and adjust the lids.
6. Process these in a boiling water bath for 35 minutes.
7. Remove the jars and cool.

107. *Chili Sauce with Garlic*

Preparation Time 35 minutes

Cooking Time: 10 minutes

Servings: 3 cups

INGREDIENTS

- 2 cups plus 1/3 cup water, divided
- 2 cups rice vinegar
- 2 cups granulated sugar
- 4 tsps. salt
- 4 minced jalapeño peppers
- 6 minced garlic cloves
- ¼ cup plus 2 tsps. canning starch

DIRECTIONS

1. Place rice vinegar, 2 cups of water, minced pepper, sugar, salt, and garlic in a sizable saucepan.
2. Mix evenly to dissolve the sugar and salt, then boil for 5 minutes.
3. Combine the canning starch into the remaining 1/3 cup of water.
4. Add the starch/water mixture into the cooking sauce.
5. Simmer for one minute as you stir thoroughly.
6. Fill the half-pint jars with the sauce, leaving some headspace.
7. Rinse the rims of the jars clean and tighten the lids.
8. Arrange the jars in a canner full of boiling water and process for 10 minutes.

108. *Hamburger Sauce Mix*

Preparation Time: 35 minutes

Cooking Time: 20 minutes

Servings: 4

INGREDIENTS

- 2 lbs. ground beef
- 3 cups chopped onions
- 12 oz tomato puree
- 1 1/3 cups water
- ½ tbsp pepper

DIRECTIONS

1. Brown beef and onions in a stockpot and skim off any fat.
2. Add all the remaining ingredients and boil, then simmer for 5 minutes.
3. Scoop the hot mixture into hot pint jars. Leave a 1-inch headspace.
4. Wipe the rims of the jars using a clean, damp paper towel and apply the 2-piece metal caps.
5. Arrange the jars in a pressure canner and process for about 75 minutes at 10 pounds of pressure, adjusting for altitude.
6. Switch off the heat and let the pressure drop naturally. Remove the lid and cool the jars in the canner for 5 minutes.
7. Take out the jars and cool further. Inspect lids for sealing after 24 hours.

PRESSURE CANNING RECIPES: MEAT, POULTRY AND SEAFOOD

109. *Simple Canned Salmon*

Preparation Time: 20 minutes (+ 1 hour to brine)

Cooking Time: 1 hour 40 minutes

Servings: 4 pints

INGREDIENTS

- 2 pounds salmon fillets, skin-on or skinless
- 1 cup Diamond Crystal kosher salt
- 1 gallon water

DIRECTIONS

1. If you caught your own salmon, gut it within 2 hours of being caught. Remove the head, tail, and scales, but leave the skin on. Wash the fish and remove any blood. Keep the fish clean and refrigerated, or on ice, until you are ready to process it.
2. In a large food-safe container, dissolve the salt in the water to make a brine (it should dissolve without needing to heat the water).
3. Cut the salmon into 3-inch pieces, add to the brine, and refrigerate for 1 hour.
4. Prep 4-pint jars and your pressure canner according to the instructions in Pressure Canning, Step-by-Step.
5. Drain the fish and pack it into the hot jars, skin-side facing the glass, leaving 1 inch of headspace.
6. Remove any air bubbles, wipe the jar rims, secure the lids and rings finger-tight, and load the jars into the pressure canner. Process the jars at 10 pounds pressure for 1 hour 40 minutes, adjusting for altitude.
7. Switch off the heat and let the pressure drop naturally.
8. Remove the lid and cool the jars in the canner for 5 minutes.
9. Take out the jars and cool further.
10. Inspect lid seals after 24 hours.

Try This Instead: Add ½ tsp. per jar of one of the following: Dijon mustard, fresh or dried dill, lemon pepper, or an Italian seasoning blend.

If you fish, this is a great way to preserve your catch instead of packing your freezer. It makes a quick and healthy source of protein that can be used in a few ways.

110. *Chili Beef*

Preparation Time: 20 minutes

Cooking Time: 35 minutes

Processing Time: 75 minutes for pints; 90 minutes for quarts

Servings: 8 pints or 4 quarts

INGREDIENTS

- 6 pounds ground beef
- 3 cups chopped yellow or white onion
- 3 garlic cloves, minced
- 2 (32-oz.) cans crushed tomatoes
- ½ cup plus 2 tablespoons chili powder
- 2 tablespoons ground cumin
- 1½ tablespoons Diamond Crystal kosher salt, divided

DIRECTIONS

1. In a large Dutch oven over medium heat, brown the meat for about 15 minutes, breaking up clumps, until no pink remains. Drain off any fat.
2. Add the onion and garlic. Cook for about 5 minutes until the onion is tender.
3. Stir in the tomatoes, chili powder, and cumin. Cook for 15 minutes; skim any fat from the surface of the chili. Add 1 tablespoon of salt; taste and add more salt, up ½ tablespoon more, as needed.

4. Prep 8 pint or 4-quart jars and your pressure canner according to the instructions in Pressure Canning, Step-by-Step.
5. Pack the chili into the hot jars, leaving 1 inch of headspace.
6. Remove any air bubbles, wipe the jar rims, secure the lids and rings finger-tight, and load the jars into the pressure canner.
7. Process the jars at 10 pounds pressure for 1 hour 15 minutes for pints, or 1 hour 30 minutes for quarts, according to the instructions, adjusting for altitude.
8. Switch off the heat and let the pressure drop naturally.
9. Remove the lid and cool the jars in the canner for 5 minutes.
10. Take out the jars and cool further.
11. Inspect lid seals after 24 hours.

111. *Essential Chicken Soup*

Preparation Time: 30 minutes

Cooking Time: 20 minutes

Processing Time: 75 minutes for pints; 90 minutes for quarts

Servings: 8 pints or 4 quarts

INGREDIENTS

- 1 tablespoon olive oil
- 1½ cups chopped carrot
- 1 cup chopped celery
- 1 cup chopped yellow onion
- 2 garlic cloves, minced
- 1 tablespoon ground turmeric
- 8 cups Slow Cooker Chicken Bone Broth or store-bought chicken broth
- 2 cups shredded cooked chicken
- 1 tsp. Diamond Crystal kosher salt, plus more as needed
- 2 tsp. s freshly ground black pepper, plus more as needed

DIRECTIONS

1. In a stockpot over medium heat, combine the oil, carrot, celery, onion, and garlic. Sauté for about 10 minutes until slightly browned. Add the turmeric and cook for 2 minutes, stirring.
2. Add the broth and increase the heat to bring the mixture to a simmer. Add the chicken and stir to combine. Stir in the salt and pepper, taste, and adjust the seasoning as needed.
3. Prep 8 pint or 4-quart jars and your pressure canner according to the instructions in Pressure Canning, Step-by-Step.
4. Pack the soup into the hot jars, leaving 1 inch of headspace.
5. Remove any air bubbles, wipe the jar rims, secure the lids and rings finger-tight, and load the jars into the pressure canner. Process the jars at 10 pounds pressure for 1 hour 15 minutes for pints, or 1 hour 30 minutes for quarts, adjusting for altitude.
6. Switch off the heat and let the pressure drop naturally.
7. Remove the lid and cool the jars in the canner for 5 minutes.
8. Take out the jars and cool further.
9. Inspect lid seals after 24 hours.

Chicken soup is the perfect dish to have at the ready. It will comfort, captivate, and cure in a single serving. Using cooked chicken and sautéing the vegetables makes this soup a little richer than cooking the chicken in the broth. Turmeric gives an anti-inflammatory boost, too. If you like, add cooked noodles or rice before serving.

112. Easy Venison or Beef Stew

Preparation Time: 25 minutes

Cooking Time: 1 hour 15 minutes

Servings: 9 pints

INGREDIENTS

- 1¼ cups Garlic Tomato Sauce or store-bought tomato sauce
- 4½ tsp. s taco seasoning or Chicken or Potato Herb Rub
- 4½ tsp. s Diamond Crystal kosher salt (optional)
- 4 pounds venison or beef chuck, excess fat removed, cut into 1-inch chunks or strips

DIRECTIONS

1. Prepare 9-pint jars and your pressure canner.
2. Evenly distribute the tomato sauce among the jars—2 tablespoons per jar.
3. Add ½ tsp. of seasoning to each jar and ½ tsp. of salt (if using) per pint.
4. Pack the raw meat into the jars, leaving 1-inch of headspace, pushing down on the venison to remove as much air as possible.
5. Examine the jar while you are packing it to make sure there are no large air pockets; you may need to move the meat pieces around a bit. Do not add extra liquid.
6. Remove any air bubbles, wipe the jar rims, secure the lids and rings finger-tight, and load the jars into the pressure canner.
7. Process the jars at 10 pounds pressure for 1 hour 15 minutes, adjusting for altitude.
8. Switch off the heat and let the pressure drop naturally.
9. Remove the lid and cool the jars in the canner for 5 minutes. Take out the jars and cool further. Inspect lid seals after 24 hours.

Stews usually need to simmer for hours, but pressure canning does all that cooking for you much more quickly. Just pack the raw meat and seasonings into the jars and process for long-simmered flavor.

113. Sloppy Joes

Preparation Time: 15 minutes

Cooking Time: 50 Minutes

Servings: 5-6 16 oz. jars

INGREDIENTS

- 1-cup chili sauce
- ¼-cup Worcestershire sauce
- 2 tbsps. lemon juice
- 1 ½ cups diced onion
- ¼ tsp. thyme
- 3 minced garlic cloves
- ¾-cup brown sugar
- 3 lbs. minced beef
- 2 tbsps. vegetable oil
- 2 tbsps. mustard
- 1 ½ tsps. salt
- 2 cups ketchup
- ½-cup water

DIRECTIONS

1. Melt the oil in a large pot and add the onions and garlic, softening slightly.
2. Add the ground beef, gently browning it with the garlic.
3. Drain the mixture of the oil and place aside in a bowl.
4. In a separate bowl, mix the sugar, mustard, salt, thyme, ketchup, chili sauce, water, Worcestershire Sauce, and lemon juice.
5. Combine this mixture into the cooked ground beef and heat again in a saucepan.
6. Pack the beef into the jars, leaving 1-inch of headspace, pushing down on the venison to remove as much air as possible.

7. Examine the jar while you are packing it to make sure there are no large air pockets; you may need to move the beef pieces around a bit. Do not add extra liquid.
8. Remove any air bubbles, wipe the jar rims, secure the lids and rings finger-tight, and load the jars into the pressure canner.
9. Process the jars at 10 pounds pressure for 1 hour 15 minutes, adjusting for altitude.
10. Switch off the heat and let the pressure drop naturally.
11. Remove the lid and cool the jars in the canner for 5 minutes. Take out the jars and cool further.
12. Inspect lid seals after 24 hours.

114. *Pressure Canned Venison*

Preparation Time: 15 minutes

Cooking Time: 45 Minutes

Servings: 5 pints

INGREDIENTS

- 5 lbs. cubed venison
- 1 tbsp. vinegar
- Cajun seasoning
- Canning salt
- Paper towels
- 1 box of beef broth

DIRECTIONS

1. Align a canning rack in the bottom of a 12-quart pressure canner.
2. Fill each jar halfway with meat.
3. Add ½ tsp. of canning salt and ¼ tsp Cajun seasoning.
4. Fill jars with meat the remainder of the way, to 1 inch from the top.
5. Add 1 tablespoon of beef broth.
6. Wipe rim of jar clean.
7. Heat lids in hot water for 3 minutes; place lids on jars and tighten rings on slightly.
8. Transfer the jars into the canner and fill with water up to the jar rings; add vinegar to the water.
9. Close and lock the pressure canner and bring to a boil over high heat, then add cooking weight to the top.
10. After 20 minutes, you will need to turn the heat to medium and cook for 75 minutes.
11. Turn off heat and leave the canner alone until it has cooled completely to room temperature.
12. After it has cooled, remove the jars from the canner and check for sealing.
13. If jars have sealed, store for up to 2 years; if not, use the meat right away.

115. *Ranch Chicken Pasta in a Jar*

Preparation Time: 10 minutes

Cooking Time: 5 minutes

Servings: 2 quart

INGREDIENTS

- 6 oz. cooked pasta shells
- 6 oz. chopped cooked chicken
- 1 chopped red bell pepper
- 2 cups baby spinach
- Dressing:
- ½-cup Greek yogurt
- ½-cup sour cream
- 1 lemon, juice
- 2 tbsps. minced parsley
- 2 tsps. minced fresh chives
- ½ tsp. dried dill
- ½ tsp. onion powder
- ½ tsp. garlic powder
- Salt and pepper

DIRECTIONS

1. Whisk all the dressing ingredients in a sizable bowl until thoroughly mixed, then add some seasonings.
2. Combine the pasta with the dressing and toss.
3. Arrange the pasta in 2 quart-sized canning jars.
4. Top with chicken, bell pepper, then spinach.
5. Seal and refrigerate.

116. *Pressure Canned Lamb*

Preparation Time: 10 minutes

Cooking Time: 45 Minutes

Servings: 5 pints

INGREDIENTS

- 5 lbs. cubed lamb
- 5-pint sized mason jars with lids and rings
- Canning salt

DIRECTIONS

1. Fill jars with meat to 1 inch from the top.
2. Add ½ tsp canning salt per pint.
3. Pour hot water over meat and salt.
4. Use a knife to jiggle the meat and remove any air pockets.
5. Wipe rim of jar clean.
6. Heat lids in hot water for 3 minutes; place lids on jars and tighten rings slightly.
7. Arrange the jars in the canner and fill with water up to the jar rings; add vinegar to the water.
8. Close and lock the pressure canner and bring to a boil over high heat, then add cooking weight to the top.
9. After 20 minutes, turn the heat to medium and cook for 75 minutes.
10. Turn off heat and leave the canner alone until it has cooled completely to room temperature.
11. After the canner has cooled, remove the jars from the canner and check for sealing.
12. If jars have sealed, store for up to 2 years; if not, use the meat right away.

117. *Beef Stroganoff with Mushroom*

Preparation Time: 10 minutes

Cooking Time: 15 Minutes

Servings: 5 pints

INGREDIENTS

- 5 lbs. chopped beef
- 2 chopped onions
- 4 chopped garlic cloves
- 4 cups sliced mushrooms
- 1 tbsp. butter
- 2 tbsps. Worcestershire sauce
- Water, as needed
- Salt and pepper, to taste

DIRECTIONS

1. Fry the beef, onions, garlic, and mushrooms in butter in a sizable saucepan until a brown color.
2. Mix in Worcestershire sauce, seasonings, and enough water as you stir to deglaze the stockpot.
3. Pour 2 more cups of water as you stir, then leave to boil.
4. Ladle the stroganoff into sanitized quart jars, distributing the cooking liquid evenly across the jars. Do not worry about adding more liquid—when the meat cooks, it will add flavorful juices.
5. Process in your pressure canner for 90 minutes at 10 PSI, adjusting for altitude.

6. Turn off heat and leave the canner alone until it has cooled completely to room temperature.
7. After the canner has cooled, remove the jars from the canner and check for sealing.
8. If jars have sealed, store for up to 2 years; if not, use the meat right away.

118. *Pressure Canned Tilapia*

Preparation Time: 10 minutes

Cooking Time: 45 Minutes

Servings: 5 pints

INGREDIENTS

- 5 lbs. tilapia fillets
- 5-pint sized mason jars with lids and rings
- Canning salt
- Lemon juice
- 1 jalapeño pepper

DIRECTIONS

1. Place 1 slice of jalapeño pepper into each jar.
2. Fill jars with fish to ½ inch from the top.
3. Add ¼-tsp. of canning salt and 1 tsp lemon juice per pint.
4. Use a knife to jiggle the meat and remove any air pockets.
5. Wipe rim of jar clean.
6. Heat lids in hot water for 3 minutes; place lids on jars and tighten rings slightly.
7. Arrange the jars in the canner and fill with water up to the jar rings.
8. Close and lock the pressure canner and bring to a boil over high heat, then add cooking weight to the top.
9. After 20 minutes, turn the heat to medium and cook for 75 minutes.
10. Turn off the heat and leave the canner alone until it has cooled completely to room temperature.
11. After canner has cooled, remove the jars from the canner and check for sealing.
12. If jars have sealed, store for up to 2 years; if not, use the meat right away.

119. *Canned Chicken Pieces*

Preparation Time: 10 minutes

Cooking Time: 45 Minutes

Servings: 10 pints

INGREDIENTS

- Dry chicken bouillon granules
- 20 lbs. of fresh chicken pieces
- Canning salt

DIRECTIONS

1. Remove fat from chicken.
2. Chop chicken into cubed pieces, if desired.
3. Place canning jars into the dishwasher and run through without any detergent to warm the jars.
4. Heat 3 quarts of water for your pressure canner to almost boiling.
5. Heat lids in hot water for 3 minutes.
6. Add ½ tsp. of canning salt and ½ tsp chicken bouillon granules to the bottom of each canning jar.
7. Place chicken into canning jars with one inch of space at the top.
8. Place lids on and tighten rings.
9. Place jars into the canner and fill with hot water to the jar rings.

10. Close and lock the pressure canner and bring to a boil over high heat, then add cooking weight to the top.
11. After 15 minutes, turn the heat to medium and cook for 75 minutes.
12. Turn off heat and leave the canner alone until it has cooled completely to room temperature.
13. After the canner has cooled, remove the jars from the canner and check for sealing.

120. *Canned Turkey Meat*

Preparation Time: 10 minutes

Cooking Time: 45 Minutes

Servings: 10 pints

INGREDIENTS

- Dry chicken bouillon granules
- 15 lb. fresh whole turkey or turkey pieces (not frozen)
- Canning salt

DIRECTIONS

1. If using a whole turkey, cut into manageable pieces.
2. Place canning jars into the dishwasher and run through, without any detergent, to warm the jars.
3. Heat 3 quarts of water for your pressure canner to not quite boiling.
4. Heat lids in hot water for 3 minutes.
5. Add ½ tsp. of canning salt and ½ tsp chicken bouillon granules to the bottom of each canning jar.
6. Place turkey into the canning jars with one inch of space at the top.
7. Place lids on and tighten rings.
8. Place jars into the canner and fill with hot water to the jar rings.

9. Close and lock the pressure canner and bring to a boil over high heat, then add cooking weight to the top.
10. After 15 minutes, turn the heat to medium and cook for 75 minutes.
11. Turn off the heat and leave the canner alone until it has cooled completely to room temperature.
12. After it has cooled, remove the jars from the canner and check for sealing.

121. *Canned Homemade Chili*

Preparation Time: 10 minutes (+8hours to soak beans)

Cooking Time: 15 Minutes

Servings: 12 pints

INGREDIENTS

- 3 cups kidney beans
- 5 tbsps. salt
- 3 lbs. beef, ground
- 1 ½ cups chopped onion
- 1 cup chopped bell peppers
- 6 tbsps. chili seasoning mix
- 1 tbsp. black pepper
- 8 cups chopped tomatoes
- 4 cups tomato juice
- 15 oz. tomato sauce

DIRECTIONS

1. Wash beans in clean water and rinse them. Put the beans in a stockpot and cover them with water, 2-inch above the beans.
2. Let the beans soak overnight.
3. Rinse the beans and add more water with 2 tablespoons salt. Heat the beans and water until simmering, then cook for 30 minutes. Drain the beans.

4. Brown beef, onions, and bell peppers in a large skillet. Transfer them to a large pot, then add the beans.
5. Add seasoning mix, black pepper, tomatoes, tomato sauce, and tomato juice to the pot and simmer for 5 minutes.
6. Ladle the mixture to the sterilized jars leaving a 1-inch headspace.
7. Wipe the rims and place the lid and rings on the jars.
8. Process the jars at 11 pounds of pressure for 75 minutes.
9. Wait for the canner to cool to remove the jars.
10. Place the jars on a cooling rack until the lids seal

122. *Beef Paprikash*

Preparation Time: 10 minutes

Cooking Time: 4 hours

Servings: 3 pints

INGREDIENTS

- 1 sliced onion
- 2 tbsps. flour
- ¼ tsps. black pepper
- ¼ tsp. salt
- 2 minced cloves of garlic
- 2 chopped red bell peppers
- 2 tbsps. sweet paprika
- ½-cup beef broth
- 2 tbsps. tomato paste
- ½-cup sour cream
- 1 tsp. caraway seeds
- ¼ cup chopped fresh dill
- 2 oz. canned beef

DIRECTIONS

1. Place onions in slow cooker.
2. In a sizable bowl, toss the beef in flour with salt and pepper.
3. Top onions with seasoned beef.
4. Spread over the garlic and bell peppers in slow cooker.
5. In a separate small bowl, combine paprika, broth, caraway, and tomato paste.
6. Pour the sauce over the beef.
7. Cook on high for 4 hours while covered.
8. Uncover and turn off heat; let stand for 10 minutes.
9. Stir in dill and sour cream.

123. *Chicken Jambalaya with Sausage*

Preparation Time: 10 minutes

Cooking Time: 90 Minutes

Servings: 1 quart

INGREDIENTS

- 1 tbsp. olive oil
- 4-lbs. cubed chicken thighs
- 2 cups chopped smoked sausage
- 2 cups chopped onion
- 2 cups chopped bell pepper
- 2 ribs celery
- 6 minced garlic cloves
- 2 tbsps. smoked paprika
- 2 tbsps. dried thyme
- Cayenne pepper
- 2 tbsps. Cajun spice blend
- 6 cups tomatoes with juice, divided
- ¼ tsp. hot pepper sauce
- 4 cups chicken broth
- 4 cups water
- Salt and pepper, to taste

DIRECTIONS

1. In a large stockpot, warm the olive oil and lightly brown the first 6 Ingredients.
2. In a sizable bowl, mix paprika, seasonings, thyme, cayenne, and Cajun spice blend.
3. Sprinkle the vegetable and meat mixture with the spice mixture, then add tomatoes and hot sauce, and stir well to combine.

4. Ladle the Ingredients into sanitized quart jars, filling them no more than halfway.
5. Meanwhile, place the broth, tomato juice, and water in the stockpot and bring it to a boil, deglazing the bottom of the pot.
6. Ladle 2 cups of hot liquid into each jar, allowing 1 inch of headspace. You can top up with water if you need to.
7. Process the sealed jars in a pressure canner for 90 minutes at 10 PSI, adjusting for altitude.
8. Wait for the canner to cool to remove the jars.
9. Place the jars on a cooling rack until the lids seal

124. Pressure Canned Lamb Meat

Preparation Time: 10 minutes

Cooking Time: 5 Minutes

Servings: 10 pints

INGREDIENTS

- 12 lbs. ground lamb
- Water or stock
- Salt

DIRECTIONS

1. Heat a skillet sprayed with cooking spray. Brown the ground lamb and keep it in a covered bowl to keep it hot.
2. Pack the lamb in sterilized jars while leaving a 1-inch headspace. Add a ½ tablespoon of pickling salt in each jar.
3. Add boiling water or stock, then remove the bubbles.
4. Transfer the jars to the pressure canner and process them at 10 pounds for 75 minutes.
5. Wait for the pressure canner to depressurize to zero before removing the jars.
6. Arrange the jars on a cooling rack for 24 hours, then store in a cool dry place.

125. Crumb Meatballs with Sauce

Preparation Time: 10 minutes

Cooking Time: 10 Minutes

Servings: 1 quart

INGREDIENTS

- 5 lbs. ground meat
- 2 cups very fine crumbs
- 2 tbsps. salt
- 2 tbsps. dried parsley
- 1 tbsp. garlic powder
- 1 tbsp. onion powder
- ½ batch snowfall spaghetti sauce

DIRECTIONS

1. Combine the meat, breadcrumbs, salt, parsley flakes, garlic powder, and onion powder in a large bowl, using your hands to mix well.
2. Form very firm meatballs.
3. Place 8 to 10 meatballs into each sanitized quart jar. Don't overfill the jars with meatballs because you want to leave room for the sauce.
4. Heat marinara sauce until it is simmering, about 10 minutes.
5. Cover the meatballs with hot marinara sauce.
6. Very gently use a rubber spatula to remove any air pockets so that the sauce occupies the jar, leaving some headspace.
7. Can for 90 minutes in a pressure canner at 10 PSI, adjusting for altitude.
8. Wait for the pressure canner to depressurize to zero before removing the jars.
9. Arrange the jars on a cooling rack for 24 hours, then store in a cool dry place.

126. *Pressure Canned Stewing Beef*

Preparation Time: 10 minutes

Cooking Time: 5 Minutes

Servings: 5 pints

INGREDIENTS

- 5 lbs. Stewing beef
- 10 cups stock or Water
- 5 tsps. Pickling salt

DIRECTIONS

1. Trim any gristle off the stewed beef, then cut it into strips or into cubes.
2. Heat a skillet sprayed with cooking spray. Brown the stewed beef in batches and keep it in a covered bowl to keep it hot.
3. Pack the beef in sterilized jars leaving a 1-inch headspace. Add a ½ tablespoon of pickling salt in each jar.
4. Add boiling water or stock, then remove the bubbles, leaving ½-inch headspaces.
5. Transfer the sealed jars to the pressure canner and process them at 10 pounds for 75 minutes.
6. Wait for the pressure canner to depressurize to zero before removing the jars.
7. Arrange the jars on a cooling rack for 24 hours then store in a cool dry place.

127. *Canned Mackerel*

Preparation Time: 10 minutes

Cooking Time: 100 minutes

Servings: 1 pint

INGREDIENTS

- Pickling spices, optional
- 1 tsp Sea salt
- 1 lb. Whole mackerel

DIRECTIONS

1. Remove head, tail, fins, and scales. The bones will soften.
2. Cut into 3 ½ inch pieces, then pack into jar. Add ½ tsp salt or pickling spice per jar.
3. Do not add any liquid.
4. Process jar at 10 pounds pressure (weighted gauge) or 11 (dial gauge) for 100 minutes.
5. Let cool naturally for 12 hours before removal and storage.

128. *Canned Salmon*

Preparation Time: 5 minutes

Cooking Time: 110 minutes

Servings: 8 half-pints

INGREDIENTS

- 8 tsp neutral oil, optional
- 16 peppercorns, optional
- 2 tsp kosher salt/canning salt
- 4 lbs. salmon, skinless, deboned

DIRECTIONS

1. Pack salmon into the jar, leaving 1-inch headspace. You do not need to use any brine.
2. Add ¼ tsp salt, 2 peppercorns into each jar.

3. Process jars at 10 pounds pressure for 110 minutes.
4. Then, let cool for 12 hours before removal and storage.

129. *Canned Olive oil Tuna*
Preparation Time: 5 minutes

Cooking Time: 120 minutes

Servings: 6 half-pints

INGREDIENTS

- 4 tbsps. olive oil
- 3 tsps. kosher salt
- 2 ½ lbs. boneless skinless tuna (bluefin or yellowfin)

DIRECTIONS

1. Wash tuna and discard connective tissue.
2. Cut into 2 ½ by 3-inch chunks, pack into jars, leaving 1 inch headspace.
3. Sprinkle ½ tsp kosher salt into each jar and pour olive oil in, leaving ¾ inch headspace.
4. Make sure the oil penetrates deep into the content.
5. Process jars at 11 pounds pressure for 1hr 40 minutes.
6. Let cool before removal and storage.

130. *Canned River Fish*
Preparation Time: 10 minutes

Cooking Time: 125 minutes

Servings: 4 pints

INGREDIENTS

- 8 lbs. Trout
- 16 peppercorns, optional
- 4 tsps. canning salt

DIRECTIONS

1. Process your trout by cutting off the heads, tails, and fins. Discard those.
2. Pack jars with 4 peppercorns and fish, leaving 1 inch headspace, then add ½ tbsp salt into each jar.
3. Process jars under 11 pounds pressure for 1 hour 45 minutes.
4. Let cool before removal and storage.

131. *Canned Shad*
Preparation Time: 10 minutes

Cooking Time: 120 minutes

Servings: 6 half-pints

INGREDIENTS

- 3 tsp kosher salt
- 2 ½ lbs. boneless skinless shad
- 1 gallon Water

DIRECTIONS

1. Make the brine by dissolving 1 cup salt in 1-gallon water.
2. Cut fish into jar-length pieces. Let soak for 1 hour, then drain for 10 minutes.
3. Pack fish into jars, leaving 1 inch headspace.
4. Process jars at 10 pounds pressure for 1hr 40 minutes.
5. Let cool for 12 hours before removal and storage.

132. *Raw-Pack Meat Can*
Preparation Time: 15 minutes

Cooking Time: 180 minutes

Servings: 6 half-pints

INGREDIENTS

- 5 cups Water
- 1 tsp salt
- 1 lb. Raw red meat, cubed

DIRECTIONS

1. Pack meat into jars not too tightly, leaving 1 inch headspace
2. Add salt to the jar
3. Add boiling water, maintaining ½-inch headspace
4. Process jars on 10 pounds pressure for 90 minutes.
5. Let cool for 16-24 hours, then store

133. *Venison*

Preparation Time: 5 minutes

Cooking Time: 75 minutes

Servings: 1 pint jar

INGREDIENTS

- 1 lb. venison, lean, cubed
- 1 tsp salt
- 3 onion slices
- 3 tsps. garlic, minced
- ½ tsp ground white pepper
- 1 tbsp green bell pepper, minced, optional

DIRECTIONS

1. Chop the venison into 3-inch pieces each one.
2. Place venison in a large bowl, seasoning with salt and pepper, and toss in the garlic. Combine well.
3. Put into the jar onion and bell pepper with venison, leaving ½ inch headspace.
4. Process jars under 10 pounds pressure for 75 minutes.
5. Let cool before removal and storage.

134. *Canned Pork*

Preparation Time: 10 minutes (+24-48 hour to marinate)

Cooking Time: 180 minutes

Servings: 3 pints

INGREDIENTS

- 3 tbsp caramelized onion
- 3 bay leaves
- 1 clove garlic, minced
- ½ tsp black pepper
- ½ tsp allspice
- 1 ½ tsp kosher salt
- ½ tsp curing salt
- lbs. pork butt

DIRECTIONS

1. Cut meat into 1-inch chunks, mix with curing salt.
2. Place meat in a bowl, sprinkle with kosher salt, then mix well.
3. Cover and cure for 24-48 hours.
4. Take out the meat and sprinkle with ground allspice and black pepper. Add garlic, mix well.
5. Pack meat, not very tightly, into jars, leaving ½ inch headspace. Add a bay leaf per jar, and top with caramelized onion.
6. Process jars under 15 pounds pressure for 70 minutes.
7. Let cool for 12 hours before removal and storage.

135. *Beef Pot Roast*

Preparation Time: 5 minutes

Cooking Time: 75 minutes

Servings: 1 pint jar

INGREDIENTS

- 1 lb. Beef round
- Stock or water

- 1 ½ tsps. Pickling salt

DIRECTIONS

1. Trim off the gristle, then cube the meat.
2. Brown the meat over a skillet with oil. Then, pack the meat into jars, leaving 1 inch headspace.
3. Add 1 ½ tsps. salt to 1 pint jar.
4. Top jar with boiling water, maintaining same headspace.
5. Process your jars under 10 pounds of pressure for 75 minutes.
6. Let cool before removal and storage.

136. *Moose*

Preparation Time: 5 mins

Cooking Time: 75 minutes

Servings: 4-pint jars

INGREDIENTS

- 4 lbs. moose meat, chunked
- ½ tsp salt
- 10 cups stock or water

DIRECTIONS

1. Boil the meat until done, strain liquid.
2. Boil water or stock in another pot.
3. Pack meat into the jars, then pour boiling water in, leaving 1 inch headspace.
4. Process jars under 11 pounds pressure for 75 minutes.
5. Let cool for 12-24 hours before removal and storage.

137. *Canned Meatballs*

Preparation Time: 20 min

Cooking Time: 30 Minutes

Servings: 5 half- pints

INGREDIENTS

- 2 lbs. ground meat
- 1 tsp ground cinnamon
- ¼ tsp ground cloves
- ¼ tsp ground nutmeg
- 1 tsps. garlic, minced
- 2 tsps. salt
- 2 cups tomato juice
- 3 cups water

DIRECTIONS

1. Sanitize the jars in a pot as indicated in the general guidelines of this book. Allow the jars to cool.
2. Put the meat in a bowl and stir in the herbs, garlic and salt. Mix until well combined.
3. Boil enough water in a saucepan.
4. Make balls out of the ground meat mixture and gently drop them into the boiling water. Allow them to cook for 5 minutes, then strain the meatballs.
5. Gently pack the meatballs inside the sterilized jars. Pour in enough tomato juice to cover the meatballs. Leave 1-inch of headspace.
6. Remove the air bubbles and close the lid.
7. Place the jars in the pressure canner and process for 25-30 minutes.
8. Let cool for 12-24 hours before removal and storage.

138. *Canned Chipotle Beef*

Preparation Time 15 min

Cooking Time: 30 Minutes

Servings: 5-6 half- pints

INGREDIENTS

- 2 lbs. beef brisket, cut into chunks
- 2 tsps. salt
- 8 minced garlic cloves
- 2 cups chopped onion
- 2 tsps. oregano
- ½ cup coriander
- 2 chipotle chilies
- 4 cups beef broth

DIRECTIONS

1. Sterilize the jars in a pressure canner as indicated in the general guidelines of this book. Allow the jars to cool.
2. Place the beef in a pot and season with salt. Turn on the heat and sear all sides for 3 minutes.
3. Stir in the garlic and onion. Cook for another minute. Add in the rest of the ingredients.
4. Seal the lid and allow the meat to simmer for 20 minutes on medium heat.
5. Turn off the heat and allow the mixture to slightly cool.
6. Transfer the mixture to the hot sanitized jars.
7. Remove the air bubbles and close the lid.
8. Transfer the jars to the pressure canner and process for 25 minutes.
9. Let cool for 12-24 hours before removal and storage.

139. *Pot Roast in a Jar*

Preparation Time: 10 minutes

Cooking Time: 50 Minutes

Servings: 5-6 half- pints

INGREDIENTS

- 2 lbs. stewing beef, cut into chunks
- 1 cup chopped onions
- 2 tsps. dried thyme
- 2 minced garlic cloves
- 2 bay leaves
- 1 cup beef broth
- 1 cup dry red wine
- 2 tsps. salt
- 1 tsp. black pepper
- 1 cup chopped carrots
- 1 cup diced potatoes
- ½ cup chopped celery

DIRECTIONS

1. Sterilize the jars as indicated in the general guidelines of this book. Allow the jars to cool.
2. Place the beef in a pot and add in the onions, thyme, garlic, bay leaves, broth, and wine. Season with salt and black pepper.
3. Seal the lid and turn on the heat.
4. Bring to a rolling boil and cook for 20 minutes
5. Add in the vegetables and simmer for another 5 minutes. Turn off the heat.
6. Transfer the mixture to sterilized jars.
7. Remove the air bubbles and close the lid.
8. Place the jars in the pressure canner.
9. Place it in a pressure canner and process for 25 minutes.
10. Let cool for 12-24 hours before removal and storage.

140. *Corned Beef and Potatoes*

Preparation Time: 10 minutes

Cooking Time: 30 Minutes

Servings: 8-9 half pint jars

INGREDIENTS

- 8 cups water
- 1 tbsp. pickling spice blend
- 5 lbs. brisket
- 10 cups cubed russet potatoes

DIRECTIONS

1. Boil water in a kettle.

2. In the meantime, place 1/4 tbsp of spice blend into each quart jar.
3. Layer brisket and potatoes into the jars. Leave 1-inch headspace.
4. Fill the jars with boiled water. Leave 1-inch headspace.
5. Remove air bubbles adjusting headspace.
6. Clean the rims of the jars using a clean damp towel.
7. Now apply 2-piece metal caps.
8. Process pint jars in a pressure canner for about 85 minutes at 11 pounds pressure (if using a dial-gauge canner) or 10 pounds pressure if using a weighted-gauge canner.
9. Let cool for 12-24 hours before removal and storage.

141. *Roast Beef and Potatoes*

Preparation Time: 10 minutes

Cooking Time: 25 Minutes

Servings: 4 pints

INGREDIENTS

- 7 oz. baby potatoes
- 1 tbsp. olive oil
- 8 roast beef slices
- 8 oz. halved cherry tomatoes
- 2 cups salad leaves
  Dressing
- 1 tbsp. horseradish
- 1 tbsp. red wine vinegar
- 1 tsp. Dijon mustard
- 4 tbsps. olive oil

DIRECTIONS

1. Preheat the oven to 350°F.
2. Place the potatoes on a baking sheet and drizzle olive oil to coat. Place the sheet in the oven and cook for 25 minutes or until golden brown and tender in the center.
3. Allow them to cool completely after removing from the oven.
4. Whisk together the dressing ingredients until thoroughly blended.
5. Divide the dressing into the 4 pint-sized jars, followed by a layer of potatoes.
6. Add the beef, tomatoes, and salad leaves.
7. Remove the air bubbles and close the lid.
8. Place the jars in the pressure canner.
9. Place it in a pressure canner and process for 25 minutes.
10. Let cool for 12-24 hours before removal and storage.

142. *Prawn, Rice, and Mango Salad*

Preparation Time: 15 min

Cooking Time: 50 minutes

Servings: 1 quart jar

INGREDIENTS

- ½ cup cooked brown rice
- 6 cooked prawns
- ¼ ripe cubed mango
- ½ chopped red chili
- 1 cup baby spinach
- chopped cilantro
  Dressing
- ½ tbsp. low-salt soy sauce
- 1 tsp. sesame oil
- 1 tsp. rice vinegar
- ½ tsp. honey

DIRECTIONS

1. Whisk together all the components for the dressing until well combined.
2. Spoon the mixture into a quart-sized canning jar.
3. Place the rice in the bottom of the jar before layering with the prawns, mango, chili, spinach, and cilantro (in that specific order).

4. Remove the air bubbles and close the lid.
5. Place the jars in the pressure canner.
6. Place it in a pressure canner and process for 25 minutes.
7. Let cool for 12-24 hours before removal and storage.

143. Canned Beef Stroganoff

Preparation Time 10 minutes

Cooking Time: 50 Minutes

Servings: 4-5 half pint jars

INGREDIENTS

- 2 lbs. stewing beef
- 4 cups beef broth
- 1 tsp. black pepper
- 2 tsps. salt
- 2 tsps. thyme
- 2 tsps. parsley
- 4 tbsps. Worcestershire sauce
- 2 minced garlic cloves
- 1 cup sliced mushrooms
- 1 cup chopped onion

DIRECTIONS

1. Sterilize the jars in a pot as indicated in the general guidelines of this book. Allow the jars to cool.
2. Put all components in a pot and bring to a boil for 5 minutes. Reduce the heat and allow it to simmer for another 20 mins.
3. Switch off the heat and leave to cool slightly.
4. Transfer the mixture to sterilized jars.
5. Remove the air bubbles and close the lid.
6. Place the jars in the pressure canner and process for 25 minutes.
7. Let cool for 12-24 hours before removal and storage.

144. Basic Pork and Beans

Preparation Time: 10 minutes (+2-8 hours to soak beans)

Cooking Time: 30 Minutes

Servings: 3–4-pint jars

INGREDIENTS

- 3 lbs. dried beans
- 6 cups water
- 2 lbs. pork
- ¼ tsp. salt
- 6 halved onions
- 12 bay leaves

DIRECTIONS

1. Soak beans in hot water for about 2 hours or overnight. Discard water.
2. Add fresh water to the beans and bring to boil. Drain the beans and reserve the water.
3. Distribute pork into pint jars evenly, then top with beans leaving 1-inch headspace.
4. Add 2 bay leaves, an onion, and a pinch of salt to each jar.
5. Meanwhile, boil 6 cups of the reserved liquid.
6. Scoop the hot liquid into the jars and leave 1-inch headspace while still totally covering the beans.
7. Lid the jars and place them in a pressure canner.
8. Process for about 75 minutes at 10 pounds of pressure while adjusting for altitude.
9. Let cool for 12-24 hours before removal and storage

145. Canned Goulash

Preparation Time: - 10 minutes

Cooking Time: 45 Minutes

Servings: 4–5-pint jars

INGREDIENTS

- 4 lbs. stewing beef, cut into chunks
- 20 peppercorns
- 3 bay leaves
- 2 tsps. caraway seeds
- 1/3 cup vegetable oil
- 3 chopped onions
- 1 tbsp. salt
- 6 chopped celery stalks
- 4 chopped carrots
- 2 tsps. mustard powder
- 1½ cups water
- 1/3 cup vinegar

DIRECTIONS

1. Transfer the meat to a bowl and add in the peppercorns, bay leaves, and caraway seeds.
2. Massage the beef and allow it to marinate for an hour in the fridge.
3. Add the oil in a saucepan over medium flame.
4. Sauté the onions for one minute until fragrant and stir in the seasoned beef. Add some salt then stir in the remaining ingredients.
5. Close the lid and bring to a boil for 5 minutes. Simmer for 15 minutes.
6. Turn off the heat and allow cooling slightly.
7. Transfer the mixture to the bottles.
8. Remove the air bubbles and close the lid.
9. Place the jars in the pressure canner and process for 25 minutes.
10. Let cool for 12-24 hours before removal and storage

146. Chipotle Taco Beef

Preparation Time: - 10 minutes

Cooking Time: 75 Minutes

Servings: 4 half pint jars

INGREDIENTS

- 2 lbs. cubed beef
- 8 garlic cloves
- 2 hot chili peppers in adobo sauce
- ½ cup chopped coriander
- 2 cups chopped onions
- 2 tsp. salt
- 2 tsp. dried oregano
- hot beef broth, as required

DIRECTIONS

1. Sterilize the jars.
2. Mix all the ingredients except the broth in a bowl and then distribute the mixture among the jars.
3. Pour hot beef broth into the jars, leaving one inch of headspace.
4. Get rid of any air bubbles and clean the rims.
5. Cover the jars with the lid and apply the bands, making sure that it is tightened.
6. Process the jars for 75 minutes at 10 pounds pressure in a pressure canner.
7. Remove, allow to cool, and then label the jars.

147. Pork Chops with Apple

Preparation Time: - 10 minutes

Cooking Time: 90 Minutes

Servings: 5–6-pint jars

INGREDIENTS

- 3 chopped onions
- 6 cloves garlic
- 1 tbsp. brown sugar per jar
- ¼ tsp. salt
- ⅛ tsp. ground cloves per jar
- 6 lbs. boneless pork chops

- 3 tart apples
- ¼ tsp. black pepper

DIRECTIONS

1. In each jar, layer half a cooking onion, a clove of crushed garlic, sugar, ground cloves, salt, and pepper.
2. Trim the visible excess fat off your pork and cut it into pieces that will easily fit in the jars.
3. Fill each jar halfway with pork, then layer 4 slices of apple in each.
4. Add more pork, then top off the jars with the rest of the apples. Do not add any cooking liquid.
5. Clean the jar rims with a vinegar-dampened cloth, then cap the jars.
6. Pressure can at 11 PSI for 90 minutes, adjusting for altitude.
7. Remove, allow to cool, and then label the jars

148. *Pork Goulash*

Preparation Time: 10 minutes

Cooking Time: 90 Minutes

Servings: 8 half pint jars

INGREDIENTS

- 4 lbs. cubed pork
- 3 bay leaves
- 20 peppercorns
- 2 tsp. caraway seeds
- 4 halved carrots
- 6 celery stalks
- 3 onions
- 3 tbsps. paprika
- 2 tsp. dry mustard
- 1/3 cup vegetable oil
- 1/3 cup vinegar
- 1 ½ cups water
- 1 tbsp. salt

DIRECTIONS

1. Sterilize the jars.
2. Combine the celery, carrots, and onion in a pot.
3. Mix the salt, paprika, and mustard and rub the mixture all over the pork.
4. Pour oil in a pan and brown the meat in it in batches, transferring it into the pot.
5. Deglaze the pan with the water and pour it into the pot, then combine the peppercorns, caraway seeds, and bay leaves in a spice bag and throw it into the pot. Add vinegar and bring the pot to a boil, then reduce heat and simmer for 1 hour, stirring occasionally.
6. Discard the vegetables and spice bag, and pour the mix into the sterilized jars, leaving one inch of headspace. Get rid of any air bubbles and clean the rims.
7. Cover the jars with the lid and apply the bands making sure that it is tightened.
8. Can at 10 lbs. pressure for 1 hour 30 minutes in a pressure canner.
9. Remove, allow to cool, and then label the jars.

149. *Ginger Miso Salmon Salad*

Preparation Time: - 10 minutes

Cooking Time: 90 Minutes

Servings: 2 half pint jars

INGREDIENTS

- 2 tbsps. white miso paste
- 1 tbsp. brown sugar
- 1 tsp. grated ginger
- 1 tbsp. low sodium soy sauce
- 4 oz. salmon fillet
- 2 shredded carrots
- ½ cup edamame
- ½ diced cucumber
- 8 cups chopped romaine
- ¼ cup roasted peanuts
  Dressing
- 2 tbsps. rice wine vinegar
- 1 tbsp. sesame oil

DIRECTIONS

1. Preheat the oven to 350°F.
2. Mix the miso paste, sugar, ginger, and soy sauce in a small bowl until well combined.
3. Put the salmon fillet on a baking sheet and drizzle half the miso mixture over the fish.
4. Transfer the salmon in the oven for 8-10 minutes, or until cooked. Remove from the oven for cooling.
5. Break the salmon into large flakes using a fork once cooled.
6. To make the dressing: Incorporate the rice wine vinegar and sesame oil into the remaining miso mixture. Spoon equal amounts of the dressing into 2 quart-sized canning jars.
7. Pile on the rest of the ingredients in the following order: carrots, edamame, cucumber, salmon, romaine lettuce, and peanuts. into the sterilized jars, leaving one inch of headspace. Get rid of any air bubbles and clean the rims.
8. Cover the jars with the lid and apply the bands making sure that it is tightened.
9. Can at 10 lbs. pressure for 1 hour 30 minutes in a pressure canner.
10. Remove, allow to cool, and then label the jars.

PRESSURE CANNING RECIPES: FRUITS, VEGETABLES AND LEGUMES

150. *Coriander Carrots*

Preparation Time: 15 minutes

Cooking Time: 5 minutes

Processing Time: 25 minutes for pints; 30 minutes for quarts

Servings: 4 pints or 2 quarts

INGREDIENTS

- 3 pounds carrots, cut into sticks (be sure they're trimmed to fit into the jar with 1 inch of headspace)
- 2 tsps. coriander seeds,
- 2 tsps. Diamond Crystal kosher salt

DIRECTIONS

1. Sanitize 4 pint or 2-quart jars with their lids.
2. In the meantime, bring a large pot of water to a boil, then add the carrots. Reduce the heat to maintain a simmer and cook for 5 minutes.
3. Using a slotted spoon, pack the carrots into the prepared jars, leaving 1 inch of headspace (reserve the cooking water).
4. Add ½ tsp. of coriander seeds and ½ tsp. of salt (if using) to each pint jar, or 1 tsp. of coriander seeds and 1 tsp. of salt to each quart jar.
5. Fill the jars with the reserved cooking water, covering the carrots and leaving 1 inch of headspace.
6. Remove any air bubbles, wipe the jar rims, secure the lids and rings finger-tight, and load the jars into the pressure canner.
7. Process the jars at 10 pounds pressure for 25 minutes for pints, or 30 minutes for quarts, while adjusting for altitude.
8. Let cool for 12-24 hours before removal and storage

This heart-healthy, vision-improving, all-around nutritious staple is a great snack or side. I like to use organic carrots when I can find them because the farming practices are more sustainable, or rainbow carrots for an eye-catching twist. You can easily double this recipe if you have more carrots.

151. *Essential Mixed Vegetables*

Preparation Time: 30 minutes

Cooking Time: 10 minutes |

Processing Time: 1 hour 30 minutes

Servings: 7 quarts

INGREDIENTS

- 7 cups chopped carrots (2 pounds)
- 7 cups chopped green beans (2½ pounds)
- 7 cups (2½ pounds) corn kernels (fresh or frozen) or kernels from 8 fresh ears of corn
- 1¾ tsp. s Diamond Crystal kosher salt, plus more for salting water
- 7 cups peeled, chopped potatoes (2½ pounds)

DIRECTIONS

1. Wash, dry and chop carrots, potatoes and green bean. Make sure the carrots, potatoes, and

green beans are all sliced to relatively the same size.
2. In a large pot, combine the carrots, green beans, and corn, cover with water, and bring to a boil.
3. Cook for 5 minutes.
4. Bring another large pot full of salted water to a boil and add the potatoes. Reduce the heat to maintain a simmer and cook for 5 minutes (they won't be fully cooked, just slightly softened).
5. Place ¼ tsp. of salt into each jar (if using). Fill the prepared jars with the hot vegetables and liquid, leaving 1-inch of headspace.
6. Remove any air bubbles, wipe the jar rims, secure the lids and rings finger-tight, and load the jars into the pressure canner.
7. Process the jars at 10 pounds pressure for 40 minutes, while adjusting for altitude.
8. Let cool for 12-24 hours before removal and storage

Add these all-purpose vegetables to soups or casseroles, season upon serving as a simple side dish, or add to grains for a nutritious boost.

152. *Tomato and Jalapeño Sauce*

Preparation Time: 60 min

Cooking Time: 15 Min

Servings: Makes approx. 5 (500 ml) jars

INGREDIENTS

- 2 cups sliced onions
- 7 cups seeded and sliced tomatoes (about 7medium)
- 8 jalapeño peppers, seeded and finely chopped
- 1 cup sliced green bell pepper
- 1 can tomato paste
- 3 cloves garlic, crushed
- ½ cup lightly packed chopped cilantro
- ½ tsp. ground cumin
- ¾ cup white vinegar

DIRECTIONS

1. Prepare the canning jars following the directions to sanitize them.
2. In a large saucepot, combine onions, tomatoes, jalapeño pepper, green pepper, tomato paste, garlic, cilantro, cumin, and vinegar
3. Place over medium heat and bring to a rolling boil.
4. Reduce heat and stir intermittently for about 30 minutes, or until sauce to reach the preferred consistency.
5. Ladle sauce into each canning jar. Remember to leave 1/2-inch headspace. Use spatula to remove air bubbles, then use a clean cloth to wipe jar rims, after that, adjust lids, and screw band.
6. Set the filled jars in a pressure canner at 11 pounds pressure for dial-gauge or 10 pounds for the weighted-gauge canner. Process heat jars for 20 minutes, adjusting for altitude.
7. Switch off the heat and let pressure drop naturally. Remove the lid and cool the jars in canner for 5 minutes.
8. Take out the jars and cool. Inspect lids seal after 24 hours.

Serve this hot and sweet condiment with Western or Asian dishes, from hot dogs, cold roast chicken, roast beef, and spring rolls.

Add delight to your baked potatoes and keep down the fat per serving. Rather than sour cream, top potatoes with the yummy sauce!

153. Singapore Pepper Sauce

Preparation Time: -35 minutes

Cooking Time: 10 minutes

Servings: 6-pint jars

INGREDIENTS

- 4 cups chopped hot red peppers
- 2 ½ cup granulated sugar
- White vinegar
- 1½ cups rinsed sultana raisins
- 1 tbsp. grated ginger
- ¼ cup chopped garlic
- 2 tsps. salt

DIRECTIONS

1. Place the sugar and vinegar into a large saucepot and place over medium-high heat. Bring to a boil, stirring intermittently. Reduce the heat and leave it to boil for three minutes.
2. Add ginger, garlic, red pepper, sultanas, and salt. Allow this to boil for 5 minutes. Remove from the heat.
3. Ladle hot sauce into each canning jar. Remember to leave a 1-inch headspace. Use a spatula to remove any air bubbles, then use a clean cloth to wipe the jar rims. After that, adjust the lids and screw bands.
4. Set the filled jars in a pressure canner at 11 pounds of pressure for dial-gauge or 10 pounds for the weighted-gauge canner. Process hot jars for 10 minutes, adjusting for altitude.
5. Switch off the heat and let the pressure drop naturally. Remove the lid and cool the jars in the canner for 5 minutes.
6. Take out the jars and cool further. Inspect lids for sealing after 24 hours.

154. Canned Spicy Garlic Pickled Carrots

Preparation Time: 15 minutes

Cooking Time: 25 minutes

Servings: 4-5 8 oz jars

INGREDIENTS

- 8-½ cups fresh garden carrots, small and peeled
- 5-½ cups white vinegar 5% acidity
- 2 cups sugar
- 3 Garlic cloves
- 1 cup water
- 2 tbsp canning salt
- 3 tbsp pickling spice

DIRECTIONS

1. Wash, dry and peel carrots well.
2. In the meantime, combine vinegar, sugar, garlic, water, and salt in a stockpot and bring to a gentle boil for about 5 minutes.
3. Add carrots and let boil again. Reduce heat and simmer for about 10 minutes until carrots are half-cooked.
4. Divide spice among 4 jars then fill the hot jars with hot carrots and leave 1-inch headspace.
5. Scoop pickling liquid into the jars covering the carrots. Leave ½-inch headspace.
6. Push a knife spatula through liquid and carrots to remove air bubbles adjusting headspace if necessary.
7. Wipe jar rims with a clean damp paper towel then apply 2-pieces canning lids.
8. Process the jars in a pressure canner for about 15 minutes following the manufacturer's guide and according to altitude.

9. Store the finished pickles in a glass container with a nonreactive lid in the refrigerator. For best results, use them after 3 months.

These canned pickled carrots are great as a snack all winter long. It is a delicious recipe as carrots are great vegetables to match with brine. Enjoy this great appetizer.

155. Pickled Jalapenos

Preparation Time: 50 minutes

Cooking Time: 10-15 minutes

Servings: 2-3 16 oz Jars

INGREDIENTS

- 3-½ cups white vinegar
- 1 cup water
- 1 tbsp pickling salt
- 1-½ lbs. jalapenos peppers, washed and stems cut off

DIRECTIONS

1. Combine the vinegar, water, and salt in a saucepan, medium.

2. Bring to a boil for about 5 minutes, stirring occasionally.

3. Place pepper into hot jars then ladle hot brine into the jars. Leave ½-inch headspace.

4. Remove air bubbles using non-metal utensils and add more brine but maintain headspace.

5. Wipe the jar rims using a clean damp cloth.

6. Place the jars in a pressure canner and process for about 10-15 minutes following manufacturers' guide and depending on the altitude.

7. Store the finished pickles in a glass container with a nonreactive lid in the refrigerator. For best results, use them after 3-4 months.

156. Canned Spicy Pickled Asparagus

Preparation Time: 40 minutes

Cooking Time: 10 minutes

Servings: 6-7 12 oz. Jars

INGREDIENTS

- 10-11 lbs. asparagus
- 6 cups water
- ½ cup pickling salt
- 5 tbsps. sugar
- 6 cups vinegar
- 7 halved garlic cloves, large

DIRECTIONS

1. Wash and dry asparagus and set them aside.

2. Add and stir well water, salt, sugar, and vinegar in a saucepan and bring to boil slowly. Let boil for 5-6 minutes.

3. Place garlic cloves to the jars bottom, then fill with asparagus spears. They should be packed tight. Leave 1-inch headspace.

4. Fill the hot jars with hot vinegar mixture. Leave ½-inch headspace.

5. Remove any air bubbles using a wooden spatula, and add more vinegar mixture if needed, to maintain the headspace.

6. Now wipe the jar rims using a clean damp towel.

7. Place lids and rings and tighten to fingertip tight.

8. Place the jars in a pressure canner and process for about 15-20 minutes following manufacturers' guide and according to the altitude.

9. Let cool, for 12-24 hours.

10. Store the finished pickles. For best results, use them after 3-5 days.

This is an easy recipe to make and can asparagus pickles that you can have in your salads, cheese plates, and appetizers. You will fall in love with canned asparagus.

157. *Rainbow Beets*

Preparation Time: 20 minutes, plus 10 minutes cooking time

Cooking Time: 15 minutes

Processing Time: 30 minutes

Servings: 4 pints

INGREDIENTS

- 8 to 10 medium multicolored beets (6 pounds), scrubbed
- 2 tsp. s Diamond Crystal kosher salt, divided
- 4 tsp. s apple cider vinegar or white distilled vinegar, divided
- Boiling water, for filling the jars

DIRECTIONS

1. Prep 4-pint jars and a pressure canner according to the instructions in *Sanitize Jars*.
2. In the meantime, blanch the beets to peel them: Bring a large pot of water to a boil, add the beets, and cook for 15 minutes.
3. While the beets cook, fill a large bowl with a 50-50 mix of ice and water. Using a slotted spoon or tongs, transfer the blanched beets into the ice water. Let cool, then remove the skins with a paring knife or your hands. Cut the beets into ½-inch or bite-size pieces.
4. Pack the cut beets into the prepared jars, leaving 1 inch of headspace. Add ½ tsp. of salt and 1 tsp. of vinegar to each jar. Fill the jars with boiling water, leaving 1 inch of headspace.
5. Remove any air bubbles, wipe the jar rims, secure the lids and rings finger-tight, and load the jars into the pressure canner. Process the jars at 10 pounds pressure for 30 minutes, while adjusting for altitude.
6. Let cool for 12-24 hours before removal and storage

Canning classic deep-red beets with delicate pink and yellow ones will turn them all red, so separate yellow or pink varieties from the classic deep-red ones. The vinegar helps the beets retain their color, so you'll have beautiful salads all year long.

158. *Simple Canned Tomatoes, Many Ways*

Preparation Time: 45 minutes

Cooking Time: 20 minutes

Processing Time: 15 minutes

Servings: 7 quarts

INGREDIENTS

- 21 pounds (about 36 medium) tomatoes, any variety
- 7 tsp. s seasoning of choice, such as Chicken or Potato Herb Rub, taco seasoning, Italian seasoning, dried basil, dried onion, red pepper flakes, or 7 bay leaves
- 14 tablespoons bottled lemon juice
- 7 tsp. s Diamond Crystal kosher salt (optional)

DIRECTIONS

1. In a large bowl, prepare an ice water bath.
2. Blanch the tomatoes to peel them:
3. Bring a large pot full of water to a boil.
4. Using a paring knife, cut a shallow X into the bottom of each tomato, then drop the tomatoes, a few at a time, into the water for 30 to 60

seconds, or until you see the skins starting to peel away at the X.

5. Transfer the tomatoes to the ice bath and peel off the skins.
6. At the same time, inspect the tomato and remove any pieces you don't want to preserve.
7. Halve the peeled tomatoes and place them in another large bowl.
8. Prep 7-quart jars and your pressure canner according to the instructions in Sanitize jars.
9. Place 1 tsp. of seasoning, or a bay leaf, plus 2 tablespoons lemon juice, in each prepared jar.
10. Add 1 tsp. salt per jar, if using. Fill the jars with the tomatoes, leaving 1-inch of headspace.
11. Remove any air bubbles, wipe the jar rims, secure the lids and rings finger-tight, and load the jars into the pressure canner. Process the jars at 10 pounds pressure for 25 minutes, while adjusting for altitude.
12. Let cool for 12-24 hours before removal and storage.

Pressure canning your tomatoes allows you to savor the fresh taste of summer year-round. You can any type of tomato; just be sure they're ripe and juicy. I like beefsteak tomatoes and heirloom varieties but use Roma if you prefer—just be sure to go by weight.

159. *End-of-Summer Bean and Tomato Stew*

Preparation Time: 20 minutes

Cooking Time: 30 minutes

Processing Time: 1 hour 10 minutes for pints; 1 hour 20 minutes for quarts

Servings: 10 pints or 5 quarts

INGREDIENTS

- 2 tablespoons olive oil
- 1 cup chopped celery (1 stalk)
- 1 cup minced white onion (1 onion)
- 2 garlic cloves, minced
- ½ cup chopped bell pepper, any color
- 4 (32-oz.) cans crushed tomatoes
- 4 cups water
- 4 cups cooked beans (lima, chickpeas, or white), or 3 (15-oz.) cans, drained and rinsed
- 2 tsp. s Diamond Crystal kosher salt, plus more as needed
- 2 tsp. s thinly sliced fresh basil or 1 tsp. dried, plus more as needed

DIRECTIONS

1. In a large pot over medium-high heat, heat the oil. Add the celery, onion, and garlic, and cook for about 5 minutes, stirring constantly, until soft.
2. Add the bell pepper and cook for 5 minutes until the pepper is soft.
3. Stir in the tomatoes and water and bring to a boil.
4. Add the beans to the tomato mixture and return the mixture to a boil.
5. Stir in the salt and basil. Taste and adjust the seasoning, as needed.
6. Prep 10 pint or 5-quart jars and your pressure canner according to the instructions in Pressure Canning, Step-by-Step.
7. Fill the jars with the hot tomato and bean mixture, leaving 1 inch of headspace.
8. Remove any air bubbles, wipe the jar rims, secure the lids and rings finger-tight, and load the jars into the pressure canner. Process the jars at 10 pounds pressure for 1 hour 10 minutes for pints, or 1 hour 20 minutes for quarts, while adjusting for altitude.

9. Let cool for 12-24 hours before removal and storage.
10. Other Instructions: Freeze this stew in pint or quart plastic storage cups for up to 9 months.

These delectable tomatoes and beans are so good. Taken alone, they make a great soup. Pour them over rice and grains for added bulk and enjoy a wholesome meal. Add meat for a protein boost. This hearty combo will warm you on a cold day and remind you of a warmer time. Omit the beans for a simple tomato sauce.

160. Sweet and Spicy Pickled Radishes

Preparation Time: 30 minutes

Cooking Time: 10 minutes

Servings: 6-7 12 oz. Jars

INGREDIENTS

- 2 lbs. radishes, ⅛ -inch thick
- 1-½ cups water
- 2 tbsp canning salt
- 1- ¼ cups white vinegar
- ¾ cup raw sugar
- ¼ cup red wine vinegar
- 2 tbsp mixed peppercorns
- 1 tbsp mustard seeds
- 1 tbsp red pepper flakes, dried

DIRECTIONS

1. Combine all ingredients except radishes in a saucepan, medium. Bring to a boil over high-medium heat until salt and sugar dissolves.
2. Place radishes into hot pint jars, leaving 1-inch headspace.
3. Scoop hot vinegar mixture into the jars and leave ½-inch headspace then distribute seeds, peppercorns, and flakes among the jars.
4. Wipe the jar rims with a clean damp cloth. Place lids and rings and tighten to fingertip tight.
5. Process jars in a pressure canner and process for about 10-15 minutes following manufacturers guide and according to the altitude.
6. Store the finished pickles in the refrigerator.

161. Baked Beans

Preparation Time: 30 minutes

Cooking Time: 5 hours

Processing Time: 1 hour 20 minutes for pints; 1 hour 35 minutes for quarts

Servings: 6 pints or 3 quarts

INGREDIENTS

- 2 pounds dried navy beans, rinsed and sorted
- 4 Smoked Bacon slices or store-bought bacon, diced
- 2 large yellow or white onions, chopped
- 2/3 cup packed light brown sugar, plus more as needed
- 2/3 cup molasses
- 2 tablespoons apple cider vinegar
- 1 tablespoon garlic powder, plus more as needed
- 1 tsp. ground mustard
- 2 tsp. s Diamond Crystal kosher salt, plus more as needed

DIRECTIONS

1. Preheat the oven to 350°F.
2. In a large Dutch oven or stockpot, combine the beans with enough water to cover by 3 inches. Bring to a boil over high heat, cover the pot, and cook for 1 to 1½ hours, or until tender.
3. Check the beans halfway through the cooking time and top off the water to be sure the beans are submerged. Alternatively, cook the beans in

your electric pressure cooker on bean mode, or at high pressure for 40 minutes.

4. Let the pressure release naturally.
5. Drain the beans, reserving 5 cups of cooking liquid.
6. Return the oven to 350°F if needed.
7. Place the cooked beans into a large baking dish or bean pot.
8. Stir in the bacon, onions, brown sugar, molasses, vinegar, garlic powder, ground mustard, salt, and the reserved cooking liquid. If you do not have enough cooking liquid, use water. Mix well.
9. Cover the dish and bake for 3 to 3½ hours, mixing the beans and checking the level of liquid every hour; the beans should have a soupy consistency.
10. You may need to add more liquid toward the end of the cooking time. Remove from the oven, taste, stir, and add more salt, brown sugar, or garlic powder, as needed.
11. Prep 6 pint or 3-quart jars.
12. Fill the jars with hot beans, leaving 1 inch of headspace.
13. Remove any air bubbles, wipe the jar rims, secure the lids and rings finger-tight, and load the jars into the pressure canner.
14. Process the jars at 10 pounds pressure for 1 hour 20 minutes for pints, or 1 hour 35 minutes for quarts, while adjusting for altitude.
15. Let cool for 12-24 hours before removal and storage.

Try This Instead: To make a vegetarian version, in step 5, omit the bacon and add 2 tablespoons olive oil, 1 tablespoon tamari or liquid aminos, 2 tablespoons Scratch Tomato Paste or store-bought paste, and 1 tsp. smoked paprika or liquid smoke (if desired).

If you put in the time for this recipe, you'll find it's well worth it. The slow-simmered flavor is head and shoulders above a store-bought can of beans. If you like a little bit of heat, add 2 to 3 tablespoons minced chipotle pepper to your batch. See the tip for a vegetarian version.

162. Glazed Carrots

Preparation Time: 30 minutes

Cooking Time: 50 minutes

Servings: 6-pint jars (12 cups)

INGREDIENTS

- 6-7 pounds of carrots
- 2 cups of brown sugar
- 2 cups of water
- 1 cup of orange juice
- 1 tablespoon kosher salt

DIRECTIONS

1. Wash, peel, and slice carrots. Slices should be thick 1-2-inch.
2. Mix brown sugar with water and orange juice as well as the carrots in a large saucepot. Bring to a boil. Reduce heat to medium and cook until the sugar has dissolved, and carrots are almost tender about 10-15 minutes.
3. Pack the carrots into the jars and pour the syrup over the carrots.
4. Process pints and quarts at 10 pounds each for 30 minutes for the weighted gauge of the pressure canner or 11 pounds if the pressure canner has a dial gauge, while adjusting for altitude.
5. Remove jars and let them cool completely at room temperature before storing.

163. *Green Beans*

Preparation Time: 30 minutes

Cooking Time: 20 minutes

Servings: 1 quart

INGREDIENTS

- 2 lb. green beans
- Water
- 1 tsp. salt, optional

DIRECTIONS

1. Sanitize the jar and lid.
2. In the meantime, wash and rinse beans thoroughly. Remove string, trim ends and break or cut freshly gathered beans into 2-inch pieces.
3. Place prepared beans in a large saucepan and cover with boiling water. Boil for 5 minutes.
4. Pack hot beans into hot jars leaving 1-inch headspace. Add 1 tsp. salt to each quart jar, ½ tsp. to each pint jar, if desired.
5. Ladle boiling water over beans leaving 1-inch headspace. Remove air bubbles. Wipe rim. Center hot lid on jar. Apply band and adjust until fit is fingertip tight.
6. Process filled jars in a pressure canner at 10 pounds pressure 20 minutes for pints and 25 minutes for quarts, adjusting for altitude.
7. Remove jars and cool. Check lids for seal after 24 hours. The lid should not flex up and down when the center is pressed.

*TIP: The processing time given applies only to young, tender pods. Beans that have almost reached the "shell-out" stage require a longer time for processing. Increase processing time 15 minutes for pints and 20 minutes for quarts.

164. *Tomatoes*

Preparation Time: 30 minutes

Cooking Time: 20 minutes

Servings: 7 quarts

INGREDIENTS

- 21 pounds whole tomatoes, skinned
- 4 tablespoons of salt
- ¾ cup lemon juice, optional
- Boiling water

DIRECTIONS

1. Place the tomatoes and the salt in a saucepan and cover with the water. Bring to a boil and cook for 5 minutes.
2. Pack sterilized jars with the tomatoes and the hot liquid; leaving a ½ inch headspace, remove any air bubbles, clean the rim, and adjust lids.
3. If omitting the lemon juice, process the jars for 45 minutes in a pressure canner at 10 pounds of pressure for a pressure canner with a weighted gauge or 11 pounds if the pressure canner has a dial gauge.
4. If using lemon juice, process the jars for 10 minutes in a boiling water bath.

165. *Stewed Tomatoes*

Preparation Time: 20 minutes

Cooking Time: 40 minutes

Servings: 4-pint jars or 2-quart jars

INGREDIENTS

- 4 quarts red tomatoes, around 16-18 medium-size tomatoes
- 1 yellow onion, diced
- ½ green pepper, diced
- 4 tsp. s of celery salt
- 4 tsp. s of sugar
- 1 tsp. of salt

DIRECTIONS

1. Wash and dry tomatoes.
2. Blanch the tomatoes for 1-2 minutes in boiling water. Drain the water and let cool until you can manipulate the tomatoes with your fingers.
3. Remove the skin and chop the tomatoes.
4. Combine all ingredients into the saucepan and bring to a boil.
5. Reduce the heat to low. Cover, and let simmer gently for 12-15 minutes, stirring often, until it starts to get a bit thicker.
6. Pack the mixture equally into jars, leaving 1/2 - inch. headspaces.
7. Process 15 minutes for pints at 11 pounds or 20 minutes for quarts at 10 pounds for the weighted gauge of the pressure canner or 11 pounds if the pressure canner has a dial gauge.
8. Remove the jars and let cool until at room temperature before storing.

166. *Herbed Peas*

Preparation Time: 30 minutes

Cooking Time: 20 minutes

Servings: 4 pints

INGREDIENTS

- 3 lbs. fresh peas
- A bunch Chervil
- A bunch thyme
- Water

DIRECTIONS

1. Wash and dry peas and shell and wash again.
2. Bring to a boil the peas, and let boil for 30 minutes, or until they will be cooked
3. Pack hot peas in 4 hot sanitized jars, and add seasoning. Remember to leave 1-inch headspace before close the lids.
4. Process 15 minutes for pints at 11 pounds or 20 minutes for quarts at 10 pounds for the weighted gauge of the pressure canner or 11 pounds if the pressure canner has a dial gauge.
5. Remove the jars and let cool until at room temperature before storing.

167. *Herbed Tomatoes*

Preparation Time: 30 minutes

Cooking Time: 20 minutes

Servings: 4 pints

INGREDIENTS

- 8 lbs. tomatoes, peeled
- 5 cups Water
- 1 ½ tsp. ground Parsley.
- 1 ½ tsp. ground Dill.
- 1 tsp. ground Rosemary.

DIRECTIONS

1. Wash and dry tomatoes.
2. Combine tomatoes and water in a saucepan and let boil for 30 minutes.
3. Put tomatoes in a bowl with cold water for 2 minutes, then peel them
4. Drizzle herbs into the jars, then add tomatoes leaving ½-inch headspaces.
5. Process 15 minutes for pints at 11 pounds or 20 minutes for quarts at 10 pounds for the weighted gauge of the pressure canner or 11 pounds if the pressure canner has a dial gauge.
6. Remove the jars and let cool until at room temperature before storing

168. *Asparagus*

Preparation Time: 30 minutes

Cooking Time: 20 minutes

Servings: 9 pints

INGREDIENTS

- 16 pounds asparagus spears
- 10 tablespoons salt
- Boiling water

DIRECTIONS

1. Wash and dry asparagus spears.
2. In a large pot, cover the asparagus with the boiling water and add the salt.
3. Bring to a boil and cook for 3 minutes.
4. Fill sterilized jars loosely with the asparagus and their liquid, leaving 1-inch headspace.
5. Adjust the jar lids and process the jars for 30 minutes in a pressure canner at 10 pounds of pressure for a pressure canner with a weighted gauge or 11 pounds if the pressure canner has a dial gauge.
6. Remove the jars and let cool until at room temperature before storing

169. *Marinated Mushrooms*

Preparation Time: 30 minutes

Cooking Time: 20 minutes

Servings: 9–10-pint jars

INGREDIENTS

- Pimiento, diced (1/4 cup)
- Lemon juice, bottled (½ cup)
- Basil leaves, dried (1 tablespoon)
- White vinegar, 5% (2 ½ cups)
- 9 garlic cloves
- Onions, chopped finely (½ cup)
- Mushrooms, small, whole (7 pounds)
- Oil, olive/salad (2 cups)
- Oregano leaves (1 tablespoon)
- Pickling/canning salt (1 tablespoon)
- Black peppercorns (25 pieces)
- 9 tsps. salt to taste

DIRECTIONS

1. Make sure your mushrooms are very fresh, still unopened, and have caps with a diameter of less than 1 ¼ inches.
2. Wash the mushrooms before cutting the stems but leave a quarter of an inch still attached to their caps.
3. Put in a saucepan and cover with water and lemon juice. Heat until boiling, and then simmer for 5 minutes before draining.
4. Add the vinegar, salt, basil, oregano, and olive oil to a saucepan. Stir to combine as you also add the pimiento and onions. Heat the mixture until boiling.
5. Meanwhile, fill each of your clean and hot jars with garlic clove (1 piece for jar), peppercorns (2 to 3 pieces) and 1 tsp. of salt/
6. Add the cooked mushrooms as well as the hot liquid mixture, making sure to leave ½- inch of headspace.
7. Take out any air bubbles before adjusting the lids. Place in the pressure canner and process for 20 minutes.
8. Remove the jars and let cool until at room temperature before storing

170. *Dried Beans*

Preparation Time: 4 hours (+8hours to soak beans)

Cooking Time: 30 minutes

Servings: 9 -10 half pints

INGREDIENTS

- 3 ¼ lbs. dried beans

- 3 tsps. Canning salt, optional
- Water

DIRECTIONS

1. Rinse the beans well, add to a large pot and add water until submerged under at least 2 inches of water.
2. Cover and soak for 12 hours overnight.
3. Drain the beans and rinse well, add to a clean pot with the same amount of freshwater.
4. Bring to boil, then reduce to a simmer for 30 minutes. Stir occasionally.
5. Fill jars with beans, leaving 1-inch headspace, and close the lids.
6. Process at 10 pounds pressure for 75 minutes.
7. Let cool for 12-24 hours before removal and storage.

171. *Instant Hummus*

Preparation Time: 1 hour 30 mins (+8 hours to soak garbanzo beans)

Cooking Time: -

Servings: 6 pints

INGREDIENTS

- 1 ½ cups lemon juice
- 18 large cloves garlic, peeled, lightly smashed
- 1 ½ cups sesame seeds, toasted
- 1 ½ pounds dried garbanzo beans

DIRECTIONS

1. In a pot of water, soak the beans overnight.
2. The next day, drain, rinse, transfer to a clean pot, then cover with 2 inches of water, bring to a rolling boil.
3. Add ¼ cup sesame seeds and 3 garlic cloves to each jar.
4. Pack beans into jars, leaving 1 inch headspace. Add ¼ cup lemon juice, maintaining headspace.
5. Process your jars under 10 pounds of pressure for 75 minutes.
6. Let cool for 24 hours before removal and storage.

172. *Kidney Beans*

Preparation Time: 10 minutes (+8 hours to soak beans)

Cooking Time: 30 minutes

Servings: 9-10 half pint jars

INGREDIENTS

- 3 lbs. Kidney beans, dried
- 6 cups Water
- 3 tsps. salt

DIRECTIONS

1. Soak beans overnight covered with water
2. Drain and rinse, then add to clean pot.
3. Add water and salt and bring to boil. Then cook for 30 minutes.
4. Pack in jars, leaving 1-inch headspace.
5. Process jars under 10 pounds pressure for 90 minutes.
6. Let cool before removal and storage.

173. *Dilly Pickled Snap Peas*

Preparation Time: 5 minutes

Cooking Time: 40 minutes

Servings: 4-5 half pint jars

INGREDIENTS

- 8 cups boiling Water or stock

- 4 lbs. green peas, shelled
- Black peppercorns (8-10 pieces)
- 4 tsp salt

DIRECTIONS

1. Raw pack into jars, leaving 1 inch headspace.
2. In a pot, bring to a boil stock or water.
3. Add 2 pieces of peppercorns and 1 tsp of salt to each jar, then pour over the peas, maintaining ½-inch headspace.
4. Seal the jars.
5. Process your jars under 10 pounds of pressure for 40 minutes.
6. Let cool before removal and storage.

174. *Black Eyed Peas*

Preparation Time: 5 minutes (+ 8 hours to soak peas)

Cooking Time: 35 minutes

Servings: 1 pint jar

INGREDIENTS

- 1 ½ lb. dried black-eyed peas
- ½ kosher salt
- 2 tbsp diced onions
- 10 black peppercorns
- ¼ tsp dried herb of choice

DIRECTIONS

1. Soak the peas overnight and drain them the next day.
2. Add to pot and cover with 2-inch of water. Boil for 35 minutes, stirring constantly.
3. Pack into the pint jar, leaving 1-inch headspace. Add the rest of the ingredients to each jar.
4. Process jars under 10 pounds pressure for 75 minutes.
5. Let cool before removal and storage.

175. *Chickpeas*

Preparation Time: 5 minutes (+1 hour to soak)

Cooking Time: 35 minutes

Servings: 2 pints

INGREDIENTS

- 1 tsp salt
- 3 cups water
- 1 lb. chickpeas, dried

DIRECTIONS

1. Rinse chickpeas and put in boiling water for a few minutes, then soak for 1 hour and drain.
2. Cover with fresh water and boil for another 30 minutes. Add ½ tsp salt per pint.
3. Fill jars with chickpeas and water, leaving 1 inch headspace.
4. Process jars under 10 pounds pressure for 75 minutes.
5. Let cool before removal and storage.

176. *Peas and Carrots with Chives*

Preparation Time: 10 mins

Cooking Time: 50 minutes

Servings: 2-pint jars

INGREDIENTS

- 1 tbsp. fresh chives, snipped
- Water
- 1 tbsps. salt, optional
- 1 lb. carrots per pint jar
- 1 lb. peas in pods per pint jar

DIRECTIONS

1. Wash, drain, and shell peas. Wash and drain again.
2. Wash and peel carrots, then wash again. Cut into ½-inch slices.

3. Combine peas and carrots in a saucepan, cover with boiling water. Boil for 5 minutes.
4. Pack into hot sanitized jars, leaving 1 inch headspace. Add 1 tsp salt and 1 tbsp snipped chives to each jar.
5. Process at 10 pounds pressure for 40 minutes.
6. Let cool 24 hours before removal and storage.

177. *Lima Beans*

Preparation Time: 75 minutes (+8 hours to soak)

Cooking Time: 30

Servings: 7- half- pint jars

INGREDIENTS

- Water
- 7 tsp salt
- 5 lbs. lima beans

DIRECTIONS

1. Soak overnight in water, then drain, and rinse.
2. Cover lima beans with fresh water, boil for 30 minutes.
3. Add ½ tsp salt per pint jar, then pack jars with beans and cooking water, leaving 1 inch headspace.
4. Process your jars under 10 pounds of pressure for 75 minutes.
5. Let cool 24 hours before removal and storage.

178. *Purple-hulled Field Peas*

Preparation Time: 1 hour

Cooking Time: 10 minutes

Servings: 2-3 half- pint jars

INGREDIENTS

- 2 lbs. Purple-hulled field peas
- 4 cups Water
- 1 tbsp. salt, optional

DIRECTIONS

1. Remove peas from the shell, rinse well.
2. Into saucepan with water, add peas, bring to boil for 10 minutes.
3. Pack into pint jars, topping with boiling water, leaving 1 inch headspace.
4. Process jars under 10 pounds pressure for 50 minutes.
5. Let cool before removal and storage.

179. *Pressure canned green peas*

Preparation Time: 25 minutes

Cooking Time: 35 minutes

Servings: 1-2 half pint jars

INGREDIENTS

- 1 lb. dried peas
- 2 tbsps. non-iodized salt

DIRECTIONS

1. Sort the peas to remove any debris.
2. Add the beans in a shallow saucepan and add water. Boil for 2 minutes.
3. Remove From heat and soak the beans for 1 hour while covered.
4. Drain the beans and rinse them with clean water. Add them back to the saucepan and add more water until just covered for.
5. Boil the peas for 30 minutes.
6. Use a slotted spoon to transfer the peas to the jars then add a half tablespoon of non-iodized salt.
7. Add the cooking liquid to each jet and ensure you leave a 1-inch headspace.

8. Use a clean damp cloth to wipe the jar rims then place the lid and rings. Use hands to tighten.
9. Place the jars in the canner and process them at 10 pounds for 40 minutes. Check the canner instructions guide.
10. Let the pressure canner depressurize and cool down before opening it and removing the jars.
11. Place the jars on a rack undisturbed for 24 hours before transferring them to the storage area.

Pressure canning peas is very easy, unlike beans. They also don't come out marsh and dark as many people fear. They are delicious, appealing, and simply the best compared to store-bought canned peas.

180. *Canned Garlic Beans*

Preparation Time: 45 minutes

Cooking Time: 30 minutes

Servings: 3-4 half pint jars

INGREDIENTS

- 2-1/4 lb. dried black beans
- 3 tsps. salt
- 7 cups Water
- A bunch cilantro
- 5 garlic cloves, diced

DIRECTIONS

1. Sort the beans to remove any unwanted particles.
2. Place the beans in a large pan and cover them in water, about 2 inches.
3. Place the pan on the heat and bring the water and beans to boil for 2 minutes.
4. Remove the beans from heat and let soak covered for 1 hour. Drain the water and return the pan back on the heat.
5. Add more water until just covered. Add cilantro and garlic. bring the beans and water to boil for 30 minutes.
6. Use a slotted spoon to pack the beans in jars leaving 1-inch headspace.
7. Add ½ tablespoon of salt to each jar then add the cooking liquid to cover the beans.
8. Remove the bubbles, wipe the jar rims, place the lid and rings on and use hands to tighten.
9. Process the jars for 60 minutes at 10 pounds pressure.
10. Wait for the canner to depressurize before removing the jars and storing them.

181. *Canned Garlic Garbanzo Beans*

Preparation Time: 25 minutes

Cooking Time: 2 minutes

Servings: 9 jars

INGREDIENTS

- 6 cups garbanzo beans
- 18 garlic cloves
- 3 tbsp salt

DIRECTIONS

1. Add the beans in a stockpot with salt such that the water is 2 inches above the beans. Place the pot overheat and bring the beans to boil for 2 minutes.
2. Remove the pot from heat and let the beans soak in water for 1 hour.
3. Use a slotted spoon to pack the beans in jars filling the jars up to ¾ full.
4. Add 2 garlic cloves and a 1/4 tablespoon of salt in each jar. Add the cooking liquid in each jar and if not enough add hot water.

5. Wipe the jar rims with a clean damp towel then place the lids and rings on the jars.
6. Process the jars in the pressure canner at 10 pounds for 75 minutes.
7. Wait for the pressure canner to depressurize before removing the jars.

182. Canned Mustard Pork and Beans

Preparation Time: 75 minutes

Cooking Time: 30 minutes

Servings: 3-4 -pint jars

INGREDIENTS

- 2 lb. navy beans
- 4 onions, chopped
- 8 pieces salt pork
- 1/4 cup brown sugar
- 1 tbsp yellow mustard
- 2 tbsp honey
- 30 oz tomato sauce
- 3 cups water
- 1 tbsp salt

DIRECTIONS

1. Preheat your pressure canner.
2. Place a half cup of navy beans in each jar. Divide the onions equally among the jars then add 2 pieces of pork to each jar.
3. Heat a saucepan and add sugar, mustard, honey, tomato sauce, and water. Bring the mixture to boil for 30 minutes.
4. Ladle the sauce mixture to each jar.
5. Fill the jar with boiling water ensuring you leave 1-inch headspace.
6. Wipe the jar rims and place the lids and rings on the jars. Place the jars in the pressure canner and process at 10 pounds for 75 minutes.
7. Wait for the pressure canner to depressurize before removing the jars. Store in a cool dry place for up to a year.

These beans are deliciously nice and soft. They are very easy to make and will be loved by every member of your family.

183. Canned Pumpkin

Preparation Time: 35 minutes

Cooking Time: 55 minutes

Servings: 3–4-quart jars

INGREDIENTS

- 1 ½ lbs. Pie pumpkins
- 10 cups Water
- 5 tsps. salt
- 3-4 tsps. rosemary, minced

DIRECTIONS

1. Start by cutting out the stem as if you want to use the pumpkin to curve, then cut it into 4 equal wedges.
2. Scrape out the seeds then use a knife to peel the pumpkin. Slice the pumpkin into 1-inch cubes.
3. Place the pumpkin cubes in a large pot with salt and water until the pumpkin is just covered.
4. Bring the pumpkin and water to boil for 2 minutes.
5. Carefully transfer 1 tsps. of rosemary to each jar and the pumpkin pieces, making sure you avoid smashing them.
6. Fill each jar the cooking liquid leaving 1-inch headspace. Wipe the jar rims with a clean damp piece of cloth.
7. Place the lids and rings on the jars and place them in the pressure canner.
8. Process the jars for at 15 pounds pressure for 90 minutes for quart jars and for 55 minutes for pint jars.

9. Wait until the pressure canner has depressurized to zero before removing the jars.

If you are a pumpkin puree lover, then this canned pumpkin is a great idea to add in your kitchen pantry. When you need to make a pie, just open a jar, strain the pumpkin, and there you go!

184. *Pressure Canned Hot peppers*

Preparation Time: 35 minutes

Cooking Time: 10 minutes

Servings: 2-pint jars

INGREDIENTS

- 2 lb. hot peppers
- salt

DIRECTIONS

1. Wear rubber gloves on your hands to avoid burning sensation.
2. Sort the peppers and select the fresh and firm once for maximum results.
3. Wash the hot peppers and place them on a lined baking sheet in a single layer.
4. Broil in the broiler for 5-10 minutes making sure you flip over once.
5. Transfer the hot pepper to a zip lock bag and seal tightly. Let rest for 10 minutes then remove them from the bag. Rub off as much peppers skin as much as possible.
6. Trim the tops off, scrape out the seeds, then cut the peppers into two or into sizes that will fit in the jar.
7. Pac the peppers in the jars then add a half tablespoon of salt to each jar. Add boil water to each bar leaving a 1-inch headspace.
8. Wipe the rims, close the lids, and place the rings in place. Process the jars for 35 minutes at 10 pounds pressure.
9. Wait for the scanner to depressurize before removing the jars out.

If you are a hot pepper lover and have a great harvest from your farm that can sustain you up to a year, here is a great solution. Pressure can the hot peppers and store them in a cool dry place

185. *Pressure Canned Sweet peppers*

Preparation Time: 35 minutes

Cooking Time: 3 minutes

Servings: 2-pint jars

INGREDIENTS

- 2 lb. sweet bell peppers
- 2 tsps. salt
- 2 tsps. chopped mint

DIRECTIONS

1. Thoroughly wash the sweet bell peppers then cut them into quarters.
2. Put peppers in a hot oven (400° F) for 9 minutes, or until skins burn, then let cool them completely.
3. Peel and slice all peppers.
4. Transfer the peppers in the pint jars then add a tsps. of salt and chopped mint in each jar.
5. Ladle the cooking liquid in each jar leaving 1-inch headspace. Wipe the rims and place the lids and rings.
6. Place the jars in the pressure canner and process for 35 minutes at 10 pounds pressure.
7. Let the pressure canner depressurize before removing the jars.

These sweet peppers are delicious and versatile. They can be used in stews, soups, skillet meals. canned sweet peppers will be good for up to a year even though their quality degrades with time.

186. *Pressure Canned Sweet Potatoes*

Preparation Time: 65 minutes

Cooking Time: 20 minutes

Servings: 10-quart jars

INGREDIENTS

- 10 lb. sweet potatoes
- 15 cups of Water
- 1-½ cups sugar

DIRECTIONS

1. Add the whole sweet potatoes in a stockpot, then add water until they are covered. Bring to boil for 15 minutes.
2. Remove the sweet potatoes from water and let them cool so that they are easy to peel.
3. Cut them into large chunks then pack them in the clean jars leaving a half-inch headspace.
4. Bring to boil 3 cups of water and add 1-½ cups of brown sugar until the sugar has dissolved.
5. Add boiled water to some of the jars and simple brown sugar syrup to others but maintain the headspace. Remove the bubble and add more hot water if necessary.
6. Wipe the jar rims then palace the lids and rings on.
7. Place the jars in the canner and process for at 10 pounds for 90 minutes for quart jars and 65 minutes for pint jars.
8. Let the pressure drop so that you can remove the jars from the canner.

Sweet potatoes are so yummy that you will want to eat them for breakfast, lunch and even dinner. Make sure to pack in enough in jars to take you all year long when they are on season.

187. *Pressure Canned Broccoli*

Preparation Time: 35 minutes

Cooking Time: 3 minutes

Servings: 4-pint jars

INGREDIENTS

- 4 lb. fresh broccoli
- Canning salt
- water

DIRECTIONS

1. Soak then thoroughly wash the broccoli to remove all the dirt that could be in the head.
2. Cut the head into 2-inch pieces and discard the stems. You can also can the stems if you desire.
3. Place the broccoli in boiling water and let it boil for 3 minutes.
4. Use a slotted spoon to pack the broccoli in sterilized jars then add the hot water in each jar leaving 1-inch headspace.
5. Release any air bubbles in each jar and add the water if necessary.
6. Add 1 tablespoon of canning salt to each jar then wipe the rims with a clean towel.
7. Place the lids and rings then transfer the jars to the pressure canner.
8. Process the jars at 10 pounds for 30 minutes. Let the canner depressurize before removing the jars.
9. Let the jars rest overnight to store them in a cool dry place.

It's no secret that you need to take a lot of vegetables for health purposes. Broccoli is one of the most nutritious vegetables that you need to have in your kitchen pantry all year round

188. Canned Kale

During winter, there is plenty of kale in most gardens. You make kale chips, you steam the kale and even feed the poultry, but it is still in surplus. To pave way for other crops in the garden, you need to cut the kale and preserve them in jars for later.

Preparation Time: 35 minutes

Cooking Time: 10 minutes

Servings: 5-pint jars

INGREDIENTS

- 10 lb. Kale
- 5 cups water
- 2 ½ tbsps. salt

DIRECTIONS

1. Chop the kale into bite-size pieces then remove all the hard stems and yellow parts of the kale.
2. Rinse the kale to remove any dirt then add it to the stockpot. Cover the kale with water.
3. Bring the water to boil until the kale has wilted nicely.
4. Use a slotted spoon to full the jars with kale then add ½ tablespoon salt in each jar. Add the cooking liquid and leave a 1-inch headspace.
5. Remove any air bubble and add more cooking liquid if necessary. Wipe the rims and place the lids and rings on the jars.
6. Process the jars at 10-11 pounds of pressure for 70 minutes.
7. Turn off the heat and let the canner cool before using a jar lifer to remove the jars.
8. Let rest for 24 hours undisturbed before storing them in a cool dry place.

189. Canning Turnips

Preparation Time: 35 minutes

Cooking Time: 10 minutes

Servings: 12-pint jars

INGREDIENTS

- 10 lb. turnips
- water
- 6 tbsps. salt

DIRECTIONS

1. Peel the turnips then dice them into small pieces
2. Add the turnips in a stockpot and add cold water until just covered. Drain the water to get rid of dirt and debris.
3. Cover with water once more and bring them to boil over medium-high heat. Reduce heat and let simmer for 5 minutes.
4. Use a slotted spoon to transfer the hot turnips in sterilized jars. Fill the jar with the cooking liquid leaving 1-inch headspace. Add a half tablespoon of pickling salt.
5. Remove any air bubble and add the cooking liquid if necessary. Wipe the pint jars and place the lids and rings.
6. Load the jars into the pressure canner and process at 10 pounds for 30 minutes.
7. Allow the canner to depressurize to zero before removing the jars.

Turnips are wonderfully tender and make a perfect vegetable side dish of all times of the year. All you need is to toss the canned chunks of turnips in oil and spices then bake in the oven.

190. *Pressure Canned Caramelized Onions*

Preparation Time: 35 minutes

Cooking Time: 10 hours

Servings: 6-pint jars

INGREDIENTS

- 6 lb. Onions
- 2 stick butter
- water

DIRECTIONS

1. Peel the onions and slice them into 1/4 inches slices.
2. Melt 1 stick of butter in the stockpot over high heat then add the diced onions.
3. Slice another stick of butter over the onions. Cook on high for an hour until the butter has melted and the onions were sweating a little bit.
4. Reduce the heat and let cook for 10 hours or overnight while stirring occasionally. The onions should be golden brown and well caramelized.
5. Ladle the onions in the sterilized hot jars then remove any air bubbles. Wipe the jar rims with a damp clean cloth
6. Place the lid and rings on the jars and process them at 10 pounds pressure for 70 minutes.
7. Remove the pressure canner from heat and let its pressure reduce to zero before removing the jars.

There is nothing delicious than these caramelized onions on a beef sandwich, baked potatoes or when mashed into potatoes

191. *Canned Fiddleheads*

Preparation Time: 35 minutes

Cooking Time: 10 minutes

Servings: 1-pint jars

INGREDIENTS

- 2 cups fiddleheads
- ½ cup of water
- ½ cup white vinegar
- 1 tbsp salt
- ½ tbsp peppercorns
- ½ tbsp fennel
- ½ tbsp coriander
- 1 sprig thyme
- 3 garlic cloves

DIRECTIONS

1. Trim off the cut ends then boil the fiddleheads for 10 minutes in salted water.
2. Strain the fiddleheads and rinse them with clean water. Pack the fiddleheads in the jars and leave 1-inch headspace.
3. Add the spices directly in each jar on top of the fiddleheads.
4. Boil water, vinegar, and salt in a saucepan and pour over the fiddleheads.
5. Wipe the rims, then place the lids and the rings on the jars. Place the jars in the pressure canner and process at 10 pounds pressure for 10 minutes.
6. Remove the pressure canner from heat and let its pressure reduce to zero before removing the jars.

These are delicious vegetables that are rare in the vegetable stores. They are mildly toxic when raw so need to be boiled in saltwater then rinsed well to get the last bit of the toxins

192. Pickled Garlic scrapes

Preparation Time: 5 minutes

Cooking Time: 10 minutes

Servings: 3-pint jars

INGREDIENTS

- 1 lb. garlic scrapes
- 3 tbsp dill seed
- 1-½ tbsp whole peppercorns
- 1-½ tbsp whole coriander
- 1-½ cups apple cider vinegar
- 1-½ cup water
- 2 tbsp pickling salt

DIRECTIONS

1. Trim the scrapes to remove the blossoms and the tough bottom end. Reserve the blossoms for another use.
2. Cut the scrapes to a size that will fit the jars. Pack the scrapes in the jars then add a tablespoon of dill, ½ tablespoon peppercorn, and coriander seeds in each jar. You can also add red pepper flakes for spicy pickles.
3. Mix vinegar, water, and salt in a pot then bring the mixture to boil while stirring until the salt has dissolved.
4. Pour the hot mixture over the garlic scrapes in the jars leaving 1-inch headspace.
5. Wipe the rim of the jars with a damp cloth then place the lids and rings.
6. Place the jars in the pressure canner and process for 55 minutes at 10 pounds pressure.
7. Let the canner depressurize to zero before removing the jars. Transfer the jars to a rack and let them rest for 24 hours undisturbed.
8. Store the jars in a cool dry place.

If you grow garlic, you will realize that it's hard to use all the garlic scrapes when fresh. That why you should pressure them to freshly preserve them. Garlic scrapes are perfect for scrambled eggs and make an awesome fresh garlic scrape pesto.

193. Pineapple Zucchini

Preparation Time: 5 minutes

Cooking Time: 60 Minutes

Servings: 4-pint jars

INGREDIENTS

- 3 cups granulated sugar
- 1 x 46-oz. can pineapple juice
- 1½ cups lemon juice
- 4 quarts diced or grated zucchini

DIRECTIONS

1. Remove peels and seeds from zucchini. Cube or grate the zucchini.
2. Mix all the ingredients well. Stir frequently while simmering for 20 minutes.
3. Fill hot, clean jars with the zucchini mixture. Leave ½ inch of headspace.
9. Adjust the lids and process them for 15 minutes at 10 pounds pressure.
4. Remove the jars and allow them too completely cool.
5. Test the seals. Store in a cool, dry place.

194. Sweet and Sour Pickled Zucchini Slices

Preparation Time: 5 minutes

Cooking Time: 10 Minutes

Servings: 6 half pint jars

INGREDIENTS

- 3 lbs. sliced zucchini
- 1 sliced onion
- 1 tbsp. mustard seed
- 1½ tsps. ground turmeric
- 1/3 cup canning salt

- 4½ cups white vinegar
- 3 cups sugar

DIRECTIONS

1. In a large nonreactive bowl, sprinkle zucchini and onion with salt and toss to coat.
2. Cover with water and let stand at room temperature for 2 hours. Drain and rinse thoroughly.
3. In a 6-quart stockpot, combine the remaining ingredients.
4. Bring to a boil. Stir until sugar is fully dissolved.
5. Cook on low heat for 5 minutes to allow the flavors to blend.
6. Add the zucchini mixture and return to a boil, stirring occasionally.
7. Reduce heat and let simmer, uncovered, for 4-5 minutes until heated through.
8. Carefully scoop hot mixture into hot, sterilized 1-pint jars, leaving ½-inch headspace.
9. Rinse the rims carefully. Place tops on jars and screw on bands until fingertip tight.
10. Process them for 15 minutes at 10 pounds pressure.
6. Remove the jars and allow them too completely cool.
7. Test the seals. Store in a cool, dry place.

195. *Butternut Squash and Chickpea Hash*

Preparation Time: 5 minutes

Cooking Time: 60 Minutes

Servings: 6-pint jars

INGREDIENTS

- 3 cups dried chickpeas
- 2 tbsps. olive oil
- 1 chopped yellow onion
- 2 tsps. coarse sea salt
- ¼ tsp. ground black pepper
- 12 diced Roma tomatoes
- 4 cups water
- 2 chopped zucchinis
- 1 chopped butternut squash
- 1 tbsp. ground ginger
- 1 tbsp. ground coriander

DIRECTIONS

1. Thoroughly rinse and clean the chickpeas, discarding any disfigured or shriveled beans and any rocks or debris.
2. In a large pot, add the dried chickpeas and add enough water to cover them. Bring to a boil over medium-high heat for 5 minutes, then simmer with the lid on for 15 minutes.
3. In a second, large stockpot, melt the oil then add the onion, salt, and pepper to cook for 5 minutes as you stir.
4. Add the tomatoes and mix well. Cook for 5 minutes to release the juices from the tomatoes, stirring often to avoid scorching the tomatoes. Add the water, zucchini, squash, ginger, and coriander and mix well. Cook for an additional 5 minutes.
5. Strain the chickpeas in a colander in the sink. Add the chickpeas to the stockpot and mix well, bringing back to a boil. Boil hard for 5 minutes, stirring often.
6. Ladle the hot hash mixture into hot jars, leaving a generous 1 inch of headspace. Get rid of any air bubbles. Add additional mixture if necessary to maintain the headspace.
7. Dip a warm washcloth in distilled white vinegar and wipe the rims of the jars. Set a lid and jar on each and tighten.

8. Set the jars in the pressure canner, place the lid in place, and allow to boil while on high heat. You can vent for approximately 10 minutes. Lock the vent and heat further to attain a dial gauge of 11 PSI and a weighted gauge of 10 PSI.
9. Can the quart jars for 90 minutes and pint jars for around 75 minutes.
10. Remove the jars and allow them too completely cool.
11. Test the seals. Store in a cool, dry place.

196. *Spicy Green Beans*

Preparation Time: -10 minutes

Cooking Time: 30 Minutes

Servings: 6 -7 32 oz jars

INGREDIENTS

- ¼ tsp. salt
- ¾ tsp. allspice
- ¾ tsp. cloves
- ¼ stick cinnamon
- ¼ piece mace
- 1 ½ tsps. celery seed
- 2 cups cider vinegar
- 1-cup sugar
- 2 pints green beans

DIRECTIONS

1. Tie the salt and the spices in thin cloth bag. Boil the vinegar, sugar, and spices for 15 minutes. Sterilize a quart jar for 15 minutes.
2. Pour the vinegar mixture into the jars, then adjust the lid and set aside for 2 weeks.
3. Remove the spice bag. Cook fresh beans until tender but firm and let cool.
4. Heat the vinegar and add ½ cup of the bean liquid.
5. Mix in the beans and simmer for 15 minutes.
6. Pack into sterile jars, being sure the vinegar covers the beans. Remove any air bubbles and adjust the jar lids.
7. Process the jars for 10 minutes in a boiling water bath.

197. *Simple Canned Sauerkraut*

Preparation Time: 75 minutes

Cooking Time: 20 Minutes

Servings: 6-pint jars

INGREDIENTS

- 2 chopped cabbage heads
- 6 tbsps. pickling salt
- 4 cups water

DIRECTIONS

1. Put the veggies in a pot with water and sprinkle with pickling salt. Toss well to combine and let cook for 10 minutes.
2. After the 10 minutes, gently pound the cabbage so it can release as much water as possible.
3. Drain the water to a separate container, then pack the cabbage into your prepared storage jars, leaving some space to cover with water.
4. Use the same water you drained from the cabbage to cover the cabbage in the jars, leaving a ¼-inch headspace.
5. Let it ferment for about 3 weeks or to your liking, then use a pressure canner to process your jars for around 75 minutes at 10 pounds pressure.
6. Remove the jars and allow them too completely cool.
7. Test the seals. Store in a cool, dry place.

198. *Fennel and Radish Slaw*

Preparation Time: 15 Minutes

Cooking Time: 75 minutes

Servings: 1 pint jar

INGREDIENTS

- 1 sliced fennel bulb
- 2 julienned watermelon radishes
- 2 chopped celery stalks
- 2 grated carrots
- ½ sliced onion
- 1 tbsp. kosher salt

DIRECTIONS

1. Scrub the veggies and remove the ends and any bruised or damaged skins. There isn't a right way to chop up these vegetables, but the suggested techniques listed in the left-hand column are the way I prefer to chop them.
2. In a large, nonreactive bowl, mix the salt with the prepared veggies and pack them into a glass jar, pushing down the mixture with your hands.
3. Within an hour or two, the natural liquid from the vegetables should release enough brine to cover the vegetables.
4. Cover jar with a cheesecloth or other breathable cover to keep dust and bugs from entering your ferment. If using a jar to ferment, you can also add the canning jar lid and tighten the ring, instead of cheesecloth.
5. However, adding the lid will require you to "burp" the jar daily to release the built-up gas that is created during fermentation. Store at room temperature, ideally between 60°F (16°C) and 75°F (24°C). Keep out of direct sunlight.
6. This is a 3-week ferment. Check on the ferment frequently to make sure the brine remains over the veggies and that no mold forms.
7. If the brine is low, press down the weight to bring the brine back over the ferment.
8. Once fermentation is complete, use a pressure canner to process your jars for around 75 minutes at 10 pounds pressure.
9. Remove the jars and allow them too completely cool.
10. Test the seals. Store in a cool, dry place.

199. *Fig jam*

Preparation Time: -

Cooking Time: 10 Minutes

Servings: 8- 9 8 oz jars

INGREDIENTS

- 1 cup water
- 3 cups sugar
- 6 lbs. fresh fig
- 4 tbsps. lemon juice

DIRECTIONS

1. Wash the figs, remove the stalks and remove the peel. Cut them into quarters and set aside.
2. Put the figs in a saucepan together with the water, sugar and lemon juice.
3. Bring to a boil and stir constantly for about 50 minutes, so that the mixture does not stick. When the mixture has reached a temperature of 220 ° F (which you can measure with a kitchen thermometer), turn off the heat.
4. Then put the lukewarm jam in the jars that you have previously sanitized, taking care to leave 1 / -inch headspace

5. Tightly screw the sanitized caps and place the jars in a pot full of boiling water, let it boil for about 15-20 minutes.
6. Carefully remove the jars and let them cool upside down for 3-4 hours.
7. Check the tightness of the jars and place them in the pantry.

200. *Corn on the Cob*

Preparation Time: 5 Minutes

Cooking Time: 55 minutes-

Servings: 2-pint jars

INGREDIENTS

- 2 lbs. Corn on the cob
- Water, as needed
- 2 tsps. Salt

DIRECTIONS

1. Husk the corn and remove the silk with a vegetable brush.
2. Start boiling a big pot of water and salt.
3. Slice the corn off the cob as closely as possible. It will come off in strips.
4. Fill your jars with corn, leaving 1 inch of headspace.
5. Ladle boiling water into the jars, allowing 1 inch of headspace.
6. Use a rubber spatula to remove any air pockets, and then add more water if needed.
7. Lid the jars and process them in your pressure canner for 55 minutes at 10 PSI or 85 minutes if you are using quart jars.
8. Carefully remove the jars and let them cool upside down for 3-4 hours.
9. Check the tightness of the jars and place them in the pantry

201. *Canned Caramelized Onions*

Preparation Time: 30 minutes

Cooking Time: 75 minutes

Servings: 4 pints

INGREDIENTS

- 6 lbs. Onions
- 2 sticks butter
- 5 cups sugar
- Water

DIRECTIONS

1. Peel the onions and slice them into ¼-inch slices.
2. Melt 1 stick of butter in the stockpot over high heat then add the diced onions.
3. Slice another stick of butter over the onions. Cook on high for 10 minutes until the butter has melted and the onions are sweating a little bit.
4. Add the sugar and cook for 20 minutes under reduced heat while stirring occasionally. The onions should be golden brown and well caramelized.
5. Ladle the onions in the sterilized hot jars then remove any air bubbles.
6. Rinse the jar rims with a damp, clean cloth.
7. Place the lids and rings on the jars and process them at 10 pounds of pressure for 70 minutes.
8. Remove the pressure canner from heat and let its pressure reduce to zero before removing the jars.

202. *Garlic and Tomato Peach Sauce*

Preparation Time: 20 minutes

Cooking Time: 30 Minutes

Servings: 9–10-pint jars

INGREDIENTS

- 8 cups fresh peaches
- 1-cup lime juice
- 1 ½ cups vinegar
- 6 garlic cloves
- 2 cups onion
- 2 cups chili peppers
- 4 cups diced tomatoes
- 1 tbsp. sea salt

DIRECTIONS

1. Wash, dry and chop thinly every solid ingredient, except salt.
2. Add all ingredients into the large stockpot and bring to boil over medium-low heat. Reduce heat to low and simmer for 10 minutes. Stir frequently.
3. Ladle salsa into the hot clean jars, leaving ½-inch headspace. Seal jar with lids.
4. Finish the canning process in a water bath canner for 15 minutes.
5. Remove the jars from the water bath and let them cool completely, then seal and label jars.

203. *Pressure Canned Spicy Corn*

Preparation Time: -

Cooking Time: 75 Minutes

Servings: 3–4-quart jars

INGREDIENTS

- 3 ½ lbs. corn on the cob
- 2 garlic cloves
- 1 tbsp. salt
- Pepper
- 3 ½ cups water

DIRECTIONS

1. Remove the silk and husk from the corn, then cut kernels from cob.
2. Fill quart jars with corn. Leave a 1-inch headspace.
3. Sprinkle with seasonings and garlic to taste, then add boiling water to cover the corn. Release trapped air bubbles by jiggling the jars.
4. Add 1-tablespoon of salt on each jar.
5. Rinse the rims of the jars using a paper towel, dampened and clean, and place on the lids and rings securely.
6. Arrange the jars in a pressure canner and process for about 1 hour 25 minutes at 10 pounds of pressure.

204. *Canned Three-Bean Salad*

Preparation Time: -

Cooking Time: 15 minutes

Servings: 3-pint jars

INGREDIENTS

- 1 ½ lbs. green bush beans
- 1 ½ lbs. yellow wax beans
- 3 cups cooked red kidney beans
- 1 red garden onion, sliced
- 6 peppers banana
- Boiling water
- 2 ½ cup granulated sugar
- 1 tbsp. mustard seeds
- 1 tbsp. celery seeds
- 4 tbsps. pickling salt
- 3 cups white vinegar
- 1 ¼ cup distilled water

DIRECTIONS

1. Add all the beans, onions, and peppers in a saucepan. Add water until covered, then bring to boil over medium heat.
2. Simmer for 5 minutes or until the veggies are heated through.
3. In a separate saucepan, combine sugar, mustard seed, celery seeds, salt, white vinegar, and distilled water.

4. Boil until the sugar has dissolved. Reduce the heat and simmer until all the spices have been fully infused.
5. Drain the vegetables and pack them in the sterilized pint jars, leaving a ½ inch headspace. Remove any air bubbles and add more cooking liquid if necessary.
6. Wipe the rims and place the lids.
7. Process the jars in boiling water in the pressure canner for 15 minutes.
8. Remove the jars from the canner and let rest to cool before storing in a cool, dry place.

205. *Canned Potato with Onions and Mushroom*

Preparation Time: 75 minutes

Cooking Time: 50 Minutes

Servings: 8 half pint jars

INGREDIENTS

- 4 sliced potatoes
- 2 tbsps. unsalted butter, divided
- 1 onion, chopped
- 8 oz. mushrooms, chopped
- 4 cloves garlic, minced
- 1 tbsp. fresh thyme, chopped
- ¼ tsp. pepper
- ¼ cups all-purpose flour
- ¾ cups heavy cream
- ¾ cups milk
- ½ cups parmesan, grated
- Salt and pepper, to taste
- 6 oz. Gruyere, shredded

DIRECTIONS

1. Preheat oven to 350°F.
2. In a sizable saucepan, boil 6 cups of water. Drop the sliced potatoes into the water and cook until they become tender, about 4 minutes. Strain off excess water and place in a clean bowl.
3. In a large skillet, heat 1 tablespoon of butter over medium heat. Sauté the onions and mushrooms until soft, about 5 minutes.
4. Add in the garlic, thyme, and black pepper and fry for another 2 minutes. Scoop the mushroom mixture into a clean plate.
5. To make the roux sauce, melt 1 tablespoon of butter in the same skillet over medium heat. Add the flour to the butter while stirring it constantly with a spatula to form a paste.
6. Drizzle in the cream and the milk to thin out the paste until it thickens to become a sauce.
7. Add the seasonings and cheese and cook for a few minutes.
8. Place 8 half-pint, wide mouth canning jars on a baking sheet. Scoop one tablespoon of the sauce into each jar, followed by 3 potato slices for every container.
9. Dollop another tablespoon of the sauce together with 1/3 cup of the mushroom mixture. Divide 2/3 of the shredded Gruyere among the jars, layer with more potato slices, cream sauce, mushroom, and finish off with more cheese.
10. Rinse the rims of the jars using a paper towel, dampened and clean, and place on the lids and rings securely.
11. Arrange the jars in a pressure canner and process for about 1 hour 25 minutes at 10 pounds of pressure.
12. Remove the jars from the canner and let rest to cool before storing in a cool, dry place.

206. Cabbage and Carrot Coleslaw

Preparation Time: -

Cooking Time: 10 Minutes

Servings: 6-pint jars

INGREDIENTS

- 3 heads cabbage
- 3 carrots
- 2 bell peppers (optional)
- 3 small onions
- 3 tsps. canning salt
- 3 cups white vinegar
- 1-cup water
- 2 cups sugar
- 1 tbsp. celery seeds
- 2 tsps. dry mustard

DIRECTIONS

1. Shred all the vegetables in a food processor. Toss them with salt, then put the veggies in a colander to drain.
2. Let the veggies drain for an hour.
3. Meanwhile, make your dressing by combining all remaining ingredients in a saucepan and bring mixture to a boil for a minute or two. Remove from heat.
4. In a sizable bowl, toss together your vegetables and warm dressing.
5. Place the slaw into jars, allowing a ½ inch of headspace.
6. Finish the caning process in a boiling water bath for 15 minutes for quarts, 20 minutes for pints. Be sure to adjust for your altitude.
7. Remove the jars from the pot and let rest to cool before storing in a cool, dry place

207. Tomato Bell Pepper Salsa

Preparation Time: 30 minutes

Cooking Time: 1 hour 20 minutes

Servings: 6-pint jars

INGREDIENTS

- 5 de-seeded, chopped jalapeno peppers
- 15 minced cloves of garlic
- 1 chopped rib of celery
- 1 chopped red pepper, sweet, medium
- 4 chopped green peppers, medium
- 35 peeled, quartered tomatoes, medium
- 24-oz. cans of tomato paste
- 3 chopped onions, large
- ½ cup of sugar, granulated
- 1¾ cups of vinegar, white
- ½ tsp. of pepper sauce, hot
- ¼ cup of canning salt

DIRECTIONS

1. Cook the tomatoes in an uncovered, large stockpot for 20 minutes on medium heat.
2. Drain the tomatoes. Reserve two cups of liquid. Return tomatoes to the same pot.
3. Stir in reserved tomato liquid, hot pepper sauce, canning salt, jalapenos, garlic, celery, red pepper, sugar, vinegar, tomato paste, onions, and green peppers.
4. Boil and then reduce the heat. Leave the stockpot uncovered and stir frequently while simmering for an hour.
5. Ladle the hot mixture in 10 of the 1-pint jars. Leave ½ inch headspace at the top. Jiggle jars to remove any air bubbles. Wipe the jar rims. Screw on the bands until they are tight to the feel.
6. Place jars in the canner along with simmering water. Be sure they are covered completely.
7. Bring water to boil and process for about 20 minutes. Remove the jars and allow cooling.

208. *Brandied Honey and Spice Pears*

Preparation Time: -

Cooking Time: 5 Minutes

Servings: 6-pint jars

INGREDIENTS

- 6 lbs. sliced pears
- Ascorbic acid color keeper
- 4 cups apple juice, cranberry juice, or apple cider
- ½ cup lemon juice
- 1 ½ cups honey
- 3 tbsps. crystallized ginger
- 8 inches stick cinnamon, break the sticks into halves
- ½ tbsps. whole cloves
- ¼-cup brandy

DIRECTIONS

1. Put the pear slices in the ascorbic acid to prevent the pears from discoloring. Set aside.
2. Make syrup in a 6–8-quart pot by combining apple juice, lemon juice, honey, ginger, cinnamon, and cloves.
3. Boil while constantly stirring. Reduce the heat to low.
4. Strain the pears and add them to the syrup. Stir in brandy then increase the heat until the mixture is boiling. Reduce the heat once more and simmer while stirring occasionally for 5 minutes or until the pears are almost tender.
5. Use a slotted spoon to pack the spears into clean pint canning jars, ensuring you leave a half-inch headspace.
6. Ladle the syrup over the pears and maintain the half-inch headspace. Use a clean towel to wipe the pint jar rims and put the lids on.
7. Load the jars into the pressure canner and process them at 10 pounds of pressure.
8. Remove the jars and allow cooling.

209. *Squash and Pumpkin*

Preparation Time: 15 minutes

Cooking Time: 90 Minutes

Servings: 2-quart jar s

INGREDIENTS

- 8 large summer squash
- 2 tbsps. salt
- 7 cups water

DIRECTIONS

1. Cut up your squash and remove the rind, seeds, and strings. Cut into 1-inch chunks.
2. You can raw-pack your pumpkin or squash. Fill your quart jars with cubes, leaving 1 inch of headspace.
3. Fill the jar with hot water and salt, keeping 1-inch of headspace.
4. Slide a rubber utensil around the sides of the jar to remove any air pockets.
5. Lid the jars and process them in your pressure canner 11 PSI for 90 minutes, adjusting for altitude.
6. Remove the jars and allow cooling.

210. *Glazed Sweet Carrots*

Preparation Time: 75 minutes

Cooking Time: 15 Minutes

Servings: 16 pints

INGREDIENTS

- 8 cups of sugar, brown
- 10 pounds of carrots
- 4 cups of orange juice
- 8 cups of water, filtered

DIRECTIONS

1. Wash carrots and drain them. Combine orange juice, brown sugar, and water in a large-sized

saucepan. Heat on medium heat and stir for 15 minutes until sugar dissolves. Keep mixture hot.
2. Place the raw carrots in the sterilized, hot jars. Leave 1-inch of headspace.
3. Fill the jars with the hot syrup, still leaving an inch of headspace.
4. Tap the jars to remove any air bubbles. Wipe jar rims and screw on the lids.
5. Process jars in a pressure canner for ½ hour under 10 pounds of pressure.
6. Store in a cool, dry area.

211. *Apple Pie Filling with Maple and Cinnamon*

Preparation Time: -

Cooking Time: 5 Minutes

Servings: 6 pints

INGREDIENTS

- 1 lemon, cut into halves
- 10 lbs. cooking apples, medium size
- 5 cups sugar
- 1 ½ cup regular clear jell starch
- 2 tbsps. cinnamon, ground
- 1 tbsp. salt
- 5 cups apple juice
- 2 ½ cup cold water
- 18 oz. maple syrup
- ¾ cup lemon juice

DIRECTIONS

1. Fill 2 large mixing bowls with cold water, then squeeze ½ a lemon in each bowl.
2. Put the apple slices in lemon water.
3. Drain the apples and measure 24 cups of water in a pot and boil it. Cook the apples ¼ at a time in the boiling water for 30 seconds.
4. Use a slotted spoon to remove the apples from the boiling water to another bowl. Cover the bowl to keep the apples hot and discard the cooking liquid.
5. Add sugar, clear jell starch, cinnamon, and salt into the pot. Add the apple juice, water, and maple syrup. Stir well.
6. Stir while cooking over medium heat or until the mixture bubbles and thickens. Stir in lemon juice and let boil for 1 minute.
7. Stir in apple pieces until well-coated.
8. Pack the apples in the sterilized jars leaving a 1-¼ -inch headspace.
9. Rinse the jar rims and place the lids and the rings.
10. Transfer the jars into a pressure canner and process for 70 minutes at 10 pounds of pressure.

212. *Canned Pickled Small Beets*

Preparation Time: 30 minutes

Cooking Time: 35 minutes

Servings: 2-3 Quart Jars

INGREDIENTS

- 4-5 lbs. small beets
- 2 tbsp pickling salt
- 1-½ cups white sugar
- 3 cups white 5% vinegar
- 2 tbsp pickling spice, mixed and tied in cheesecloth bag
- 1 cup water

DIRECTIONS

1. Wash and remove most beets tops. Leave ½-inch beet top.
2. Cook the beets in a boiling pot of water, large; until barely tender then remove from heat.
3. Submerge cooked beets in a bowl, large, of ice water for the skin to come off easily.
4. Completely cut off tops and roots of the beets then remove the skin. Slice into large chunks.
5. Meanwhile, combine the remaining ingredients in a pot, non-reactive, and boil the mixture. Reduce heat to low and simmer for about 10 minutes.
6. Add beets to the liquid mixture and boil again. Remove the pickling spice bag.
7. Ladle beets and pickling liquid carefully into hot pint jars, sterilized. Leave ½-inch headspace.
8. Use a non-metal utensil to remove air bubbles, if any, and add more pickling if needed but still maintain a proper headspace.
9. Wipe the pint jar rims using a damp cloth, clean, for proper sealing. Put the lids on jars.
10. Seal the jars and process in a pressure canner for about 35 minutes. For altitudes exceeding 3000ft (914m), add processing time by 5 minutes.
11. Store the finished pickles in a glass container with a nonreactive lid in the refrigerator. If they stay submerged in their brine, they will keep for months

LOW-SODIUM AND LOW SUGAR CANNING AND PRESERVING RECIPES

213. Apple Butter

Preparation Time: 10 minutes

Cooking Time: 14 minutes

Servings: 2-4 16 oz jars

INGREDIENTS

- 3 lbs. Fuji apples, cored and chopped
- ¼ cup water
- 1 tsp. ground cinnamon
- ½ tsp. ground ginger
- ¼ tsp. ground cloves

DIRECTIONS

1. In a slow cooker, place apples, water, and spices and stir to combine.
2. Set the slow cooker on Low and cook, covered, for about 6 hours.
3. Uncover the slow cooker and with an immersion blender, mash the apples until pureed.
4. With the lid, cover the pot loosely.
5. Set the slow cooker on Low and cook, covered, for about 6–8 hours.
6. In 3 (½-pint) hot sterilized jars, divide the apple butter, leaving about ½-inch space from the top.
7. Slide a small knife around the insides of each jar to remove air bubbles.
8. Wipe any trace of food off the rims of jars with a clean, moist kitchen towel.
9. Close each jar with a lid and screw on the ring.
10. Arrange the jars in a boiling water canner and process for about 10 minutes.
11. Remove the jars from water canner and place onto a wood surface several inches apart to cool completely.
12. After cooling with your finger, press the top of each jar's lid to ensure that the seal is tight.
13. Canned apple butter can be stored in the refrigerator for up to 2–3 weeks.

214. Applesauce

Preparation Time: 10 minutes

Cooking Time: 20 minutes

Servings: 3-4 16 oz jars

INGREDIENTS

- 7½ pounds apples, cored and chopped
- 1 cup water

DIRECTIONS

1. In a heavy-bottomed pot, add apples and water over medium heat and cook for about 15–20 minutes or until apples begin to soften, stirring occasionally.
2. In a high-speed blender, add apples and pulse until pureed.
3. In 4 (1-pint) hot sterilized jars, divide the applesauce, leaving about ½-inch space from the top.
4. Slide a small knife around the insides of each jar to remove air bubbles.
5. Wipe any trace of food off the rims of jars with a clean, moist kitchen towel.
6. Close each jar with a lid and screw on the ring.
7. Arrange the jars in a boiling water canner and process for about 20 minutes.
8. Remove the jars from water canner and place onto a wood surface several inches apart to cool completely.
9. After cooling with your finger, press the top of each jar's lid to ensure that the seal is tight.

10. Canned applesauce can be stored in the refrigerator for up to 2–3 weeks.

215. *Pear Sauce*

Preparation Time: 10 minutes

Cooking Time: 30 minutes

Servings: 4-5 16 oz. jars

INGREDIENTS

- 12 ripe pears, cored and quartered
- 6 cups water
- 1 tsp. ground cinnamon

DIRECTIONS

1. In a large stainless-steel pan, add pears, water, and cinnamon over medium heat and cook for about 25–30 minutes, stirring occasionally.
2. In a high-speed blender, add apples and pulse until pureed.
3. In 5 (1-pint) hot sterilized jars, divide the pear sauce, leaving about ½-inch space from the top.
4. Slide a small knife around the insides of each jar to remove air bubbles.
5. Wipe any trace of food off the rims of jars with a clean, moist kitchen towel.
6. Close each jar with a lid and screw on the ring.
7. Arrange the jars in a boiling water canner and process for about 15 minutes.
8. Remove the jars from water canner and place onto a wood surface several inches apart to cool completely.
9. After cooling with your finger, press the top of each jar's lid to ensure that the seal is tight.
10. Canned pear sauce can be stored in the refrigerator for up to 2–3 weeks.

216. *Blueberry Jam*

Preparation Time: 10 minutes

Cooking Time: 8 minutes

Servings: 4-5 16 oz. jars

INGREDIENTS

- 7 cups fresh blueberries
- 1 cup unsweetened apple juice
- 1 (1¾-oz.) package no-sugar-added pectin
- 1½ tsp. s liquid stevia

DIRECTIONS

1. In a heavy-bottomed saucepan, add blueberries, apple juice, and pectin and stir to combine.
2. Add the stevia and mix well.
3. Place the pan over medium heat and cook until boiling, stirring continuously.
4. Boil for about 3 minutes.
5. Remove the pan of jam from heat and immediately skim off foam from the top.
6. In 5 (½-pint) hot sterilized jars, divide the jam, leaving about ½-inch space from the top.
7. Slide a small knife around the insides of each jar to remove air bubbles.
8. Wipe any trace of food off the rims of jars with a clean, moist kitchen towel.
9. Close each jar with a lid and screw on the ring.
10. Arrange the jars in a boiling water canner and process for about 10 minutes.
11. Remove the jars from water canner and place onto a wood surface several inches apart to cool completely.
12. After cooling with your finger, press the top of each jar's lid to ensure that the seal is tight. The canned jam can be preserved in the pantry for up to 1 year.

217. Raspberry Jelly

Preparation Time: 10 minutes

Cooking Time: 6 minutes

Servings: 48

INGREDIENTS

- 4 cups fresh raspberries, crushed
- 1 cup water
- 4½ tablespoons no-sugar-added pectin

DIRECTIONS

1. In a heavy-bottomed stainless-steel saucepan, add raspberries, water, and pectin and stir to combine well.
2. Place the pan over medium heat and cook until boiling, stirring continuously.
3. Boil for about 1 minute.
4. Remove the saucepan of jelly from heat and immediately skim off foam from the top.
5. In 6 (½-pint) hot sterilized jars, divide the jelly, leaving about ½-inch space from the top.
6. Slide a small knife around the insides of each jar to remove air bubbles.
7. Wipe any trace of food off the rims of jars with a clean, moist kitchen towel.
8. Close each jar with a lid and screw on the ring.
9. Arrange the jars in a boiling water canner and process for about 10 minutes
10. Remove the jars from water canner and place onto a wood surface several inches apart to cool completely.
11. After cooling with your finger, press the top of each jar's lid to ensure that the seal is tight.
12. The canned jelly can be preserved in the pantry for up to 1 year.

218. Strawberry & Lemon Concentrate

Preparation Time: 15 minutes

Cooking Time: 5 minutes

Servings: 3-4 8 oz jars

INGREDIENTS

- 3 cups fresh strawberries, hulled
- 1½-2 cups erythritol
- 2 cups fresh lemon juice

DIRECTIONS

1. In a high-powered blender, place hulled strawberries and pulse until smooth.
2. In a heavy-bottomed stainless-steel saucepan, add pureed strawberries, erythritol, and lemon juice over medium-high heat and cook for about 3–5 minutes, stirring continuously.
3. Remove the pan of the strawberry mixture from heat and immediately skim off foam from the top.
4. In 7 (½-pint) hot sterilized jars, divide the strawberry mixture, leaving about ½-inch space from the top.
5. Slide a small knife around the insides of each jar to remove air bubbles.
6. Wipe any trace of food off the rims of jars with a clean, moist kitchen towel.
7. Close each jar with a lid and screw on the ring.
8. Arrange the jars in a boiling water canner and process for about 15 minutes.
9. Remove the jars from water canner and place onto a wood surface several inches apart to cool completely.
10. After cooling with your finger, press the top of each jar's lid to ensure that the seal is tight.

11. The canned preserve can be stored in the refrigerator for up to 3 weeks.

219. Pickled Beets

Preparation Time: 15 minutes

Cooking Time: 45 minutes

Servings: 2-4 16 oz. jars

INGREDIENTS

- 3 pounds beets, trimmed
- 1 tsp. allspice berries
- 6 whole cloves
- 1 cinnamon stick
- 2 cups apple cider vinegar
- ¼ tsp. stevia extract

DIRECTIONS

1. In a saucepan of boiling water, cook the beets for about 20–25 minutes.
2. Drain the beets, reserving 1 cup of cooking liquid.
3. Set the beets aside to cool.
4. Remove the skin of beets and then cut into slices.
5. In a cheesecloth, tie all the spices.
6. In a large nonreactive saucepan, add vinegar, reserved cooking liquid, stevia, and spice bag over medium-high heat and cook until boiling.
7. Now set the heat to low and cook for about 15 minutes.
8. In the bottom of 3 (1-pint) hot sterilized jars, divide the beet slices.
9. Now pack each jar with pickling liquid, leaving about ½-inch space from the top.
10. Slide a small knife around the insides of each jar to remove air bubbles.
11. Wipe any trace of food off the rims of jars with a clean, moist kitchen towel.
12. Close each jar with a lid and screw on the ring.
13. Arrange the jars in a boiling water canner and process for about 15 minutes.
14. Remove the jars from water canner and place onto a wood surface several inches apart to cool completely.
15. After cooling with your finger, press the top of each jar's lid to ensure that the seal is tight.
16. Place the jars in refrigerator for up to 1 month.

220. Healthy Hot Sauce

Preparation Time: 15 minutes

Cooking Time: 45 minutes

Servings: 5-6 32 oz jars

INGREDIENTS

- 6 tablespoons pickling spices
- 6 tbsps. hot peppers; stemmed, seeded, and chopped
- 6 lbs. chopped tomatoes
- 4 cups white vinegar
- 6 tsp. pickling salt

DIRECTIONS

1. In a cheesecloth, tie the pickling spices.
2. In a large saucepan, add spice bag and remaining ingredients over medium-high heat and cook until boiling.
3. Now set the heat to low and cook for about 20 minutes.
4. Through a food mill, press the mixture.
5. Return the mixture into the same saucepan and again bring to a boil.
6. Cook for about 15 minutes.
7. Divide the sauce into hot sanitized jars, leaving about ½-inch headspace
8. Slide a small knife around the insides of each jar to remove air bubbles.

9. Wipe any trace of food off the rims of jars with a clean, moist kitchen towel.
10. Close each jar with a lid and screw on the ring.
11. Arrange the jars in a boiling water canner and process for about 10 minutes.
12. Remove the jars from water canner and place onto a wood surface several inches apart to cool completely.
13. After cooling with your finger, press the top of each jar's lid to ensure that the seal is tight.
14. The canned sauce can be preserved in the pantry for up to 1 month.

221. BBQ Sauce

Preparation Time: 10 minutes

Cooking Time: 1 hour 5 minutes

Servings: 3-4 8oz jars

INGREDIENTS

- 6 oz. sugar-free, low-sodium tomato paste
- ¾ cup water
- 1/3 cup apple cider vinegar
- 3 tablespoons white wine vinegar
- 2 tablespoons Worcestershire sauce
- 2 tsp. s red chili powder
- ½ tsp. onion powder
- ½ tsp. garlic powder
- 1/4 tsp. ground cinnamon
- ⅛ tsp. salt
- ½ tsp. ground black pepper

DIRECTIONS

1. In a nonreactive saucepan, add all Ingredients over medium-high heat and cook until boiling.
2. Now set the heat to low and cook for about 1 hour, stirring occasionally.
3. In 3 (½-pint) hot sterilized jars, divide the sauce, leaving about ½-inch space from the top.
4. Slide a small knife around the insides of each jar to remove air bubbles.
5. Wipe any trace of food off the rims of jars with a clean, moist kitchen towel.
6. Close each jar with a lid and screw on the ring.
7. Arrange the jars in a boiling water canner and process for about 10 minutes.
8. Remove the jars from water canner and place onto a wood surface several inches apart to cool completely.
9. After cooling with your finger, press the top of each jar's lid to ensure that the seal is tight.
10. The canned sauce can be preserved in the pantry for up to 1 month.

222. Canned Apple Slices

Preparation Time: 15 minutes

Cooking Time: 10 minutes

Servings: 6 half pint jars

INGREDIENTS

- 1 tsp. citric acid
- 5 pounds apples; peeled, cored, and cut into slices
- 2 cups water
- 1 tsp. ground cinnamon

DIRECTIONS

1. In a nonreactive saucepan, place the acid.
2. Add apple slices and water and mix well.
3. Place the pan over medium-high heat and cook until boiling.
4. Boil for about 5 minutes.
5. In the bottom of 4 (1-pint) hot sterilized jars, divide the apple slices.
6. Now pack each jar with cooking liquid, leaving about ½-inch space from the top.
7. Add in the cinnamon in each jar.
8. Slide a small knife around the insides of each jar to remove air bubbles.
9. Wipe any trace of food off the rims of jars with a clean, moist kitchen towel.
10. Close each jar with a lid and screw on the ring.
11. Arrange the jars in a boiling water canner and process for about 20 minutes.
12. Remove the jars from water canner and place onto a wood surface several inches apart to cool completely.
13. After cooling with your finger, press the top of each jar's lid to ensure that the seal is tight.
14. These canned apples can be preserved in refrigerator for up month

223. *Light Turkey Tortilla Soup*

Preparation Time: 20 min

Cooking Time: 75 minutes

Servings: 6-pint jars

INGREDIENTS

- 1 ½ tbsps. extra virgin olive oil
- 2 cups onions
- 8 oz. green chilies
- 2 ½ oz. taco seasoning
- 2 cans crushed tomatoes
- 16 cups turkey broth
- 20 oz. corn kernels
- 6 cups cooked turkey

DIRECTIONS

1. Heat oil in a sizable pan, add the onion, and cook until translucent in color. Add the chilies and taco seasoning to the onions and cook for a further two to three minutes.
2. Add the tomatoes and slowly stir in the chicken stock, little by little, and then bring it to a boil.
3. Take the cooked turkey and cut into bite-sized cubes.
4. Add the corn kernels and turkey to the pot and simmer the mixture on low heat for 10 minutes, at which point it should be done.
5. Start the canning process.
6. Leave a 1-inch headspace.
7. Pressure the canner at 10 lbs. pressure.

224. *Canned Chicken Stock*

Preparation Time: 20 min

Cooking Time: 2 hours 20 minutes

Servings: 4- 5 16 oz jars

INGREDIENTS

- 16 cups water
- 4 lbs. chicken, pieces cut
- 2 stalks celery
- 2 quartered onions, medium
- 1 tbsp. salt
- 10 peppercorns

DIRECTIONS

1. Prepare your pressure canner and heat your jars with simmering water. Wash the lids with warm, soapy water and set the bands aside.
2. Place the water and chicken in a large saucepan, then bring to a boil.

3. Reduce the heat and simmer for about 2 hours until chicken becomes tender. Now remove from heat and skim off the foam.
4. Remove and reserve the chicken for other use.
5. Meanwhile, strain the stock through several cheesecloth layers or a sieve, and allow it to cool for the fat to solidify. Now skim the fat off.
6. Heat the stock to boiling and scoop hot stock into hot pint jars. Leave a 1-inch headspace.
7. Rinse the rims of the jars using a clean, damp paper towel.
8. Center lid on jars, then apply band, adjusting until fingertip-tight fit.
9. Can pint jars in a pressure canner for 20 minutes at 11 pounds of pressure if using a dial-gauge canner or 10 pounds of pressure if using a weighted-gauge canner.

225. *Potato and Chicken Stew*

Preparation Time: 20 min

Cooking Time: 1 hour

Servings: 9-10 quarts jars

INGREDIENTS

- 1-quart cubed beef
- 1-quart cubed lamb
- 1½ quarts cubed chicken
- 4 quarts cubed potatoes
- 1-cquart cubed carrots
- 3 cups chopped onions
- 4 slices bacon
- 1 green bell pepper
- 1 red bell pepper
- 3 minced garlic cloves
- 1 tbsp. black pepper
- 1 tbsp. paprika
- 1 tbsp. salt
- 1-pint tomato sauce
- ¾-cup tomato juice

DIRECTIONS

1. In a large pot, add meat, quartered onion, and carrot cut into thirds; cover with water and simmer for about 1 hour.
2. Discard the carrots and onion pieces.
3. Cook bacon and pour off the grease. Add to the pot of meat. Add remaining ingredients to the pot, cover, and simmer gently until mixture is hot. Ladle hot stew into hot jars, leaving a 1-inch headspace.
4. Following the "Pressure Canning" directions, process quarts for 90 minutes and pints for 75 minutes at 10 PSI, adjusting the PSI as necessary for your altitude according to the altitude adjustment directions.
5. Makes about 9 to 10 quarts.

226. *Pressure Canned Turkey Broth*

Preparation Time: - 10 minutes

Cooking Time: 45 minutes

Servings: 2 -quart jars

INGREDIENTS

- Turkey carcass bones, meat removed
- 2 quartered onions
- 2 sliced celery stalks
- 2 bay leaves
- 3 minced garlic cloves (optional)
- 1 tbsp. black pepper
- 1 tbsp. paprika (optional)
- 1 tbsp. salt
- Salt
- 14 cups Water

DIRECTIONS

1. Place turkey bones and all optional ingredients in a large stockpot, then add water to cover everything.

2. Cover the pot and simmer for about 30-45 minutes until remaining meat tidbits fall off easily.
3. Remove and discard the bones, then strain the broth and discard the bay leaves and vegetables.
4. Cool the broth then skim off the fat and discard it. Season with salt, if desired.
5. Reheat your broth to boiling.
6. Scoop broth into quart jars. Leave 1-inch headspace.
7. Wipe the jar rims using a clean, damp paper towel, and then apply the 2-piece metal caps.
8. Can the quart jars in a pressure canner for 25 minutes at 11 pounds of pressure if using a dial-gauge canner or 10 pounds of pressure if using a weighted-gauge canner.

227. *Chicken Broth with Chile and Corn*

Preparation Time: 10 minutes

Cooking Time: 36 minutes

Servings: 5-quart

INGREDIENTS

- 2 tbsps. veggies oil
- 1 cup sliced celery (about 2 stalks)
- 1½ sliced onions, (about 3 medium)
- 2 poblano chili pepper, seeded and sliced
- 2 tsps. mild chili powder or ground chili peppers
- 12 cups chicken stock
- 4 cups sliced chicken, cooked
- 5 cups freshly picked corn kernels
- ½ tsp black pepper, freshly ground

DIRECTIONS

1. Prepare the canning jars.
2. Melt the oil over medium-high heat in a large saucepot. Add celery, onions, and chiles, then cook and stir for 5 minutes or until softened. Add chili powder, stirring frequently, and cook for one minute.
3. Add chopped chicken, stock, corn, and black pepper. Allow it to boil for 30 minutes.
4. Ladle vegetables and chicken into each canning jar by filling halfway and adding broth. Remember to leave a 1-inch headspace. Use a spatula to remove any air bubbles, then use a clean cloth to wipe jar rims. After that, adjust the lids, and screw the bands.
5. Set the filled jars in a pressure canner at 11 pounds of pressure for dial-gauge or 10 pounds for the weighted-gauge canner. Process hot jars for 75 minutes, adjusting for altitude. Switch off the heat and let the pressure drop naturally.
6. Remove the lid and cool the jars in the canner for 5 minutes.
7. Take out the jars and cool. Inspect lids for sealing after 24 hours.

228. *Chicken Stew with Carrot*

Preparation Time: 10 minutes

Cooking Time: 40 minutes

Servings: 1 pint

INGREDIENTS

- 3 tbsps. butter
- 1½ cups diced onion
- ½ cup diced fresh mushrooms
- 1½ cups diced carrot
- 1 cup diced Yukon gold potatoes
- ½ cup diced celery
- 5 cups chicken stock
- 1-cup dry white wine
- 1 tsp. dried thyme
- 1 tsp. salt
- ½ tsp. ground black pepper
- 1 bay leaf
- 3 cups cubed skinned and boned raw chicken
- ½ cup frozen baby sweet peas, thawed
- 1 tbsp. bottled lemon juice

DIRECTIONS

1. Heat the butter in a large stainless steel or enameled Dutch oven over medium heat. Add onion and mushrooms.
2. Sauté for 3 minutes or until mushrooms are lightly browned.
3. Add the carrot and next 2 ingredients, and sauté 2 minutes.
4. Stir in stock and the next 5 ingredients.
5. Boil uncovered for 10 minutes or until vegetables are tender, stirring occasionally. Remove from the heat.
6. Stir in chicken, peas, and lemon juice. Remove and discard bay leaf.
7. Ladle hot stew into a hot jar, leaving a 1-inch headspace.
8. Rinse jar rim and place jar on rack in a pressure canner containing 2 inches of simmering water 180°F. Repeat until all jars are filled.
9. Process 1-pint jars in a pressure canner for 90 minutes at 11 PSI. Be sure to adjust for altitude.

229. *Bean and Tomato Chicken Soup*

Preparation Time: 10 minutes

Cooking Time: 45 minutes.

Servings: 1 quart

INGREDIENTS

- 3 cans diced tomatoes; juice reserved
- 6 cups chicken broth
- 3 tbsps. chili powder
- 1 tbsp. cilantro
- 1 tbsp. ground cumin
- 3 cups chicken, cooked and shredded
- 3 cups black beans, rinsed, sorted, and pre-soaked
- 2 cups corn kernels
- 1 onion, finely diced
- 4 cloves garlic, minced
- 1 bell pepper, diced
- Salt and pepper, to taste

DIRECTIONS

1. In a large stockpot, stir together all the ingredients.
2. Bring this mixture to a boil for 45 minutes.
3. Layer the other ingredients evenly in your jars.
4. Top the layered ingredients with your hot broth mixture, leaving 1 inch of headspace.
5. Can the sealed jars in a pressure canner for 90 minutes at 11 PSI. Be sure to adjust for altitude.

230. *Texas Chili*

Preparation Time: 10 minutes

Cooking Time: 50 minutes

Servings: 9 pints

INGREDIENTS

- 3 lbs. stewing beef, cut into small bite-size cubes
- 2 tbsps. vegetable oil
- 3 cups dried red kidney beans
- 5 ½ cups water
- 5 tsps. salt, divided
- 1 ½ cups onions, chopped
- 1 cup red bell peppers, chopped
- 1 tsps. black pepper
- 4 tbsps. chili powder
- 1 tbsp. cumin
- 2 quarts crushed tomatoes

DIRECTIONS

1. In a sizable pot, combine the beans with the water and salt.
2. Simmer for 30 minutes then strain.
3. Warm the oil on medium-high heat. Add the beef cubes by batch and brown on all sides. Do not overcrowd the meat. Place browned meat on plate covered with paper towels to absorb the excess fat. Pat dries the browned beef.
4. Clean skillet with a paper towel and add 1 tablespoon of oil. Sauté the onions and peppers

for 2 minutes until tender fragrant and tender. Drain excess liquids if necessary.

5. Add beef, onions and peppers mixture, salt, chili powder, tomatoes, and beans. Let simmer for at least 5 minutes.
6. Pour the chili into sterile jars, leaving a 1-inch headspace.
7. Rinse the jar rims clean and adjust the lids. Process the jars in a pressure canner for 75 minutes at 10 pounds of pressure for a pressure canner.

231. *Carrot, Coriander, and Ginger Soup*

Preparation Time: 10 minutes

Cooking Time: 75 minutes

Servings: 4-pint jars

INGREDIENTS

- 1 big onion, chopped
- 3 tbsps. butter
- 2 whole cloves peeled garlic
- 3 pounds carrots, chopped
- 2 ribs celery, chopped
- 3 tbsps. fresh ginger, chopped
- 8 cups vegetable or chicken broth
- 1 tsp. ground coriander
- ½-cup honey
- 1 tsp. ground ginger
- Fresh ground black pepper and salt

DIRECTIONS

1. Melt the butter in a large saucepot over medium-high heat.
2. Add onion, garlic, carrot, ginger root, and celery to butter and cook for 10 minutes with frequent stirring.
3. Add the broth to the veggies and allow it to boil. Reduce heat and leave to cook for about 30 minutes so the carrots are tender.
4. Take it out of heat sauce. Add ground ginger, honey, and coriander.
5. Puree the soup in the pot in batches with either a regular blender or using an immersion blender.
6. Ladle the hot soup into each canning jar. Remember to leave 1-inch headspace. Use a spatula to remove any air bubbles, then use a clean cloth to wipe jar rims. After that, adjust lids and screw band.
7. Set the filled jars in a pressure canner at 11 pounds of pressure for dial-gauge or 10 pounds for the weighted-gauge canner.
8. Process heat jars for 75 minutes, adjusting for altitude. Switch off the heat and let pressure drop naturally. Remove the lid and cool the jars in canner for 5 minutes. Take out the jars and cool.
9. Inspect lids for seal after 24 hours.

232. *Mexican Chicken Soup*

Preparation Time: 10 minutes

Cooking Time: 75 minutes

Servings: 4-pint jars

INGREDIENTS

- 1 large boneless chicken breast (boiled, cubed, or shredded)
- ¼ cup chopped carrots
- 2/3 cup chopped celery
- 1 medium onion, sliced
- 2/3 can of tomatoes
- 2/3 can of kidney beans
- 1 cup cubed tomatoes
- 2 cups chicken stock
- 2 cups water
- 1 cup corn (fresh or frozen)
- 1 garlic clove (crushed)
- 1/3 tsp. ground cumin
- 1/3 tbsp. canning salt
- 1 chicken bouillon cube

DIRECTIONS

1. Combine all ingredients in a large saucepot.

2. Place over medium-high heat, bring to a boil, cover, and boil for three minutes.
3. Reduce heat and chicken, then cook slowly for 5 minutes.
4. Ladle hot soup into canning jars. Remember to leave 1-inch headspace. Use a spatula to remove any air bubbles, then use a clean cloth to wipe jar rims. After that, adjust lids and screw band.
5. Set the filled jars in a pressure canner at 11 pounds of pressure for dial-gauge or 10 pounds for the weighted-gauge canner.
6. Process hot jars for 75 minutes, adjusting for altitude. Switch off the heat and let the pressure drop naturally.
7. Remove the lid and cool the jars in canner for 5 minutes.
8. Take out the jars and cool. Inspect lids seal after 24 hours.

233. *Five-Bean Medley*

Preparation Time: 10 minutes

Cooking Time: 90 minutes

Servings: 6 pints

INGREDIENTS

- 12 cups hot water
- 3 cups dried pinto beans
- 2 ½ cups dried kidney beans
- 2 ¼ cups dried black beans
- 2 ¼ cups dried split peas
- 2 ½ cups dried great northern beans
- 7 tsps. coarse sea salt

DIRECTIONS

1. Add the water to the stockpot and bring to a boil on high heat.
2. Thoroughly rinse and clean the dried beans, discarding any disfigured or shriveled beans and any rocks or debris.
3. If using, add 1-tsp. salt per quart jar or ½-tsp. salt per pint jar before filling with dried beans.
4. Using a ladle and funnel, fill each quart jar with 1½ cups clean dried beans and each pint jar with ¾ cup. Next, ladle the hot water over the beans, leaving 1 inch of headspace.
5. Dip a warm washcloth in distilled white vinegar and wipe the rims of the jars. Set a lid on each jar and tighten.
6. Set the jars in the pressure canner, place the lid in place, and allow to boil while on high heat. You can vent for approximately 10 minutes. Lock the vent and heat further to attain dial gauge of 11 PSI and a weighted gauge of 10 PSI.
7. Can the quart jars for 90 minutes and pint jars for around 75 minutes.

234. *Chicken & Veggie Soup*

Preparation Time: 10 minutes

Cooking Time: 1 hour

Servings: 8 pints

INGREDIENTS

- 4 cups of chopped cooked chicken
- 4 quarts of broth, chicken – homemade, if possible
- 4 cups chopped mixed veggies, like onions, carrots, and celery
- 1 garlic clove
- Kosher salt
- Ground pepper

DIRECTIONS

1. Place cooked chicken and broth in large sized stockpot. Bring to a boil.
2. Add the vegetables to the pot. Bring back to a boil.
3. Add salt and ground pepper.

4. Mix in the garlic and any other seasonings you would like.
5. Use a slotted spoon to add the solid ingredients to the jars. The solids should not fill any more than ½ of each jar. Then top the jars off with the broth. Leave an inch at the top.
6. Place lids on the jars. Process using the instructions from the pressure canner.

235. *Black Bean Chili with Potato*

Preparation Time: 20 min

Cooking Time: 2 hours

Servings: 7 pints

INGREDIENTS

- 4 cups dried black beans
- 2 tbsps. olive oil
- 6 minced garlic cloves
- 2 diced bell peppers
- 1 diced onion
- 1 diced sweet potato
- 2 minced jalapeños
- 2¼ tsp. salt
- 1 tbsp. ground cumin
- 1 tbsp. chili powder
- 1 tbsp. dried oregano
- Crushed red pepper or cayenne, to taste
- Juice of 1 lime
- ½-cup tomato purée

DIRECTIONS

1. Soak the beans for 18 hours. Drain off the soaking water and transfer to a large soup or stockpot.
2. Boil the beans while covered with water for an hour.
3. In a sizable skillet with olive oil, sauté the bell pepper, garlic, hot peppers, onions, sweet potato, and salt for 15 minutes.
4. Stir in the spices, sautéed vegetables, lime juice, and tomato purée to the cooked beans.
5. Simmer for 45 minutes while stirring often.
6. Fill the jars, leaving a 1-inch of headspace.
7. Rinse the rims of the jars and seal.
8. Can in a pressure canner according to the manufacturer's instructions.

236. *Onion Soup with Butter*

Preparation Time: 20 min

Cooking Time: 1 hour 30 minutes

Servings: 1 pint

INGREDIENTS

- 1 tbsp. butter
- 4 lbs. onions, thinly sliced
- 1 tbsp. salt
- 1 tsp. ground black pepper
- 1 tsp. dried thyme
- 3 cups dry white wine, divided
- 3-quart beef bone broth, or commercial canned chicken, beef, or vegetable stock

DIRECTIONS

1. Place the butter in a stainless steel or enameled Dutch oven over medium-low heat. Stir in onion, next 3 ingredients, and 2 cups (500 mL) white wine. Cover and cook for 1 hour or until onion is very tender, stirring occasionally.
2. Cook as you stir constantly while uncovered.
3. Add the other 1-cup wine and cook 2 minutes as you stir.
4. Mix in the broth and simmer for 15 minutes while uncovered.
5. Fill the hot soup into a hot jar, leaving a 1-inch headspace.
6. Rinse jar rims and arrange them on a rack in a pressure canner.
7. Can for 1 hour 15 minutes.

237. Chicken Soup with Tomato

Preparation Time: 20 min

Cooking Time: 5 minutes

Servings: 7 quarts

INGREDIENTS

- 1 tbsp. salt
- 1½ cups sliced carrots
- 6 cups diced tomatoes
- 3 minced garlic cloves
- 6 diced jalapeno peppers,
- 3 cooked and shredded chicken breasts
- 12 cups chicken broth
- 3 cups corn
- 2 cups chopped celery
- 2 cans kidney beans
- 1 tsp. ground cumin

DIRECTIONS

1. Boil all the ingredients in a sizable pot except for the cooked chicken; cover and simmer for 5 minutes.
2. Stir in the cooked chicken and continue to simmer until chicken is hot.
3. Ladle hot soup into jars, leaving a 1-inch headspace. Following the "Pressure Canning" directions, process quarts for 90 minutes and pints for 75 minutes at 10 PSI, adjusting the PSI as necessary for your altitude according to the altitude adjustment directions.

238. Venison & Tomato Chili

Preparation Time: 20 min

Cooking Time: 30 Minutes

Servings: 8-pint jars

INGREDIENTS

- 6 lbs. chopped venison
- 6 cups canned tomatoes
- ½ cup chili powder
- 2 cups chopped onions
- 4½ tsp. salt
- 1 tsp. cumin seeds
- 2 minced jalapeno peppers
- 2 minced garlic cloves

DIRECTIONS

1. Sterilize the jars.
2. Brown the meat in a skillet in batches and then transfer it into a pot.
3. Stir fry the garlic and onions in a skillet and add it to the pot with the remaining ingredients.
4. Bring to a boil and then cook for 20 minutes at reduced heat.
5. Ladle the mix immediately into the sterilized jars, leaving one inch of headspace.
6. Get rid of any air bubbles and clean the rims.
7. Cover the jars with the lid and apply the bands, making sure that it is tightened.
8. Process the jars for 75 at 10 pounds pressure in a pressure canner.
9. Remove, allow to cool, and then label the jars.

239. Pickled Kimchi Soup

Preparation Time: 20 min

Cooking Time: 10 Minutes

Servings: 6-pint jars

INGREDIENTS

- 3 heads napa cabbage, chopped
- 12 garlic cloves
- ¼ cup dried salted shrimp
- 2 tbsps. minced ginger
- 1 yellow onion
- 3 tbsps. sweet rice flour
- 4 cups coarse sea salt
- 2 tbsps. brown sugar
- 3 cups water
- ½ cup fish sauce
- 2 cups sliced Korean radish
- 6 chopped green onions
- 4 cups Korean red chili flakes
- 1 tbsp. sesame seeds

DIRECTIONS

1. Divide 3 cups of water among 3 large bowls and stir 1 cup of sea salt in each bowl of water. Sprinkle the remaining 1 cup of salt over the chopped cabbage.
2. Divide the salted cabbage in the 3 bowls until partially submerged and let sit for 12 hours.
3. Rinse cabbage thoroughly in a colander then then let drain for 1 hour to get rid of excess water.
4. Combine the rice flour and 3 cups of water in a pot over medium heat and bring to a boil, heating the mixture until you get a glue-like consistency, which should be about 5 minutes.
5. Remove pot from heat and cool rice mixture to room temperature.
6. Combine garlic, 1 tablespoon of water, ginger, and onion in a food processor: pulse until smooth, adding more water if too dry.
7. Combine the chili flakes, onion mixture and rice flour mixture, fish sauce, shrimp, brown sugar, and sesame seeds in a large bowl until well mixed.
8. Toss in the radish and green onions and toss well to combine.
9. Rub the cabbage with the chili mix, ensuring the cabbage is well coated, and pack into storage jars and tightly cover. L
10. Leave the jars at room temperature for 3 days for the fermentation to occur.
11. Process the jars for 75 at 10 pounds pressure in a pressure canner.
12. Remove, allow to cool, and then label the jars.

240. *Carrot Soup*

Preparation Time: 20 min

Cooking Time: 1 Hour 35 Minutes

Servings: 12 pint

INGREDIENTS

- 4 lbs. sliced carrots
- 1 lb. chopped fennel bulb
- 1 tsp. dried thyme
- 2 tsps. onion powder
- 12 cups vegetable stock
- 1 tbsp. olive oil
- ½ tsp. ground cumin
- 1 tsp. black pepper
- 1 tsp. ground coriander
- 1 tsp. ground ginger
- 2 tbsps. salt

DIRECTIONS

1. Pour oil in a saucepan to heat over medium heat.
2. Add fennel and sauté until translucent.
3. Add carrots and 4 cups of stock and let it simmer for 30 minutes.
4. Remove saucepan from heat and, using a blender, puree the carrots until smooth.
5. Return the saucepan to the heat.
6. Add the remaining ingredients and stir well. Cook on low heat for 20-30 minutes.
7. Ladle soup into the clean jars. Leave a 1-inch headspace.
8. Seal the jar with the lids and prepare in a water bath canner for 40 minutes.
9. Allow the jars from the water bath to cool completely.
10. Check the seals of jars. Label and store.

241. *Squash Soup with Chiles*

Preparation Time: 20 min

Cooking Time: 25 Minutes

Servings: 3-pint jars

INGREDIENTS

- 8 cups chicken or vegetable broth
- ½ tsp. ground red pepper
- 3 minced garlic cloves
- 2 minced Thai chiles
- 1 quartered lemongrass stalk
- 1 grated ginger
- 1½ lbs. cubed butternut
- 2 tbsps. sugar
- 2 tsps. salt
- 1 tsp. lime zest
- 2 tbsps. lime juice
- 4 chopped shallots
- 1 chopped red bell pepper
- ½ cup coconut milk
- 2 tbsps. red onion slivers
- 1 tbsp. chopped cilantro
- lime wedges

DIRECTIONS

1. Boil the broth in a 6-quart stainless steel or enameled Dutch oven. Stir in ground red pepper and the next 4 ingredients; cover, reduce heat, and simmer 20 minutes, stirring occasionally.
2. Remove lemongrass. Add squash and the next 6 ingredients. Simmer for 5 minutes as you stir.
3. Ladle hot soup into a hot jar, leaving 1-inch) headspace.
4. Remove air bubbles. Wipe jar rim. Center lid on jar. Apply band and adjust to fingertip tight. Place jar on rack in a pressure canner containing 2 inches of simmering water 180°F.
5. Repeat until all jars are filled.
6. Tighten the lid on canner, and switch to locked position.
7. Set the heat to medium-high. Vent steam for 10 minutes. Place the counterweight or weighted gauge on vent; bring pressure to 10 pounds (psi) for a weighted-gauge canner or 11 pounds (psi) for a dial-gauge canner.
8. Process 1-pint jars for 1 hour and 15 minutes or 1-quart jars for 1 hour and 30 minutes.
9. Cool jars in canner 10 minutes. Remove jars and cool.
10. Serve with lime wedges.

242. *Black Bean Soup*

Preparation Time: 20 min

Cooking Time: 40 Minutes

Servings: 6-pint jars

INGREDIENTS

- 1 lb. dried black beans
- 2 diced onions
- 4 diced carrots
- 4 minced garlic cloves
- 1 diced poblano pepper
- 2½ quarts chicken stock
- 2 cups diced ham
- 2 tsps. ground cumin
- 3 tsps. kosher salt
- 1½ tsps. black pepper
- ½ tsps. cayenne pepper
- 2 tsps. Mexican oregano

DIRECTIONS

1. Transfer the beans to a large pot and cover with enough cold water to cover the beans by 3 inches.
2. Add the onion that is cut in half and bring to a boil. Reduce the heat and let this simmer for 30 minutes.
3. In another pot, add the chicken stock, spices, and vegetables and let it simmer for at least 5 minutes.

4. Strain the beans and discard the liquid and the onion. Strain the vegetables out of the stock, reserving both.
5. In sterile jars, fill the jars ¼ full of the beans, the vegetables, the ham, and the stock, leaving a 1-inch head space.
6. Wipe the rims clean and adjust the lids.
7. Can in a pressure canner for 75 minutes at 10 pounds of pressure for a pressure canner with a weighted gauge or 11 pounds if the pressure canner has a dial-gauge.

243. *Pea Soup with Carrot*

Preparation Time: 20 min

Cooking Time: 1 Hour 30 Minutes

Servings: 6 -7-pint jars

INGREDIENTS

- 6 quarts dried split peas
- 6 quarts water
- 4½ cups diced carrots
- 3 cups chopped onion
- 3 cups cooked and diced ham
- ½ tsp. allspice
- salt & black pepper, to taste

DIRECTIONS

1. Mix the split peas and water in a large pot and boil.
2. Simmer for 1 hour while covered or until peas are soft. Mash peas, if desired, with a potato masher.
3. Mix in the remaining ingredients and simmer for 30 minutes. Adjust consistency of soup by adding boiling water or broth if needed.
4. Add hot soup into hot jars, leaving 1-inch headspace. Following the "Pressure Canning" directions, process quarts for 90 minutes and pints for 75 minutes at 10 psi, adjusting the psi as necessary for your altitude according to the altitude adjustment directions.

244. *Chicken Soup*

Preparation Time: 20 min

Cooking Time: 20 Minutes

Servings: 8-pint jars

INGREDIENTS

- 3 cups diced chicken
- salt, to taste
- 6 cups chicken broth
- 10 cups water
- 1 cup diced onion
- Black pepper to taste
- 1½ cups diced celery
- 1½ cups sliced carrots
- 3 chicken bouillon cubes

DIRECTIONS

1. Sterilize the jars.
2. Boil all the ingredients in a sizable pot except for the seasonings and bouillon cubes.
3. Reduce the flame and simmer for 30 minutes.
4. Stir in the remaining ingredients and stir while cooking until the bouillon cubes dissolve.
5. Turn off the flame and skim off any visible foam.
6. Ladle the mix immediately into the sterilized jars, leaving one inch of headspace.
7. Get rid of any air bubbles and clean the rims.
8. Cover the jars with the lid and apply the bands, making sure that it is tightened.
9. Process the jars for 1 hour 15 minutes at 10 pounds pressure in a pressure canner.
10. Remove; allow cooling, and then labeling the jars.

245. Bean and Bacon Soup

Preparation Time: 20 min

Cooking Time: 2 Hours

Servings: 8-pint jars

INGREDIENTS

- 2 lbs. dried navy beans, soaked in water overnight
- 8 cups tomato juice
- 8 cups chicken or vegetable stock
- 2 cups carrots
- 4 cups white potatoes
- 3 cups chopped celery
- 1 tbsp. salt
- 2 tsps. black pepper
- 2 bay leaves
- 3 cups diced onion
- 2 lbs. bacon
- water

DIRECTIONS

1. Slice carrots and celery. Dice onions, potatoes, and bacon.
2. Boil all ingredients, except for the bacon and onions, in a large stockpot over medium heat. Let it simmer.
3. Sauté the bacon in a sizable skillet over medium heat until golden brown, about 10 minutes. Add the onions. Sauté for an additional 10 minutes.
4. Add bacon and onions to the bean mixture.
5. If the soup is thick, add some water until you get the preferred consistency. Heat it until it simmers, about 30-35 more minutes.
6. Remove bay leaves with tongs and pour equal amounts of the soup into jars.
7. Cook under pressure for 1 hour at 10 pounds for the weighted gauge of the pressure canner, or 11 pounds if the pressure canner has a dial-gauge.
8. Allow the jars cool at room temperature before storing. This can take about a day.

246. Mexican Beef and Sweet Potato Soup

Preparation Time: 20 min

Cooking Time: 80 Minutes

Servings: 8-pint

INGREDIENTS

- 1 tbsp. vegetable oil
- 2½ quarts beef broth
- 2 ½ lbs. beef chuck roast
- 4 sliced Roma tomatoes
- 1 sliced sweet potato
- 8 sliced carrots
- 1 cup whole kernel corn
- 1 sliced onion
- 2 sliced jalapeño peppers
- 2 sliced poblano peppers
- 1 tbsp. salt
- 6 minced garlic cloves
- ½ tbsp. ground black pepper
- ½ tbsp. chili powder

DIRECTIONS

1. Pour ½ tbsp veggie oil in a 6-quart pot and place over medium-low heat. Add half of the beef cubes.
2. Fry while stirring to turn brown. Move beef into a small bowl. Do the same with the remaining ½ tbsp oil and beef. Transfer all the meat to the pot and add broth.
3. Reduce heat and allow to it boil. Simmer covered until beef is soft.
4. Add sweet potatoes, carrots, tomatoes, onions, corn, garlic, jalapeno peppers, poblano peppers, salt, black pepper, and chili powder to beef mixture in the pot.
5. Cover and leave it to boil for 5 minutes.
6. Ladle vegetables and beef into the canning jars by filling each halfway. Pour hot broth into every jar and leave a 1-inch headspace.
7. Remove air bubbles, clean the jar rims, adjust lids, and screw band.

8. Set the filled jars in a pressure canner at 11 pounds pressure for dial-gauge or 10 pounds for the weighted-gauge canner.
9. Process heat jars for 75 minutes, adjusting for altitude.
10. Switch off the heat and let the pressure drop naturally.
11. Remove the lid and cool the jars in canner for 5 minutes.
12. Take out the jars and cool. Inspect lids seal after 24 hours.

247. *Tomato Soup with Celery*

Preparation Time: 20 min

Cooking Time: 25 Minutes

Servings: 8 Pints

INGREDIENTS

- 6 sliced onions
- 1 bunch sliced celery
- 5-quarts tomato juice
- 1 cup sugar
- ¼ cup salt
- 1 cup butter
- 1 cup flour

DIRECTIONS

1. Add chopped celery and onions in a large pot with a little amount of water to prevent them from burning.
2. Place pot over medium heat. Bring to a boil.
3. While boiling, add tomatoes to the pot and cook to become softened.
4. Pour the combination all through a strainer and then return to the pot. Add salt and sugar.
5. Combine flour and butter. Mix evenly and add 2 cups of cold juice until well blended. Add flour and butter mixture to warm juice (before it is hot to prevent flour lumps).
6. Stir well. The flour can turn lumpy if it reaches a boil, so only heat to hot and turn off the heater before boiling. It will keep thickening as it cools.
7. Ladle hot soup into each canning jar. Remember to leave a 1-inch headspace. Use spatula to remove air bubbles, then use a clean cloth to wipe jar rims. After that, adjust lids and screw band.
8. Set the filled jars in a pressure canner at 11 pounds pressure for dial-gauge or 10 pounds for the weighted-gauge canner.
9. Process heat jars for 25 minutes, adjusting for altitude.
10. Switch off heat and let the pressure drop naturally.
11. Remove the lid and cool the jars in the canner for three minutes. Take out the jars and cool. Inspect lids seal after 24 hours.

248. *Green Lima Vegetable Soup*

Preparation Time: 20 min

Cooking Time: 55 Minutes

Servings: 7-pint

INGREDIENTS

- 4 cups sliced tomatoes
- 3 cups chopped carrots
- 3 cups cubed potatoes
- salt and black pepper, to taste
- 2 cups uncooked corn kernels
- 2 cups green lima beans
- 1 cup sliced onions
- 1 cup chopped celery
- 3 cups water

DIRECTIONS

1. In a medium saucepot, combine all the vegetables. Pour water and allow it to boil.

2. Cook for 5 minutes on reduced heat. Add pepper and salt if you wish.
3. Ladle hot veggie soup into each canning jar. Remember to leave a 1-inch headspace. Use a spatula to remove air bubbles, then use a clean cloth to wipe jar rims. After that, adjust lids and screw band.
4. Set the filled jars in a pressure canner at 11 pounds pressure for dial-gauge or 10 pounds for the weighted-gauge canner.
5. Process heat jars for 55 minutes, adjusting for altitude. Switch off the heat and let pressure come down naturally.
6. Remove the lid and cool the jars in the canner for ten minutes.
7. Take out the jars and cool.
8. Inspect lids seal after about 24 hours.

249. *Cabbage and Corned Beef Soup*

Preparation Time: 20 min

Cooking Time: 80 Minutes

Servings: 8-pint

INGREDIENTS

- 1 sliced onion
- 1½ cups sliced carrot
- 1½ cups chopped celery
- 1½ cups tomato sauce
- 1/3 tsp. ground allspice
- 5 cups beef stock
- 2 cups diced potatoes
- 1 sliced head cabbage
- ½ lb. corned beef
- ½ tsp. black pepper
- 1 tsp. canning salt
- 2 cups water

DIRECTIONS

1. Layer equal quantities of carrots, onions, celery, cabbage, corned beef, and potatoes to each cleaned canning jar to around ¾ full.
2. In a medium saucepot, add tomato sauce or juice, beef stock, allspice, pepper, salt, and water. Allow it to boil and remove from the heat source.
3. Ladle the mixture into each canning jar. Remember to leave a 1-inch headspace. If necessary, add more hot water or stock to each canning jar.
4. Use a spatula to remove air bubbles, then use a clean cloth to wipe jar rims. After that, adjust lids and screw band.
5. Set the filled jars in a pressure canner at 11 pounds pressure for dial-gauge or 10 pounds for the weighted-gauge canner. Process heat jars for 75 minutes, adjusting for altitude.
6. Switch off the heat and let the pressure drop naturally.
7. Remove the lid and cool the jars in canner for 5 minutes.
8. Take out the jars and cool. Inspect lids seal after 24 hours.

250. *Split Pea Soup*

Preparation Time: 20 min

Cooking Time: 90 Minutes

Servings: 2-pint jars

INGREDIENTS

- 1 lb. yellow, dry split peas
- 2 quarts water
- 4 tsps. lime juice
- ¾ cups sliced carrots

- 1 cup chopped onions
- 2 minced garlic cloves
- ½ tsp. cayenne pepper
- 1 tsp. cumin seed and coriander
- 1 tsp. salt

DIRECTIONS

1. Allow the water with split peas in it to come to a boil in a large stockpot.
2. Let it gently simmer without covering until the peas become soft; this will take about an hour.
3. Add the other ingredients and allow it to continue simmering for 30 minutes more. Check the consistency and thin out the water if necessary.
4. Ladle it into jars and leave a headspace of 1 inch. Put cap on and seal.
5. Set the filled jars in a pressure canner at 11 pounds pressure for dial-gauge or 10 pounds for the weighted-gauge canner. Process heat jars for 75 minutes, adjusting for altitude.
6. Switch off the heat and let the pressure drop naturally.
7. Remove the lid and cool the jars in canner for 5 minutes.
8. Take out the jars and cool. Inspect lids seal after 24 hours.

OTHER WAYS TO PRESERVE YOUR FOOD

Freezing: What Is and How to Do It Right

Freezing and refrigeration are the most common types of preservation in homes around the world today. Where refrigeration slows bacterial action, freezing comes close to totally stopping microbes' development. This happens because the water in frozen food turns to ice, in which bacteria cannot continue to grow. Enzyme activity, on the other hand, isn't completely deterred by freezing, which is why many vegetables are blanched before being packaged. Once an item is defrosted completely, however, any microbes still within will begin to grow again.

What Can Be Frozen?

Except for eggs in the shell, nearly all foods can be frozen raw, after blanching and/or cooking. So, the real question here is what foods don't take well to freezing. The following list includes the foods you generally cannot freeze:

- Cream sauces separate even when warmed completely after being frozen.

- Mayonnaise, cream cheese, and cottage cheese don't hold up well, often losing textural quality.

- Milk seems to be a 50-50 proposition. While it can be frozen quite safely, it sometimes separates after being frozen. If remixed, this milk is an option for cooking and baking.

- Precooked meat can be frozen, but it doesn't have as much moisture as raw and will often dry out further if left frozen for more than four weeks.

- Cured meats do not last long in the freezer and should be used in less than four weeks.

If you are in doubt about the process or how to best prepare an item for freezing (or even if you should), the National Center for Home Preserving (www.uga.edu/nchfp) is a great online resource. It offers tips on how to freeze various items ranging from pie and prepared food to oysters and artichokes.

Frosty Facts

In freezing, zero is your magic number. At 0°F, microbes become dormant. The food won't spoil, and any germs therein will not breed until you defrost the food. Bear in mind, however, that the longer the food remains frozen the more it tends to lose certain qualities such as vivid flavor and texture. Always try to freeze things when they're at their peak and remember that cooking your defrosted food as soon as it's thawed will also stop microbial growth.

The first step in freezing is keeping those items cold until you're ready to prepare them. This is very important with meat, but it also makes a difference in how fruits and vegetables come out of the freezer.

Canning and Preserving Food for Beginners

1. **Equipment**

Once you're ready to begin, assemble all the items you need. For example, if you're freezing fruit, you'll want a clean cutting board, a sharp knife, and your choice of storage containers. If you're doing any preparation on the fruit before freezing it, you'll also need cooking pans. Stainless steel is highly recommended; galvanized pans may give off zinc when the fruit is left in them because of the fruit's acid content. Additionally, there's nothing like stainless steel for easy cleanup.

If it's in your budget, a vacuum sealer is another great piece of equipment to consider. Vacuum sealers come in different kinds of sizes with a similar variety of bags that are perfect for preservers who like freezing and drying methods. They're cost-effective when compared to freezer bags or plastic containers, and they eliminate the excess air that contributes to ice crystals.

A third item that you shouldn't be without is a freezer-proof label system. If you double-wrap your frozen items, put a label on each layer. If one gets knocked off, the other remains.

2. **Help and Hints**

Freezing, like any other method of preservation, requires some observation and annotation to achieve success. As you're working with recipes, remember that practice really does make perfect. For example, you may follow a recipe for frozen butter pickles exactly, but you find you'd like the cucumbers sliced more thinly for greater flavor. Make a note of that and change it next time.

As you note changes, you'd like to make, also consider if that means getting different types of equipment for your kitchen. In the case of the cucumbers and other thinly sliced vegetables, a mandolin might be the perfect fix. Put it on a wish list. Being prepared saves a lot of last-minute headaches, and having the right tools is always a great boon.

3. **Vegetables**

Vegetables should be chosen for crispness and freshness. Home gardeners should pick their items a few hours before packing them for the ultimate in organic goodness. The next step for vegetables is blanching, which will improve the lifespan of your frozen goods.

If there's no specific blanching time provided in your preserving recipe, here's a brief overview to get you started. Remember to move your vegetables into an ice bath immediately after blanching until they're totally cooled.

Timing and Techniques for Blanching Vegetables

- Asparagus. Remove the tough ends from the asparagus. Depending on the storage container, you may need to cut the stems in half. If your stalks are thin, they'll only need 2 minutes of blanching; thick stalks require twice as much.
- Beans (green or wax). Remove any tips. Leave the beans whole and blanch them for 3 minutes.
- Brussels sprouts. Clean off outer leaves, then soak the sprouts in cold salty water for 30 minutes. Drain and blanch for 4 minutes.

- Cabbage. Remove the outer leaves. Shred the cabbage and blanch for just over 1 minute and leave in the water for another 30 seconds before icing.
- Carrots. Clean the skins, then slice them into ¼ pieces. Blanch for 3 minutes. Whole baby carrots need 5 minutes of blanching.
- Cauliflower and broccoli. Break off the pieces from the central core and clean well (a spray nozzle at the sink works very well). Soak in a gallon of salty water (3–4 tsp. s salt) for 30 minutes. Pour off the liquid. Rinse and blanch for 3 minutes.
- Corn. Rinse, remove from the cob, and blanch for 5 minutes.
- Mushrooms (small). These can be frozen whole. Toss with a little fresh lemon juice and blanch for 4 minutes.
- Greens (including spinach). Rinse. Remove any leaves that have spots or other damage. Blanch for 3 minutes.
- Peas. Blanch out of the husk for 90 seconds.
- Peas in the pod. Trim the ends and remove strings. Blanch for 1–2 minutes, depending on the size of the pod.
- Peppers. Slice open and remove the seeds. Cut into the desired size and blanch for 2 minutes.
- Potatoes. Wash and scrub thoroughly. Remove the peel and blanch for 4 minutes.
- Tomatoes. To easily peel the skins, use a straining spoon and dip the tomatoes in boiling water for 30 seconds. Peel and remove the core. These can be stored whole or diced to the desired size.
- Zucchini and squash. Peel. Cut into ½-inch slices and blanch for 3 minutes.

Fruit

Do small batches of fruit so it doesn't brown while you're packing. Fruit need not be packed in syrup, but many people do prefer the texture and taste that sugar or sugar syrup adds to frozen fruit. Some folks use sugar substitutes for dietary reasons. In any case, small fruits such as berries take well to a simple sprinkling. Larger chunks such as peaches do well in syrup. The average ratio is ½ cup of syrup to every pint of fruit. Some preservers like to use ascorbic acid to improve the quality of frozen fruit. Adding about ½ tsp. of this per pint is sufficient; just mix it into the syrup or a little water.

Packaging

Since 95 percent of American homes freeze some of their food regularly, it's not surprising to find people have a lot of questions on the best type of storage containers to use and how to prepare food for the table after it's been frozen. Plastic bags are the most common receptacles, followed by plastic containers. While some people have been known to use glass, this is a bit risky since the glass may crack and break when the food inside expands in the freezing process. Additionally, slippery glass jars coming out of the freezer are easily dropped.

Overall, it's always a good idea to use bags and containers that are rated for freezing. Avoid using waxed cartons; they don't retain the food's quality very well and defrosted food often becomes limp and unstable for handling. Your packaging materials should also be leak and oil-resistant, and all packing materials should be able to withstand freezing.

1. **Size Counts**

Another consideration with your containers is size. Think about how many people you plan to serve and choose freezing containers accordingly. If you're going to put several servings in one large container, separate them with a piece of aluminum foil or plastic wrap so you can take them out one at a time easily.

2. **Space Constraints**

When you're packing food into a container, always leave a little room for expansion. Let the food achieve room temperature before you freeze it (right out of the ice bath is a perfect time with vegetables). Putting food that is hot or warm in the freezer creates a temperature variance for all the food inside the freezer.

Most importantly, remember to label and date everything. This will help you gauge what should be eaten first so it retains the greatest quality.

3. **Wrap It Up**

Many preservers wrap the meat with aluminum foil or freezer wrap, then transfer it into another freezer bag or container. This decreases the chance that water crystals will form and protects the foil from being accidentally torn. Note, however, that waxed paper isn't a good choice for freezing because it doesn't resist moisture.

4. **Stews and Leftovers**

If you know in advance that you'd like to set aside some of what you're cooking for the freezer, it's a good idea to leave it a little undercooked. Freeze the goods as soon as they reach room temperature. When you warm it up, you will finish the cooking process and can also doctor the flavor a bit at that time. Your frozen foods need not be defrosted before you start cooking them. Just remember to get all the packing materials off the item first—you would not be the first person to forget this step and find unpleasant paper or wrapping in a meat serving!

CONCLUSION

Canning and preserving food are a well-known activity that is relatively easy to master. It can be a very common desire to preserve our food if we want it to last, and of course, we want to use all of our food while it is fresh. That is why these techniques allow you to have healthy food for your family, and can last from a few days up to a few months. In this overall discussion, I gave you a great overview of canning and preserving foods as well as what to do with the many fruits and vegetables that are available in the world. Ultimately, my goal was to make it easier for you by giving you some quick tips on how to preserve your crops the fastest way possible.

Together we learned that there are many benefits to storing your food at home, including saving money and having high quality food carefully made for your family.

We have clarified what exactly a canning is, briefly outlining the main types of canning and associated techniques, focusing on the pressure canning method and how it compares to that of canning water bath. In addition, we talked about some of the basics of food safety in food preservation, and then reveal my best recipes to begin your personal journey through the world of preserves.

I hope you enjoyed this book and that you liked this journey exploring different ways to store your food for future use.

Writing this guide was a wonderful adventure but it wasn't easy: if you liked even a small part of what I wrote, please leave an honest review on Amazon.

I wish you the best!

Printed in Great Britain
by Amazon